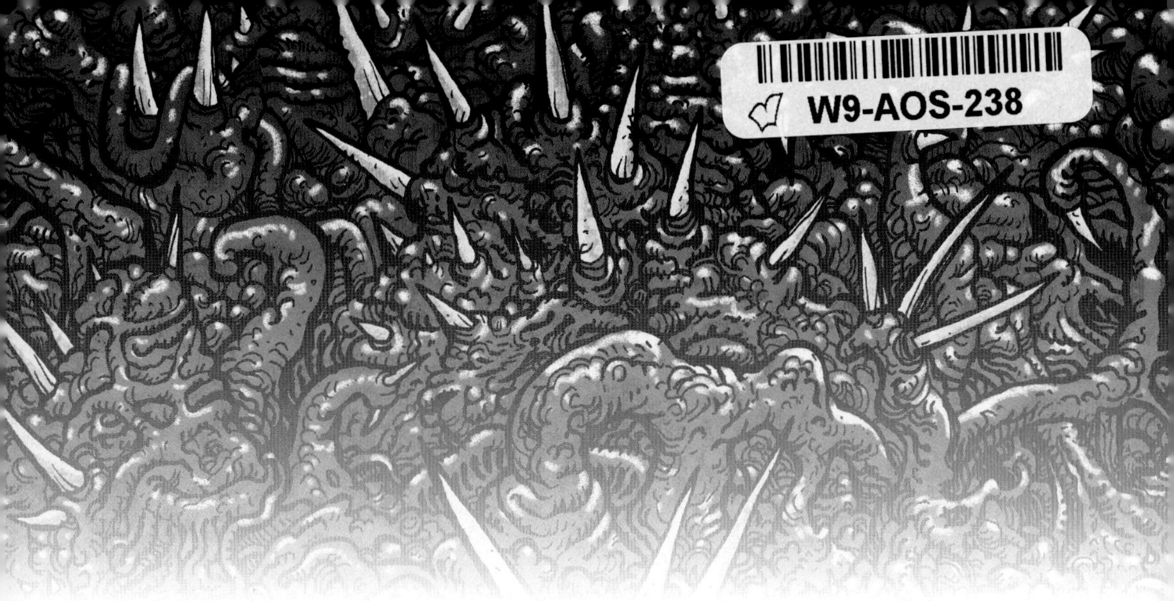

SPREAD™

VOL. 2: THE CHILDREN'S CRUSADE

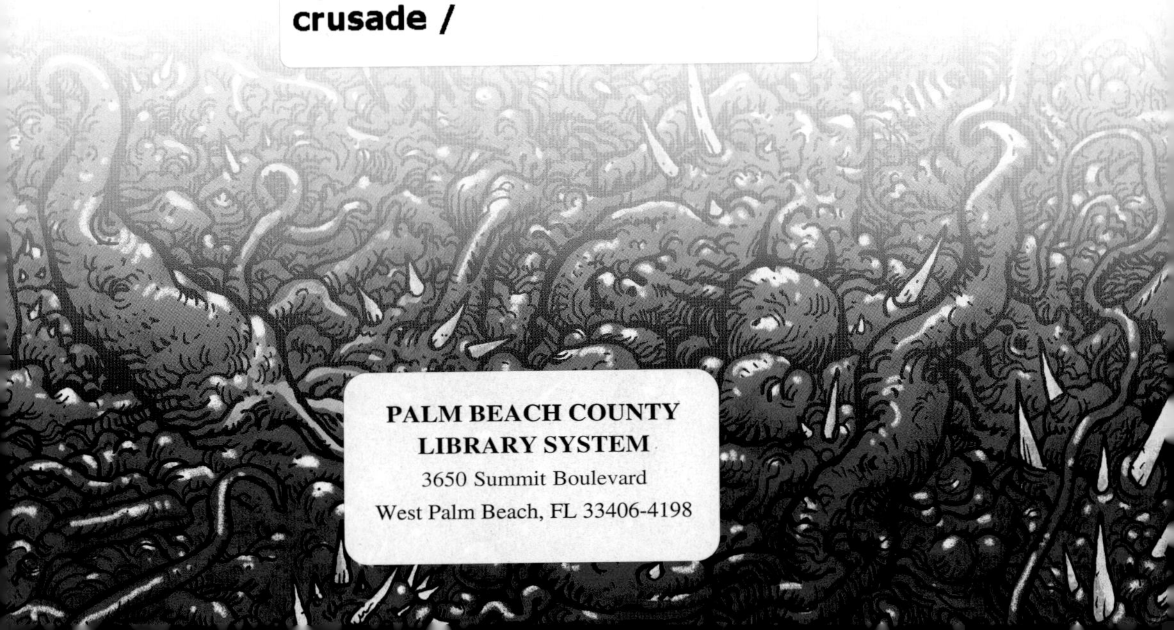

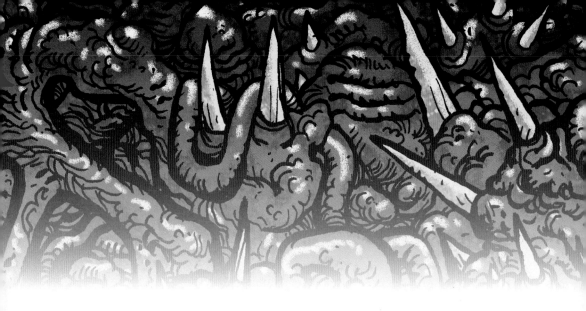

IMAGE COMICS, INC.
Robert Kirkman – Chief Operating Officer
Erik Larsen – Chief Financial Officer
Todd McFarlane – President
Marc Silvestri – Chief Executive Officer
Jim Valentino – Vice-President

Eric Stephenson – Publisher
Corey Murphy – Director of Sales
Jeff Boison – Director of Publishing Planning & Book Trade Sales
Jeremy Sullivan – Director of Digital Sales
Kat Salazar – Director of PR & Marketing
Emily Miller – Director of Operations
Branwyn Bigglestone – Senior Accounts Manager
Sarah Mello – Accounts Manager
Drew Gill – Art Director
Jonathan Chan – Production Manager
Meredith Wallace – Print Manager
Briah Skelly – Publicity Assistant
Randy Okamura – Marketing Production Designer
David Brothers – Branding Manager
Ally Power – Content Manager
Addison Duke – Production Artist
Vincent Kukua – Production Artist
Sasha Head – Production Artist
Tricia Ramos – Production Artist
Jeff Stang – Direct Market Sales Representative
Emilio Bautista – Digital Sales Associate
Chloe Ramos-Peterson – Administrative Assistant
IMAGECOMICS.COM

SPREAD VOL. 2. FIRST PRINTING. DECEMBER 2015.
ISBN# 978-1-63215-562-7

Published by Image Comics, Inc. Office of publication: 200█
Center Street, 6th Floor, Berkeley, CA 94704. Copyright © 201█
Justin Jordan & Kyle Strahm. All rights reserved. Original█
published in single magazine form as Spread #7-11. SPREAD█
(including all prominent characters featured herein), its logo an█
all character likenesses are trademarks of Justin Jordan & Ky█
Strahm, unless otherwise noted. Image Comics® and its logo█
are registered trademarks of Image Comics, Inc. No part of th█
publication may be reproduced or transmitted, in any form █
by any means (except for short excerpts for review purposes█
without the express written permission of Image Comics, In█
All names, characters, events and locales in this publication a█
entirely fictional. Any resemblance to actual persons (living █
dead), events or places, without satiric intent, is coincidenta█
PRINTED IN THE U.S.A. For information regarding the CPSIA o█
this printed material call: 203-595-3636 and provide reference █
RICH – 654448.

For international rights, contact:
foreignlicensing@imagecomics.com

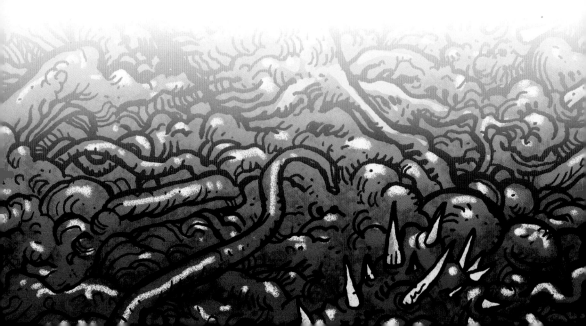

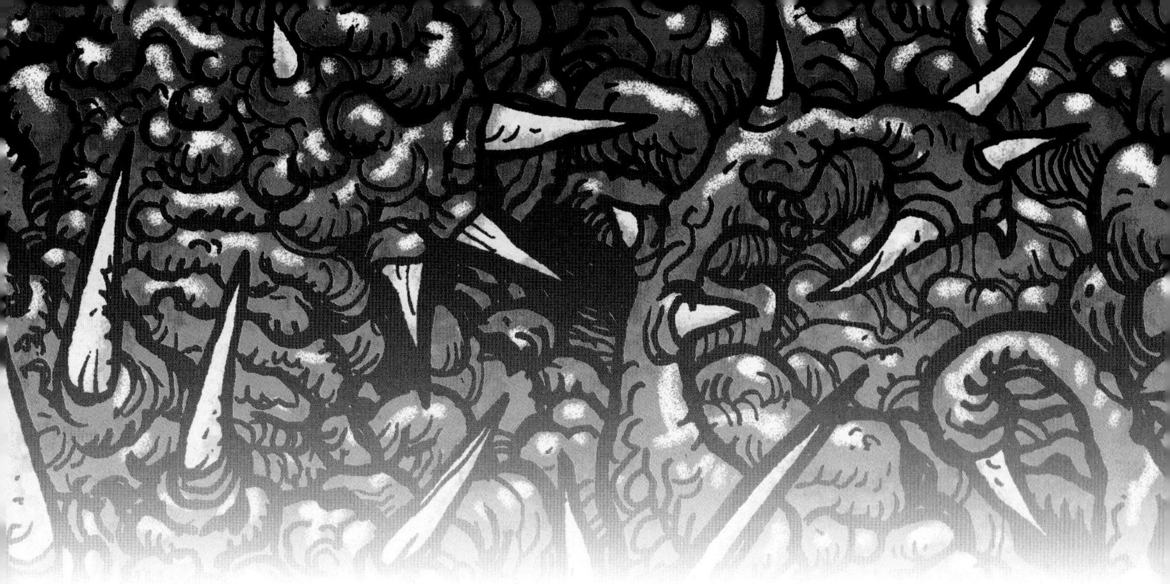

CO-CREATED BY

JUSTIN JORDAN and KYLE STRAHM

SCRIPT BY
JUSTIN JORDAN

ISSUE #7 ART BY
LIAM COBB

ISSUE #8-11 ART BY
KYLE STRAHM

COLOR BY
FELIPE SOBREIRO

LETTERS BY
CRANK!

EDITED BY
SEBASTIAN GIRNER

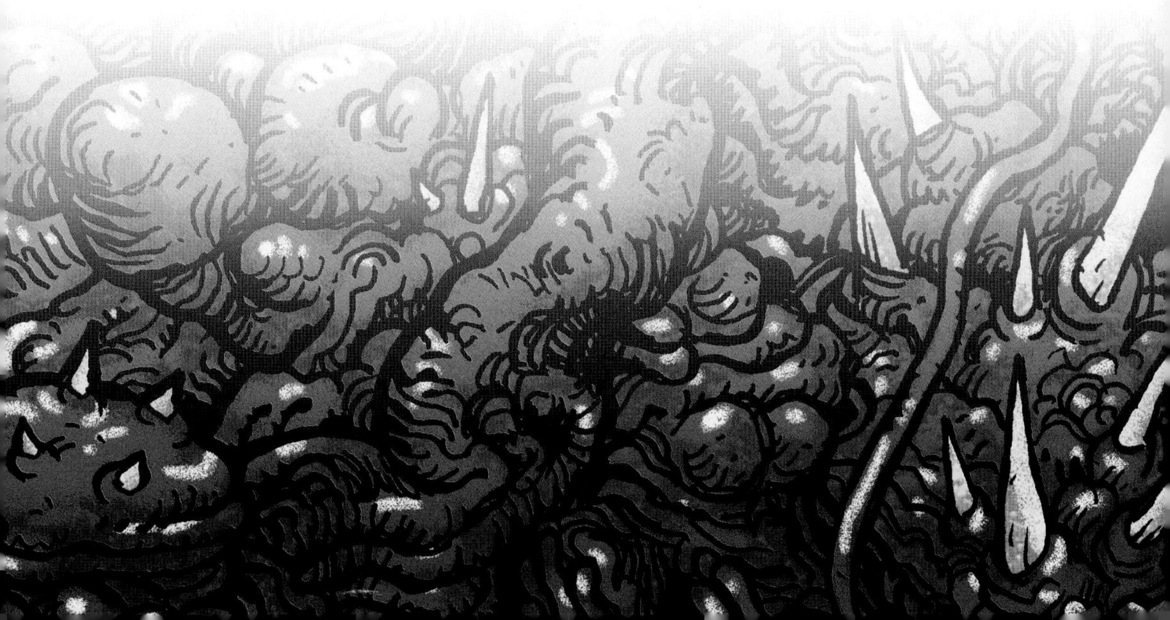

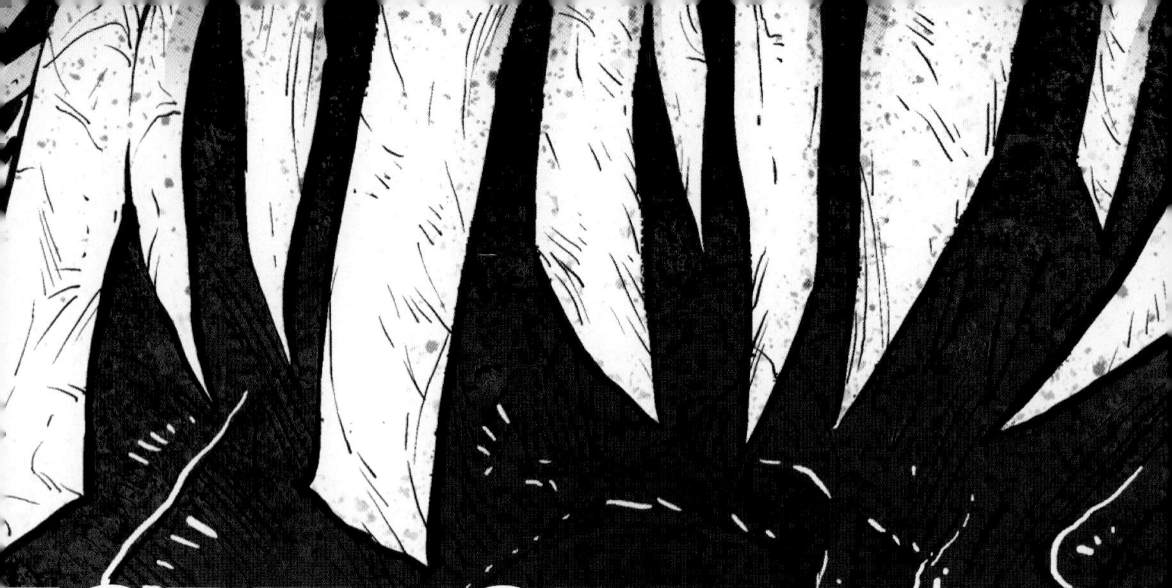

FOREWORD
Good God, We Did It Again

So, welcome to the second volume of *Spread*. In which you will find more of the same, and not more of the same. Also, apparently, a writer who speaks in weird pseudo zen koans.

What I mean by the same/not the same is the essential difficulty of doing long form work. You want the book (or television show) to fundamentally BE what made people like the work to begin with, without also being the same thing over and over.

This volume, hopefully, has what brought you to the dance to begin with; babies, badasses and monsters, while not being the first story again. You'll notice this volume includes a story taking place before the main timeframe and it focuses on people other than No.

Because that is the fun of an ongoing series, especially when you're creating a world from scratch. In *Spread*, we've got a pretty big sandbox, so we're working hard to show you a lot of it. The first volume had a pretty tight focus on No, but we're expanding that focus as the series goes.

But fear not, there is still going to be plenty of fights and body horror and monsters. More so, even, as time goes on.

So thank you for reading, and I hope you follow us deeper into the world of *Spread*.

-Justin Jordan

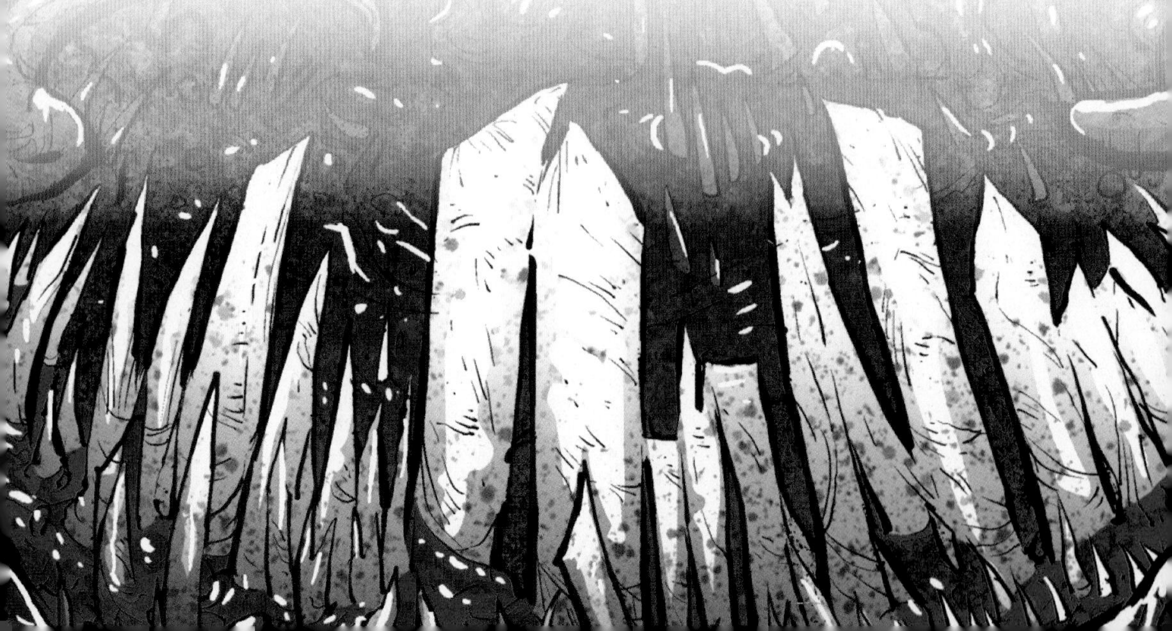

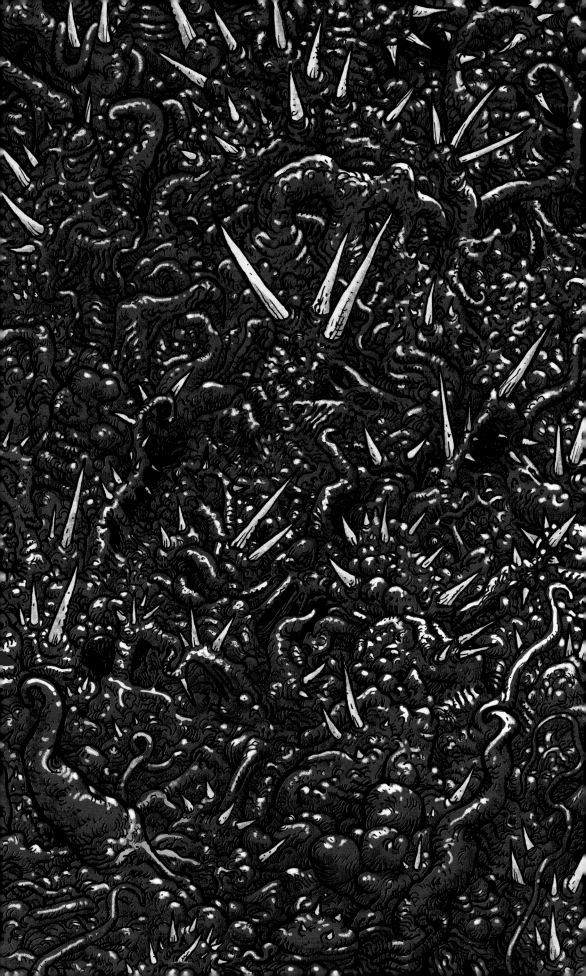

CHAPTER ONE

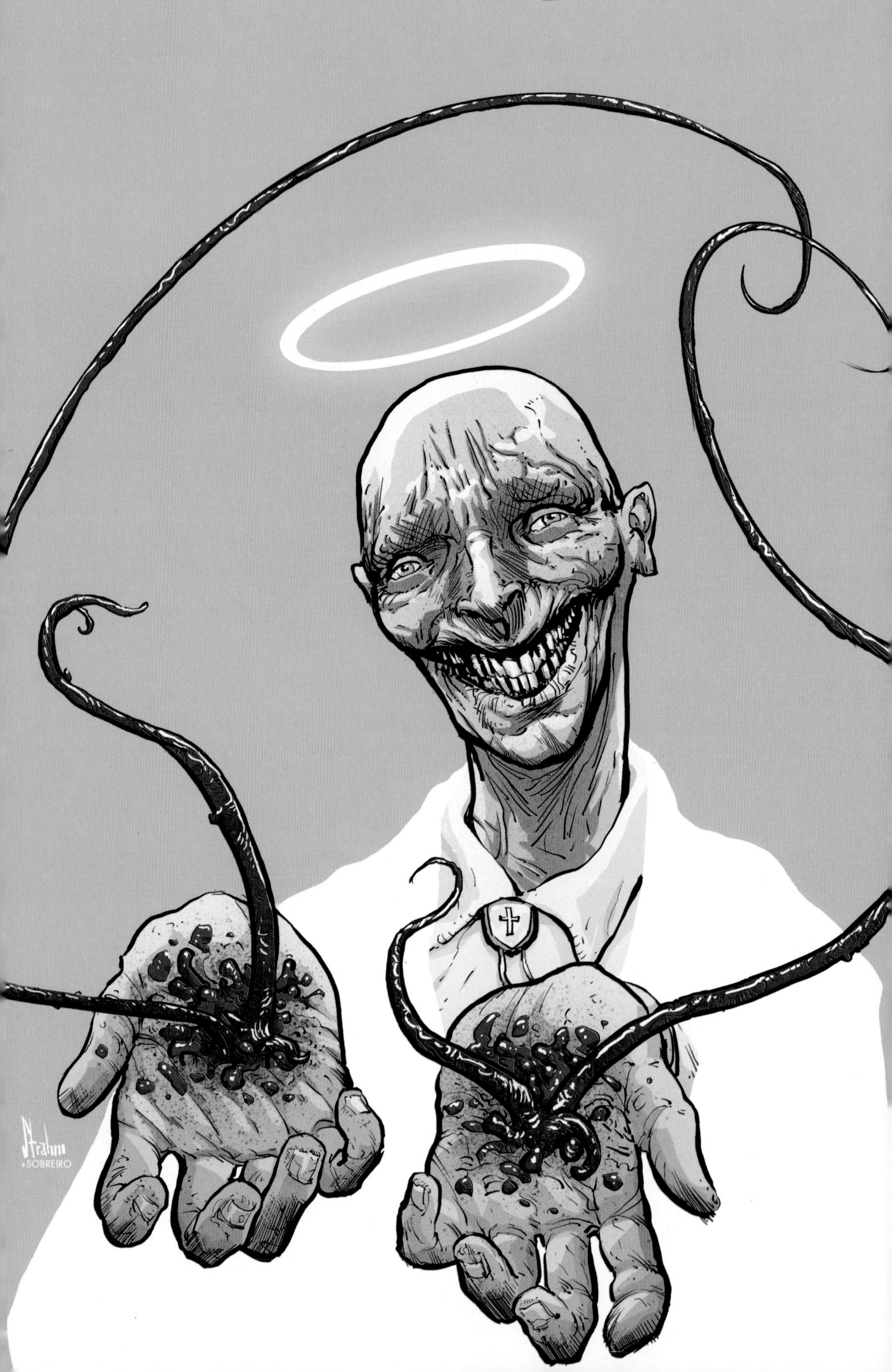

Strahm
+SOBREIRO

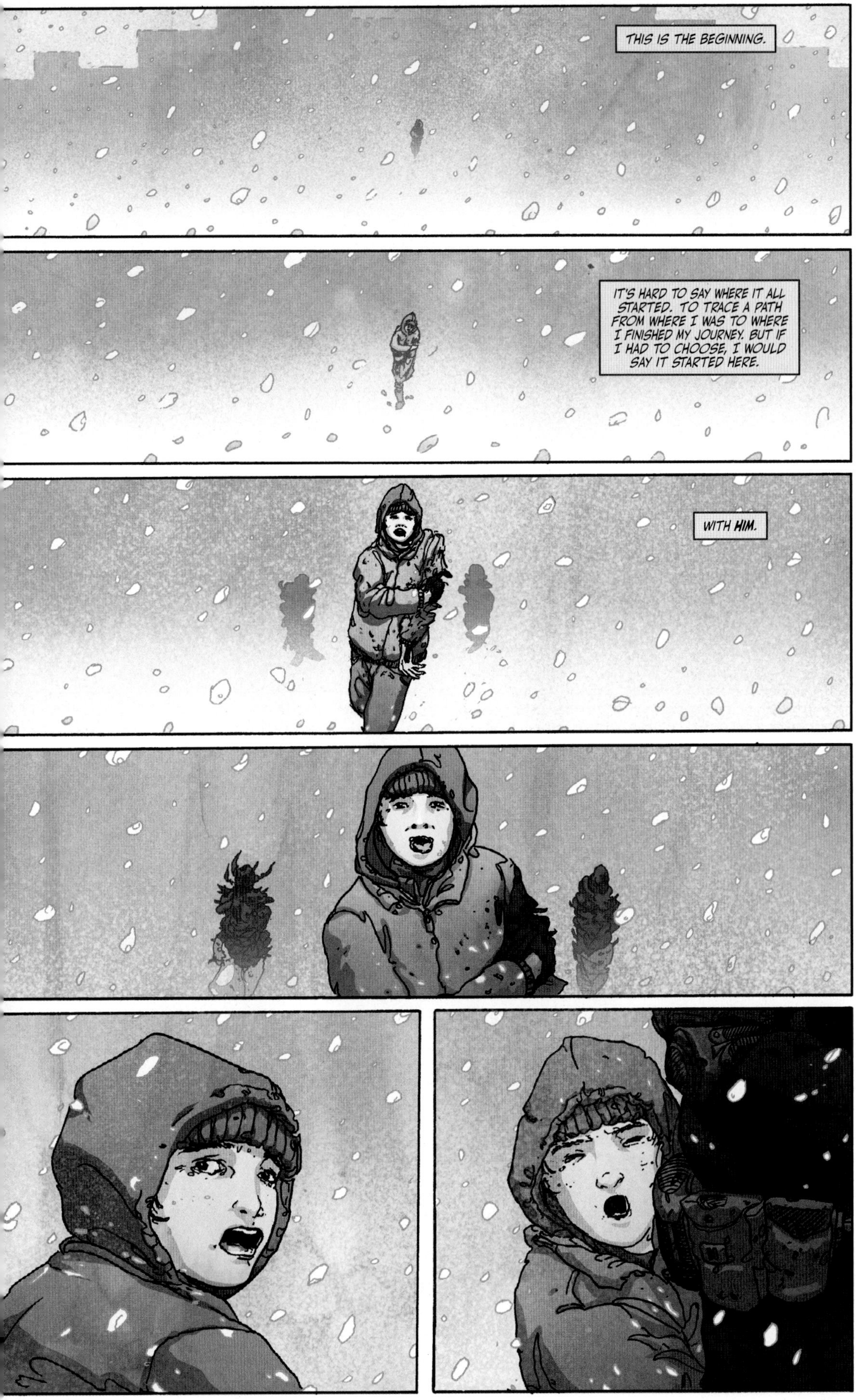
THIS IS THE BEGINNING.
IT'S HARD TO SAY WHERE IT ALL STARTED. TO TRACE A PATH FROM WHERE I WAS TO WHERE I FINISHED MY JOURNEY. BUT IF I HAD TO CHOOSE, I WOULD SAY IT STARTED HERE.
WITH **HIM**.

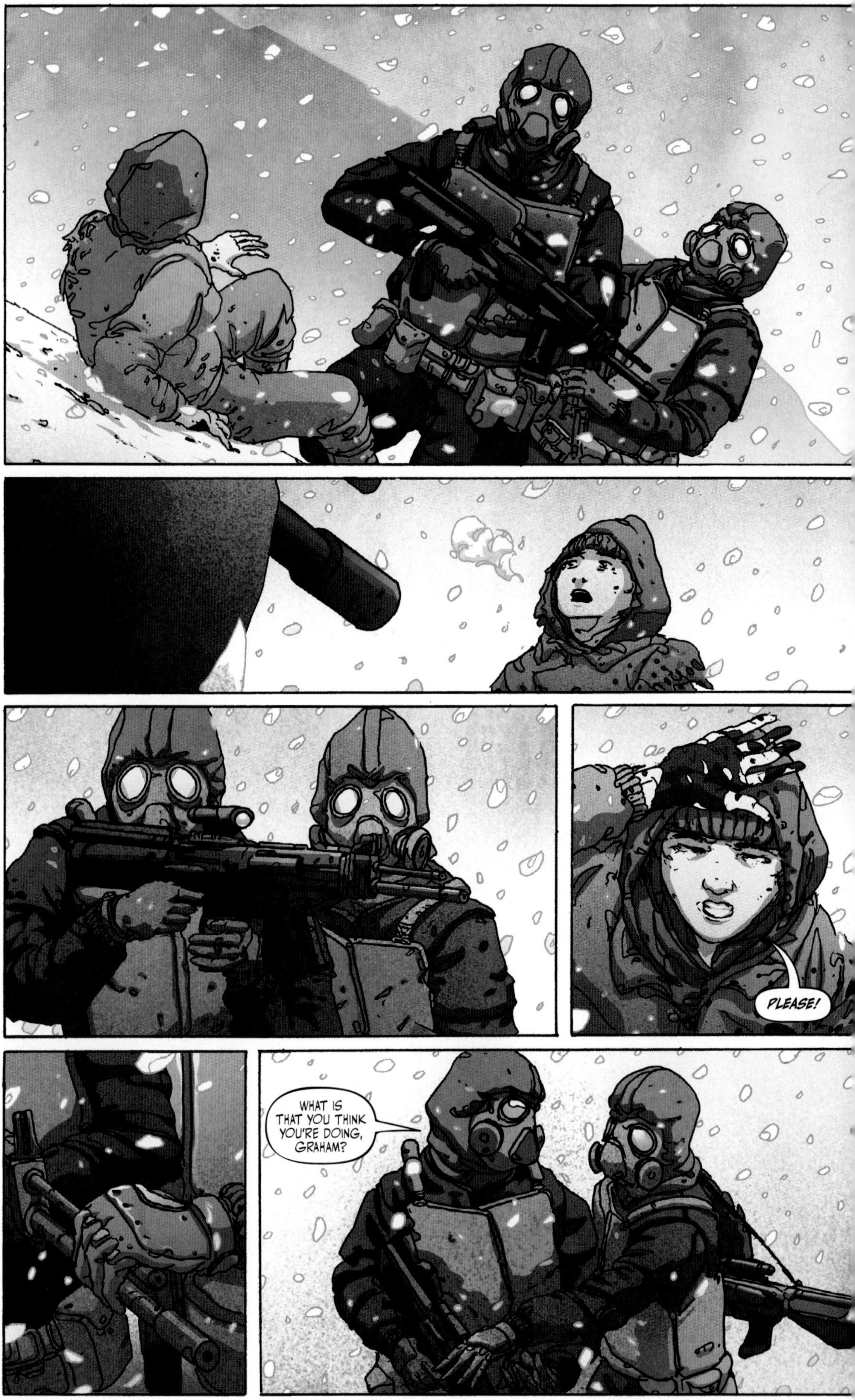
PLEASE!
WHAT IS THAT YOU THINK YOU'RE DOING, GRAHAM?

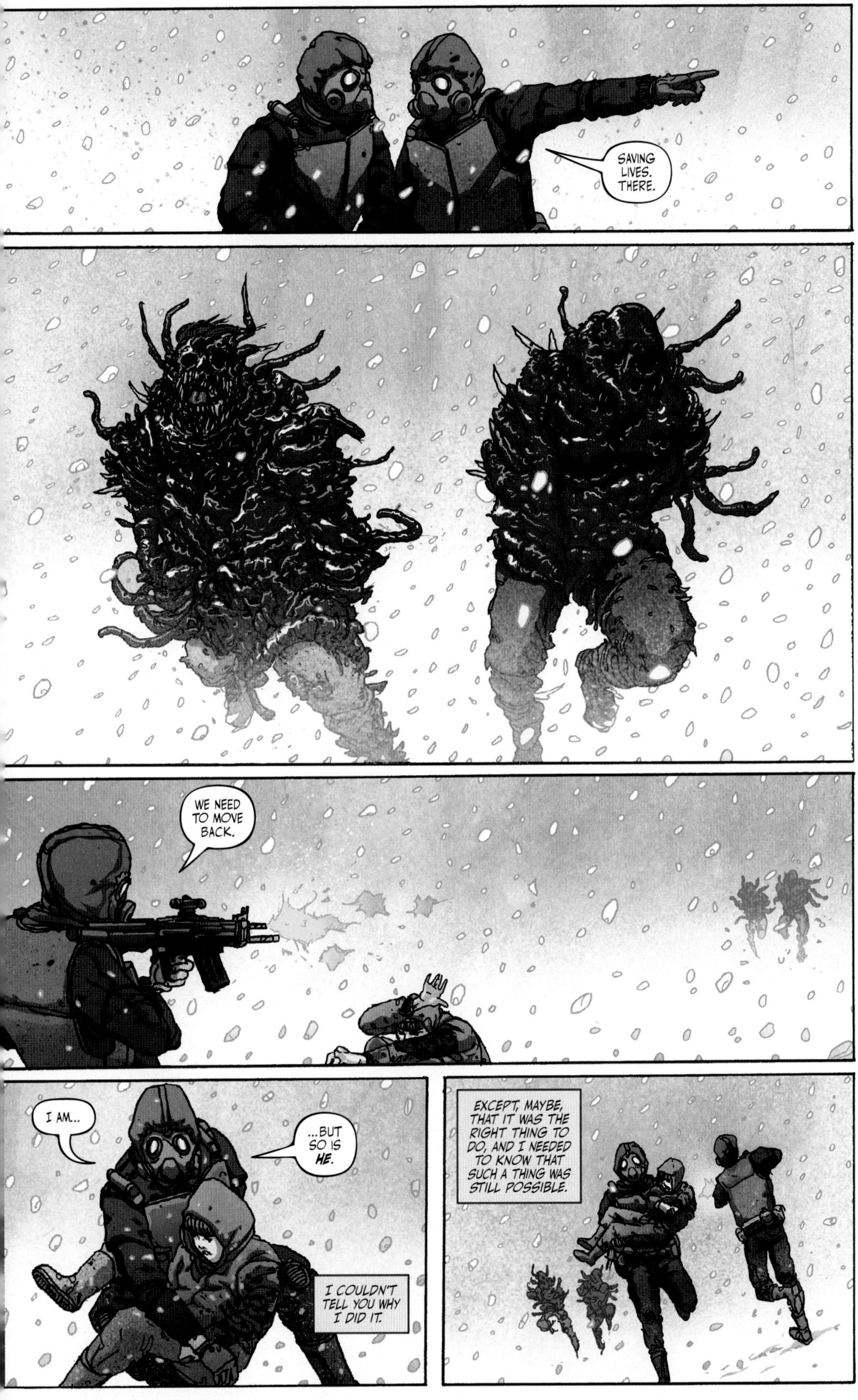

SAVING LIVES. THERE.
WE NEED TO MOVE BACK.
I AM...
...BUT SO IS HE.
I COULDN'T TELL YOU WHY I DID IT.
EXCEPT, MAYBE, THAT IT WAS THE RIGHT THING TO DO, AND I NEEDED TO KNOW THAT SUCH A THING WAS STILL POSSIBLE.

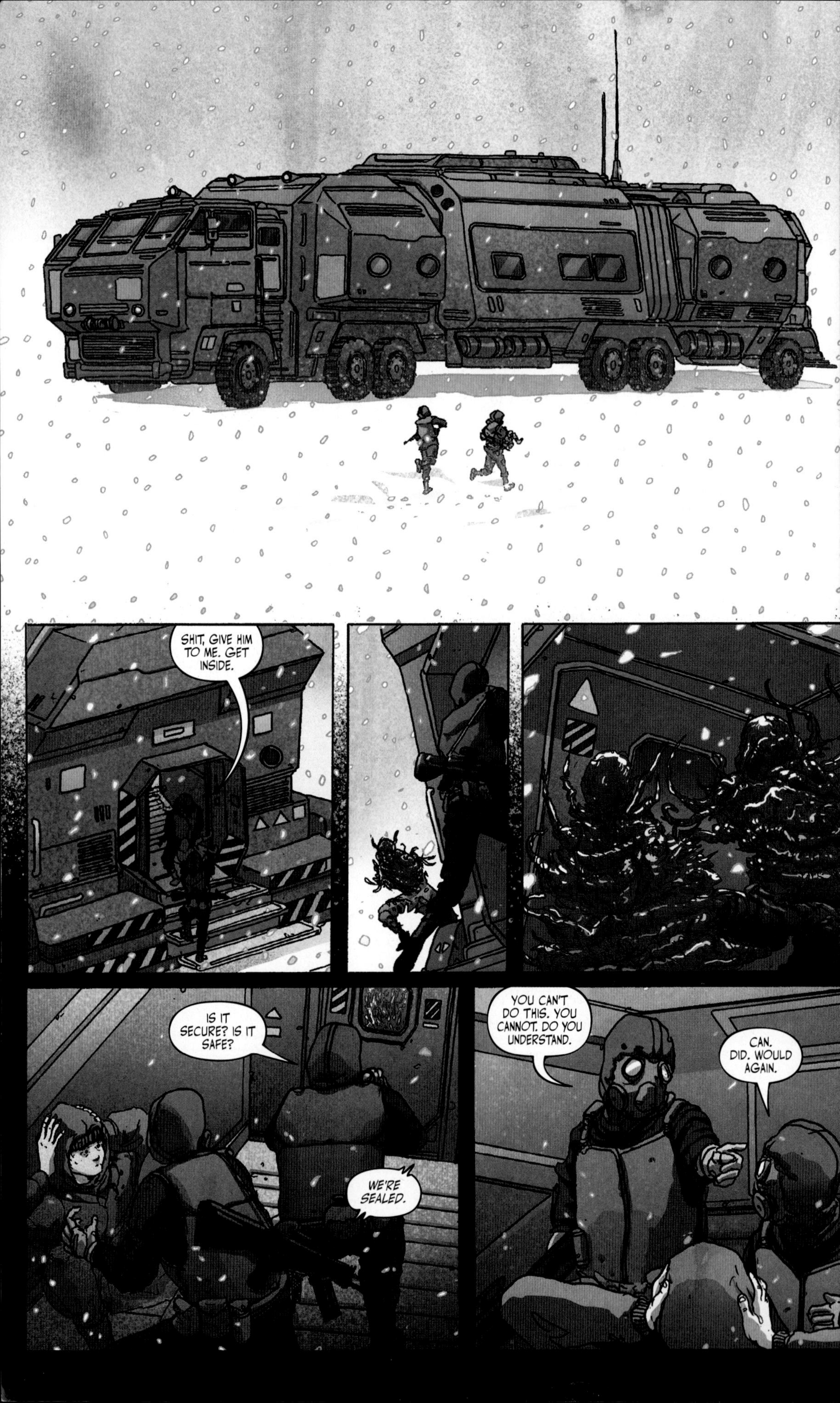
SHIT, GIVE HIM TO ME. GET INSIDE.
IS IT SECURE? IS IT SAFE?
WE'RE SEALED.
YOU CAN'T DO THIS. YOU CANNOT. DO YOU UNDERSTAND.
CAN. DID. WOULD AGAIN.

HEY, HEY, IT'S OKAY. *OKAY?* WE'RE HERE TO HELP?

NNNNN.

MOM... DADDY?

SHHHH, IT'S OKAY. I JUST NEED TO CHECK YOU OUT, OKAY? AND THEN I'LL GET YOU SOME PLACE WARM.

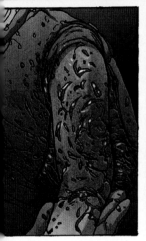

WELL, EXCELLENT WORK DR. SUNDERLAND.

YOU'VE SAVED HIM FROM... *NOT A FUCKING THING.*

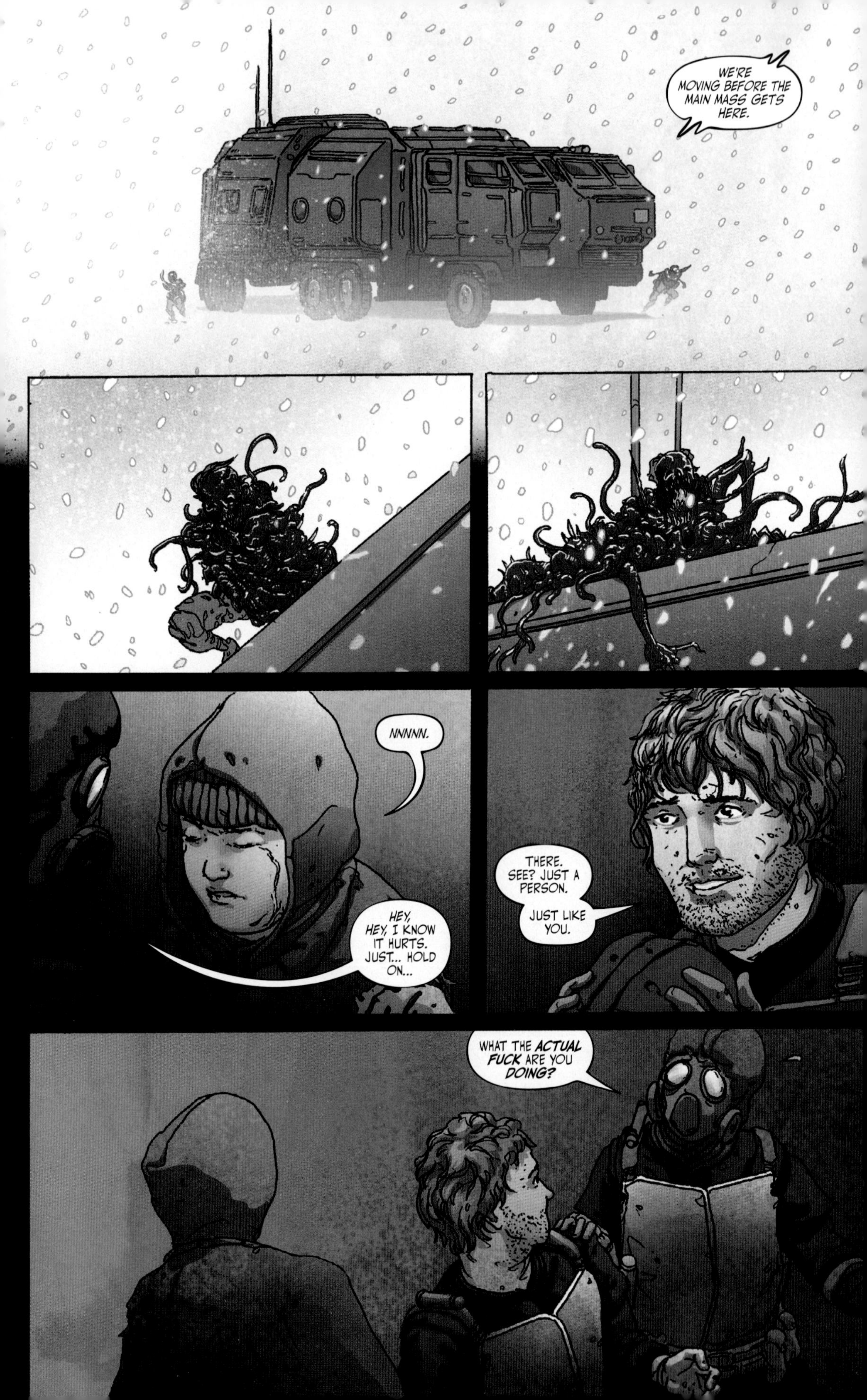
WE'RE MOVING BEFORE THE MAIN MASS GETS HERE.
NNNNN.
HEY, HEY, I KNOW IT HURTS. JUST... HOLD ON...
THERE. SEE? JUST A PERSON.
JUST LIKE YOU.
WHAT THE ACTUAL FUCK ARE YOU DOING?

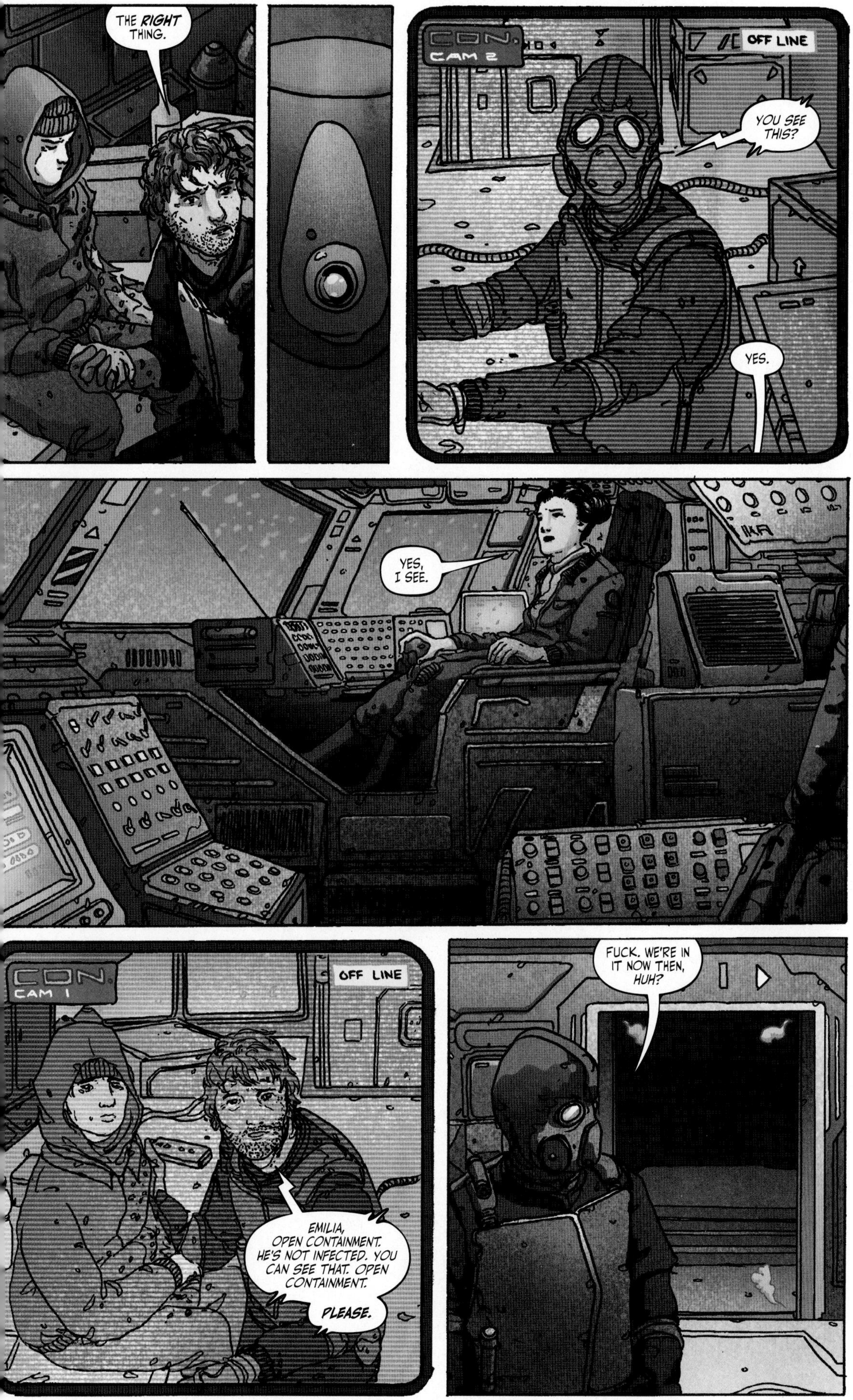
THE RIGHT THING.
CON.
CAM 2
OFF LINE
YOU SEE THIS?
YES.
YES, I SEE.
CON
CAM 1
OFF LINE
EMILIA, OPEN CONTAINMENT. HE'S NOT INFECTED. YOU CAN SEE THAT. OPEN CONTAINMENT.
PLEASE.
FUCK. WE'RE IN IT NOW THEN, HUH?

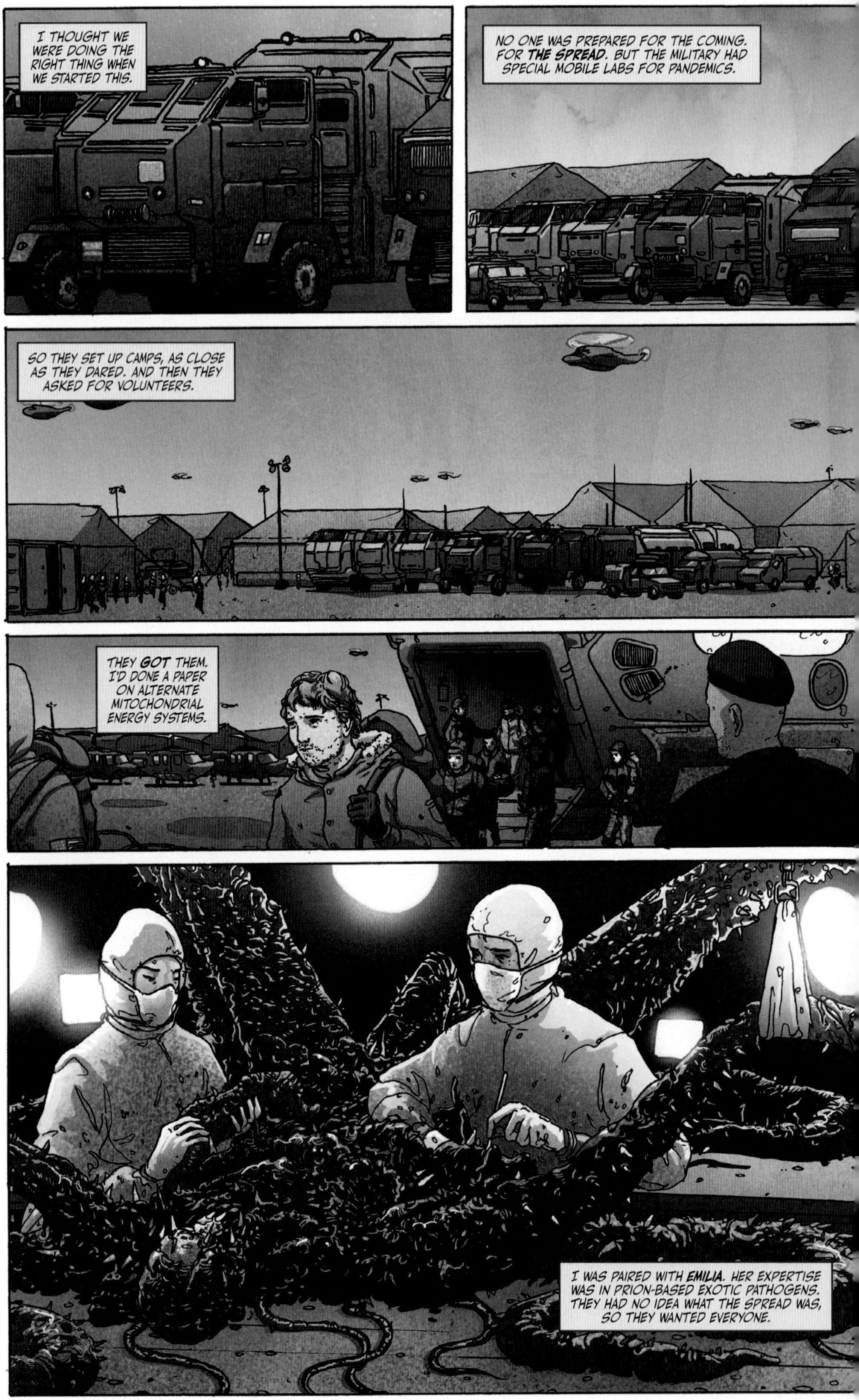
I THOUGHT WE WERE DOING THE RIGHT THING WHEN WE STARTED THIS.
NO ONE WAS PREPARED FOR THE COMING. FOR THE SPREAD. BUT THE MILITARY HAD SPECIAL MOBILE LABS FOR PANDEMICS.
SO THEY SET UP CAMPS, AS CLOSE AS THEY DARED. AND THEN THEY ASKED FOR VOLUNTEERS.
THEY GOT THEM. I'D DONE A PAPER ON ALTERNATE MITOCHONDRIAL ENERGY SYSTEMS.
I WAS PAIRED WITH EMILIA. HER EXPERTISE WAS IN PRION-BASED EXOTIC PATHOGENS. THEY HAD NO IDEA WHAT THE SPREAD WAS, SO THEY WANTED EVERYONE.

BUT WE DIDN'T HAVE ENOUGH TIME. IF WE'D JUST HAD A LITTLE MORE, WE MIGHT HAVE...

I THOUGHT THAT. I DIDN'T REALIZE HOW **FOOLISH** I WAS. BUT IT DIDN'T MATTER.

THEY DECIDED **CONTAINMENT** WAS THE ONLY OPTION. THE ENTIRE AREA WAS TO BE QUARANTINED. IT WAS THE LARGEST MASS EVACUATION IN HUMAN HISTORY.

WE WERE EVACUATED TOO. OR...

...WE WERE **SUPPOSED** TO BE. WE DECIDED THAT WE **WOULD** HAVE MORE TIME.

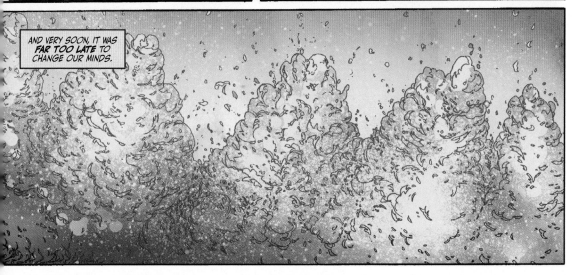

AND VERY SOON, IT WAS **FAR TOO LATE** TO CHANGE OUR MINDS.

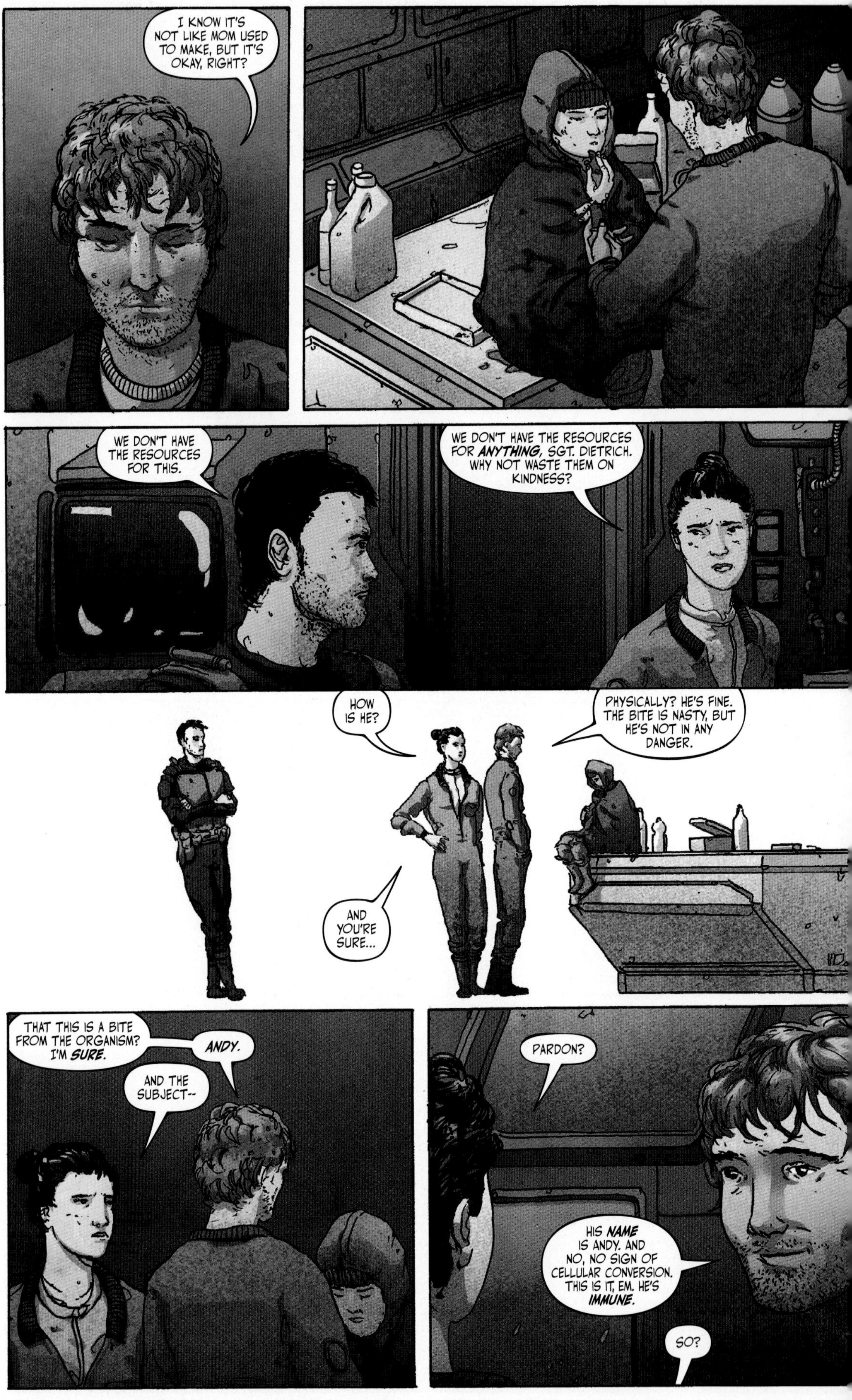

I KNOW IT'S NOT LIKE MOM USED TO MAKE, BUT IT'S OKAY, RIGHT?
WE DON'T HAVE THE RESOURCES FOR THIS.
WE DON'T HAVE THE RESOURCES FOR ANYTHING, SGT. DIETRICH. WHY NOT WASTE THEM ON KINDNESS?
HOW IS HE?
PHYSICALLY? HE'S FINE. THE BITE IS NASTY, BUT HE'S NOT IN ANY DANGER.
AND YOU'RE SURE...
THAT THIS IS A BITE FROM THE ORGANISM? I'M SURE.
ANDY.
AND THE SUBJECT--
PARDON?
HIS NAME IS ANDY. AND NO, NO SIGN OF CELLULAR CONVERSION. THIS IS IT, EM. HE'S IMMUNE.
SO?

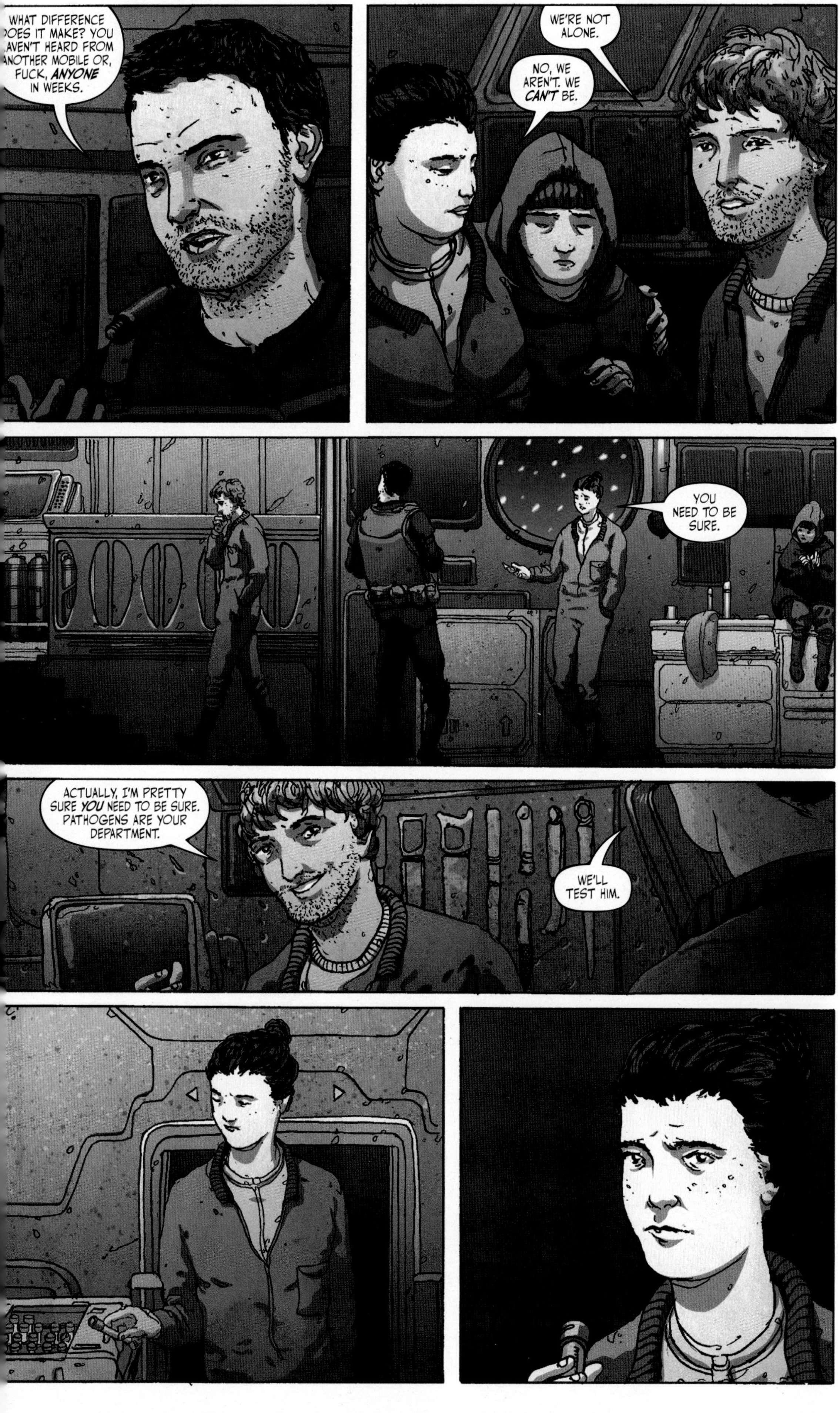
WHAT DIFFERENCE DOES IT MAKE? YOU HAVEN'T HEARD FROM ANOTHER MOBILE OR, FUCK, ANYONE IN WEEKS.
WE'RE NOT ALONE.
NO, WE AREN'T. WE CAN'T BE.
YOU NEED TO BE SURE.
ACTUALLY, I'M PRETTY SURE YOU NEED TO BE SURE. PATHOGENS ARE YOUR DEPARTMENT.
WE'LL TEST HIM.

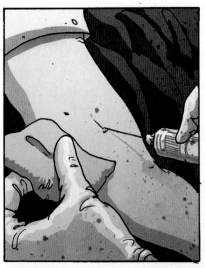

I HAD SPENT MY LIFE TURNING AWAY FROM *FAITH*.

LOOKING FOR ANSWERS THAT MY PARENTS AND MY PASTORS COULDN'T GIVE ME.

I WAS LOOKING IN THE WRONG PLACE. SCIENCE IS JUST QUESTIONS. EVERY ANSWER BIK'THS MORE UNCERTAINTY. PERHAPS THAT WAS THE *OPPOSITE* OF FAITH. I WAS NOT SURE.

BUT I WAS SURE WHAT SHE WOULD SEE. I WAS SURE WHAT WE HAD FOUND, JUST WHEN WE WERE ALMOST OUT OF OPTIONS AND ODDS.

HOPE.

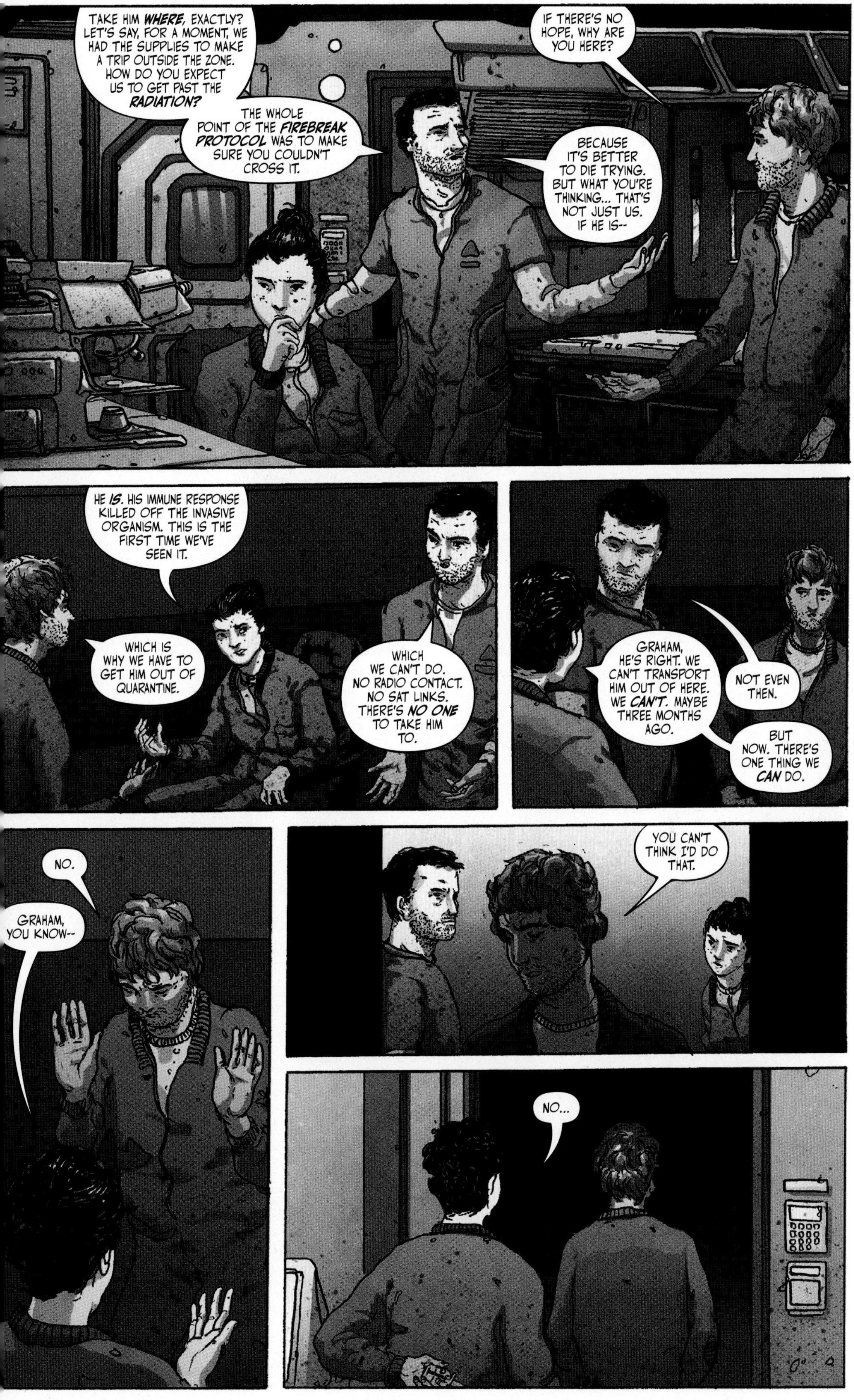

TAKE HIM *WHERE*, EXACTLY? LET'S SAY, FOR A MOMENT, WE HAD THE SUPPLIES TO MAKE A TRIP OUTSIDE THE ZONE. HOW DO YOU EXPECT US TO GET PAST THE *RADIATION?*
THE WHOLE POINT OF THE *FIREBREAK PROTOCOL* WAS TO MAKE SURE YOU COULDN'T CROSS IT.
IF THERE'S NO HOPE, WHY ARE YOU HERE?
BECAUSE IT'S BETTER TO DIE TRYING. BUT WHAT YOU'RE THINKING... THAT'S NOT JUST US. IF HE IS--
HE *IS*. HIS IMMUNE RESPONSE KILLED OFF THE INVASIVE ORGANISM. THIS IS THE FIRST TIME WE'VE SEEN IT.
WHICH IS WHY WE HAVE TO GET HIM OUT OF QUARANTINE.
WHICH WE CAN'T DO. NO RADIO CONTACT. NO SAT LINKS. THERE'S *NO ONE* TO TAKE HIM TO.
GRAHAM, HE'S RIGHT. WE CAN'T TRANSPORT HIM OUT OF HERE. WE *CAN'T*. MAYBE THREE MONTHS AGO.
NOT EVEN THEN.
BUT NOW. THERE'S ONE THING WE *CAN* DO.
NO.
GRAHAM, YOU KNOW--
YOU CAN'T THINK I'D DO THAT.
NO...

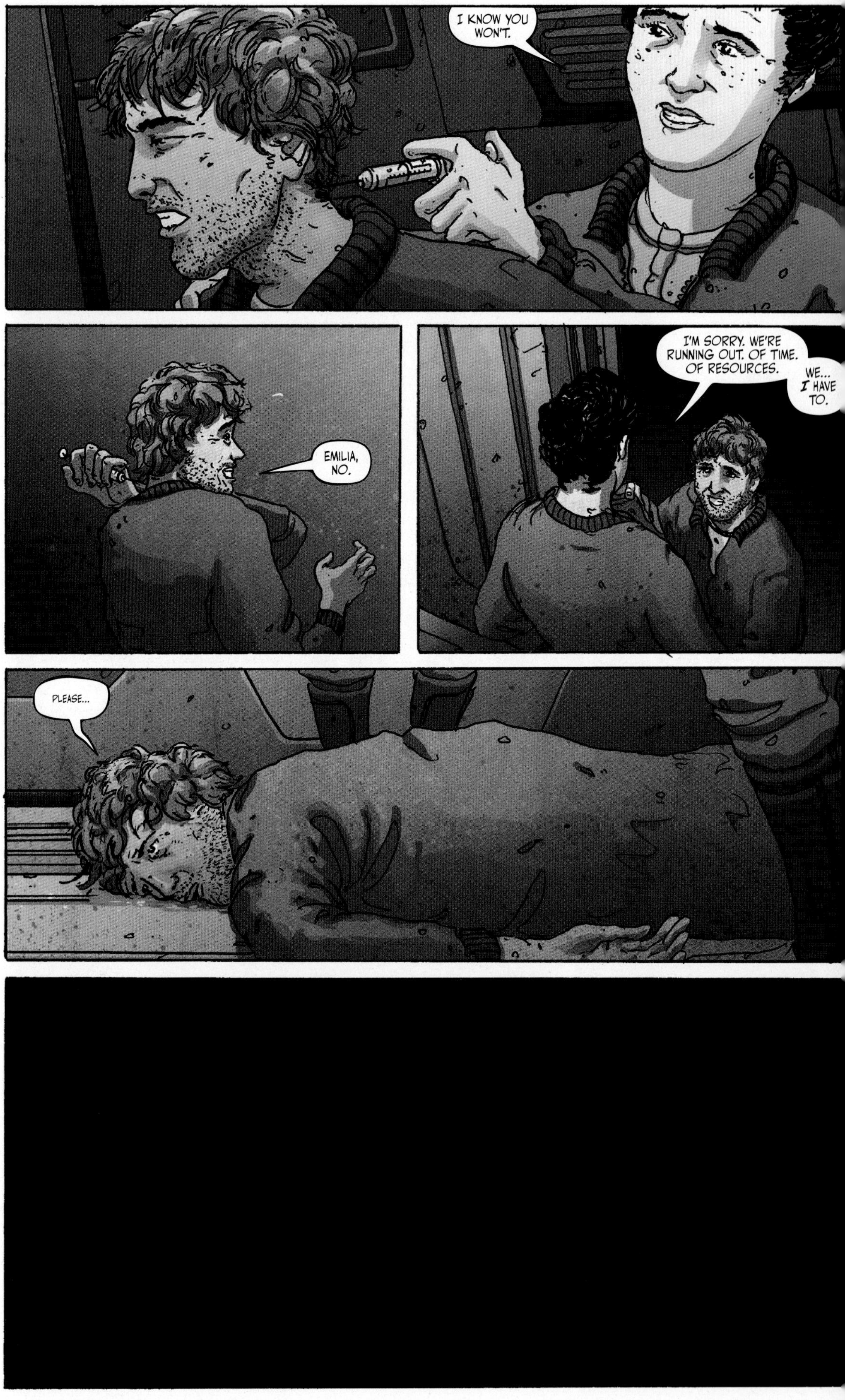
I KNOW YOU WON'T.
EMILIA, NO.
I'M SORRY. WE'RE RUNNING OUT. OF TIME. OF RESOURCES.
WE... I HAVE TO.
PLEASE...

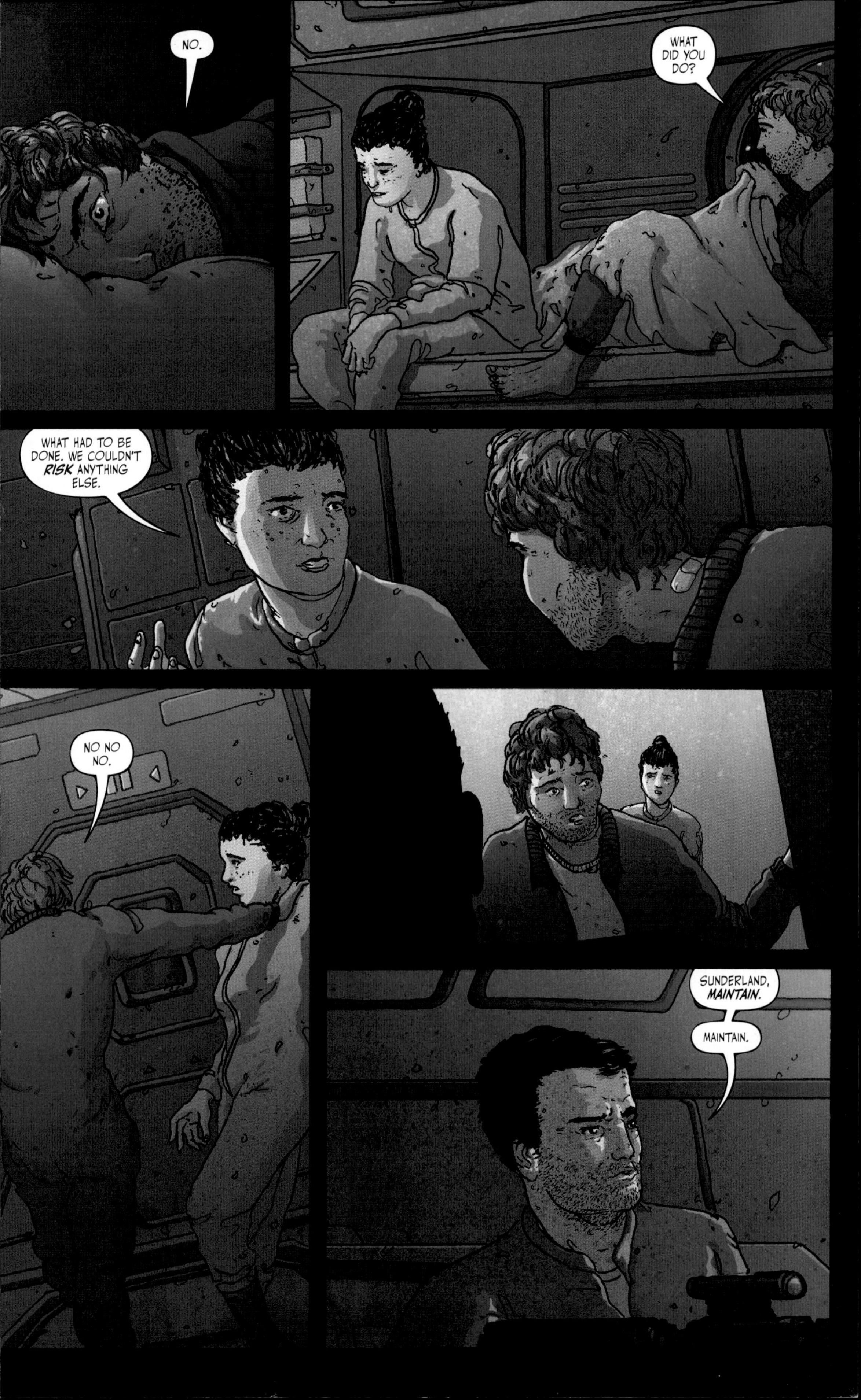
NO.
WHAT DID YOU DO?
WHAT HAD TO BE DONE. WE COULDN'T RISK ANYTHING ELSE.
NO NO NO.
SUNDERLAND, MAINTAIN.
MAINTAIN.

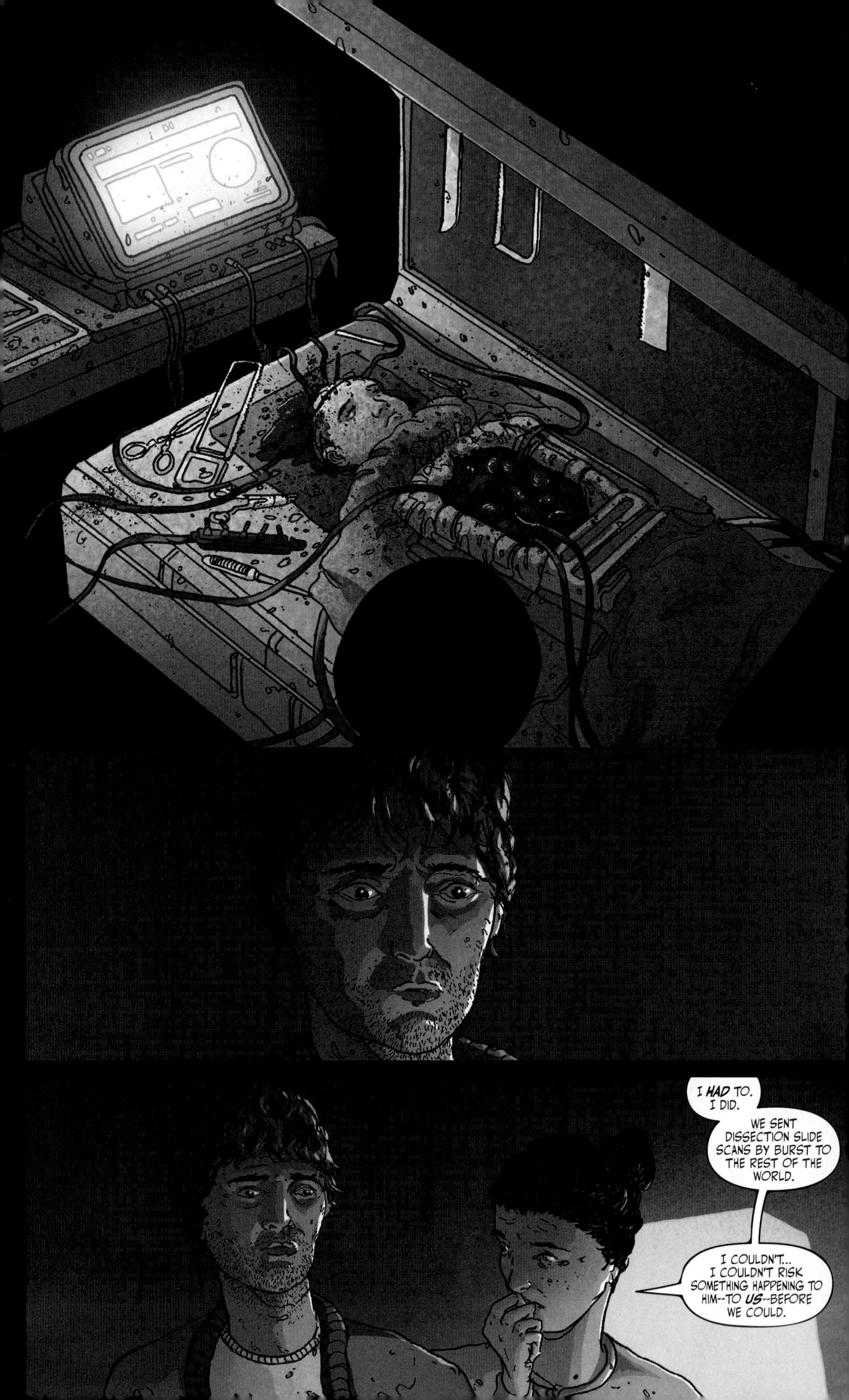
I HAD TO.
I DID.
WE SENT DISSECTION SLIDE SCANS BY BURST TO THE REST OF THE WORLD.
I COULDN'T... I COULDN'T RISK SOMETHING HAPPENING TO HIM--TO US--BEFORE WE COULD.

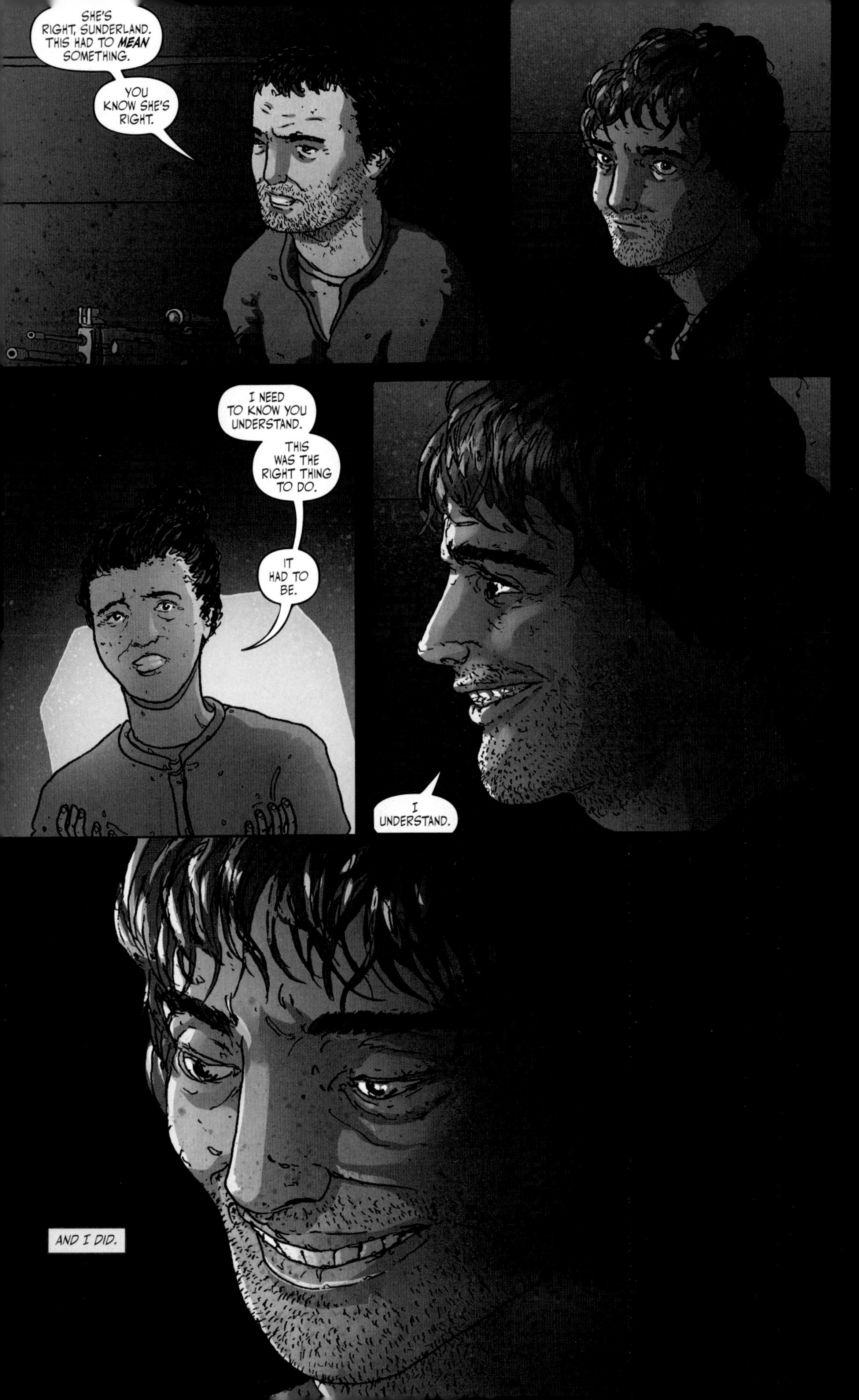

SHE'S RIGHT, SUNDERLAND. THIS HAD TO *MEAN* SOMETHING.
YOU KNOW SHE'S RIGHT.
I NEED TO KNOW YOU UNDERSTAND.
THIS WAS THE RIGHT THING TO DO.
IT HAD TO BE.
I UNDERSTAND.
AND I DID.

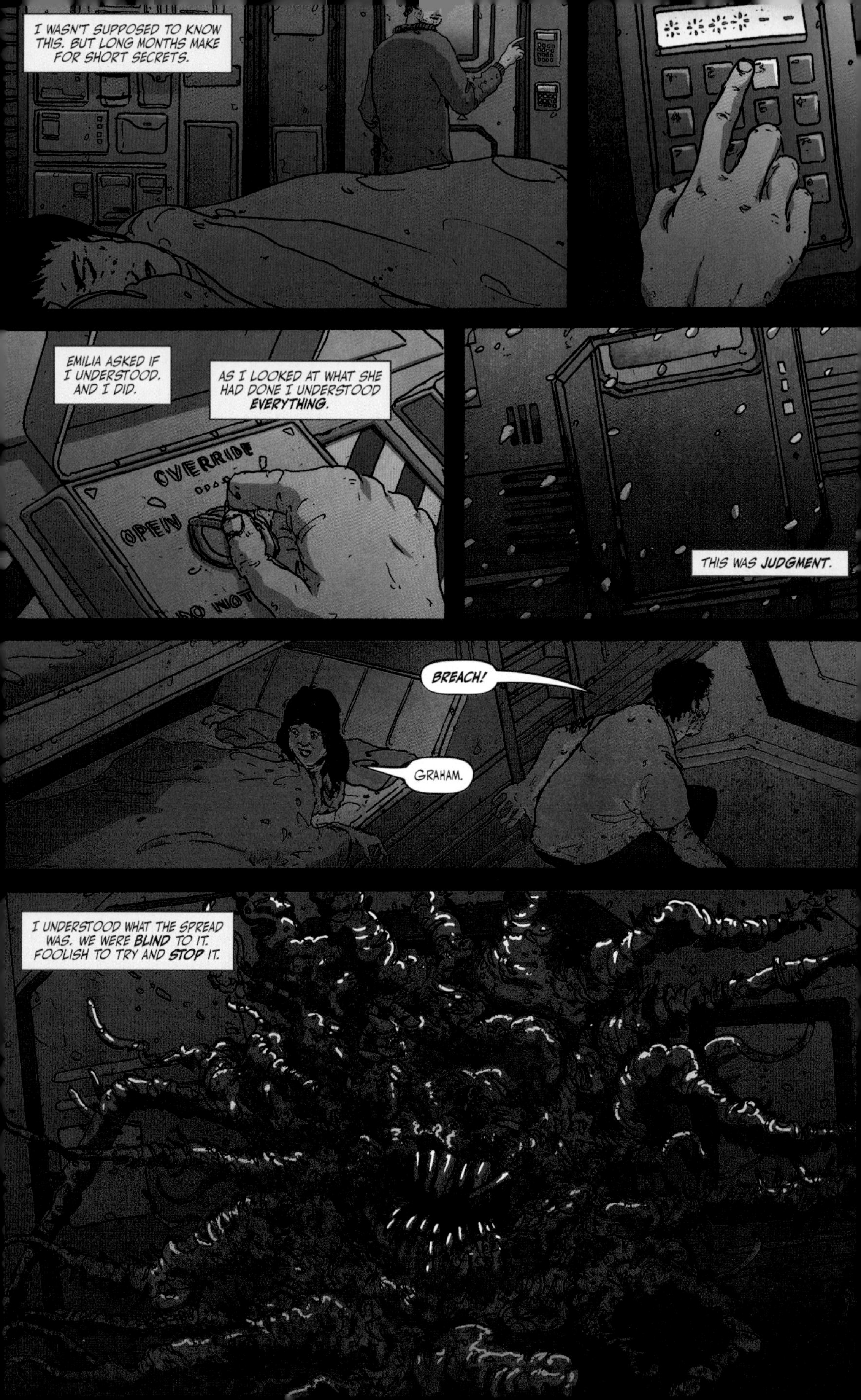
I WASN'T SUPPOSED TO KNOW THIS. BUT LONG MONTHS MAKE FOR SHORT SECRETS.
EMILIA ASKED IF I UNDERSTOOD. AND I DID.
AS I LOOKED AT WHAT SHE HAD DONE I UNDERSTOOD EVERYTHING.
OVERRIDE
OPEN
DO NOT
THIS WAS JUDGMENT.
BREACH!
GRAHAM.
I UNDERSTOOD WHAT THE SPREAD WAS. WE WERE BLIND TO IT. FOOLISH TO TRY AND STOP IT.

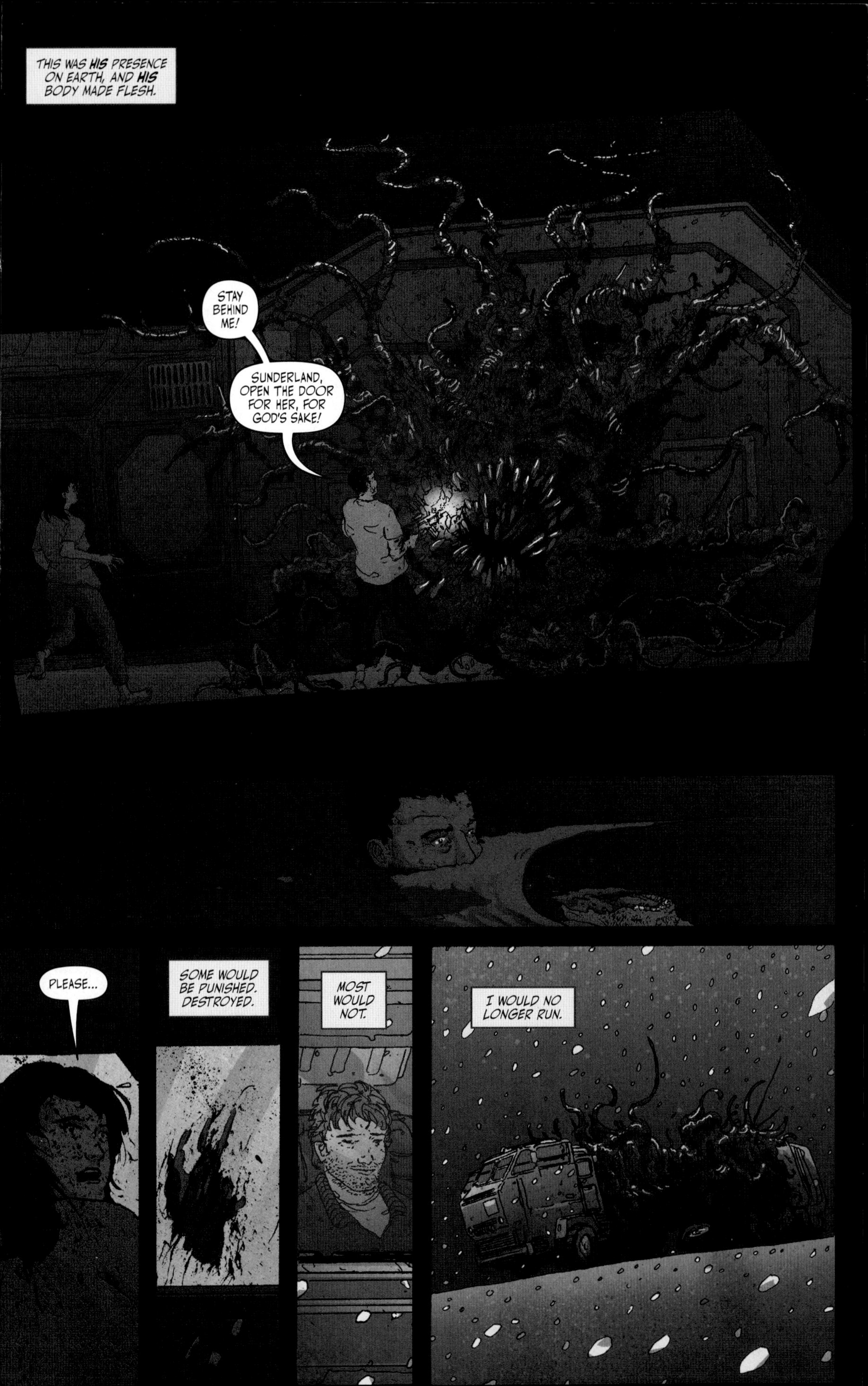
THIS WAS HIS PRESENCE ON EARTH, AND HIS BODY MADE FLESH.
STAY BEHIND ME!
SUNDERLAND, OPEN THE DOOR FOR HER, FOR GOD'S SAKE!
PLEASE...
SOME WOULD BE PUNISHED. DESTROYED.
MOST WOULD NOT.
I WOULD NO LONGER RUN.

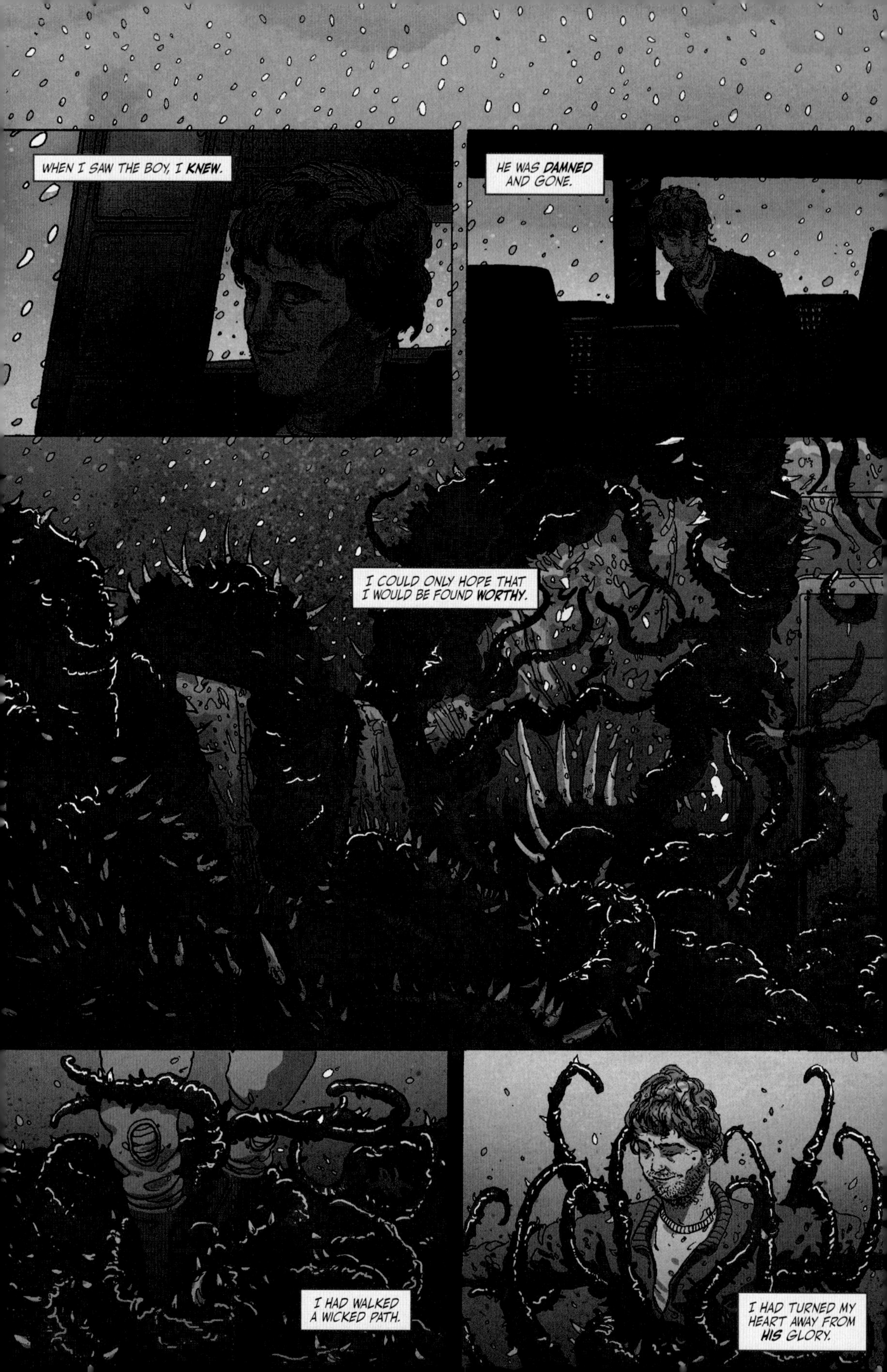
WHEN I SAW THE BOY, I KNEW.
HE WAS DAMNED AND GONE.
I COULD ONLY HOPE THAT I WOULD BE FOUND WORTHY.
I HAD WALKED A WICKED PATH.
I HAD TURNED MY HEART AWAY FROM HIS GLORY.

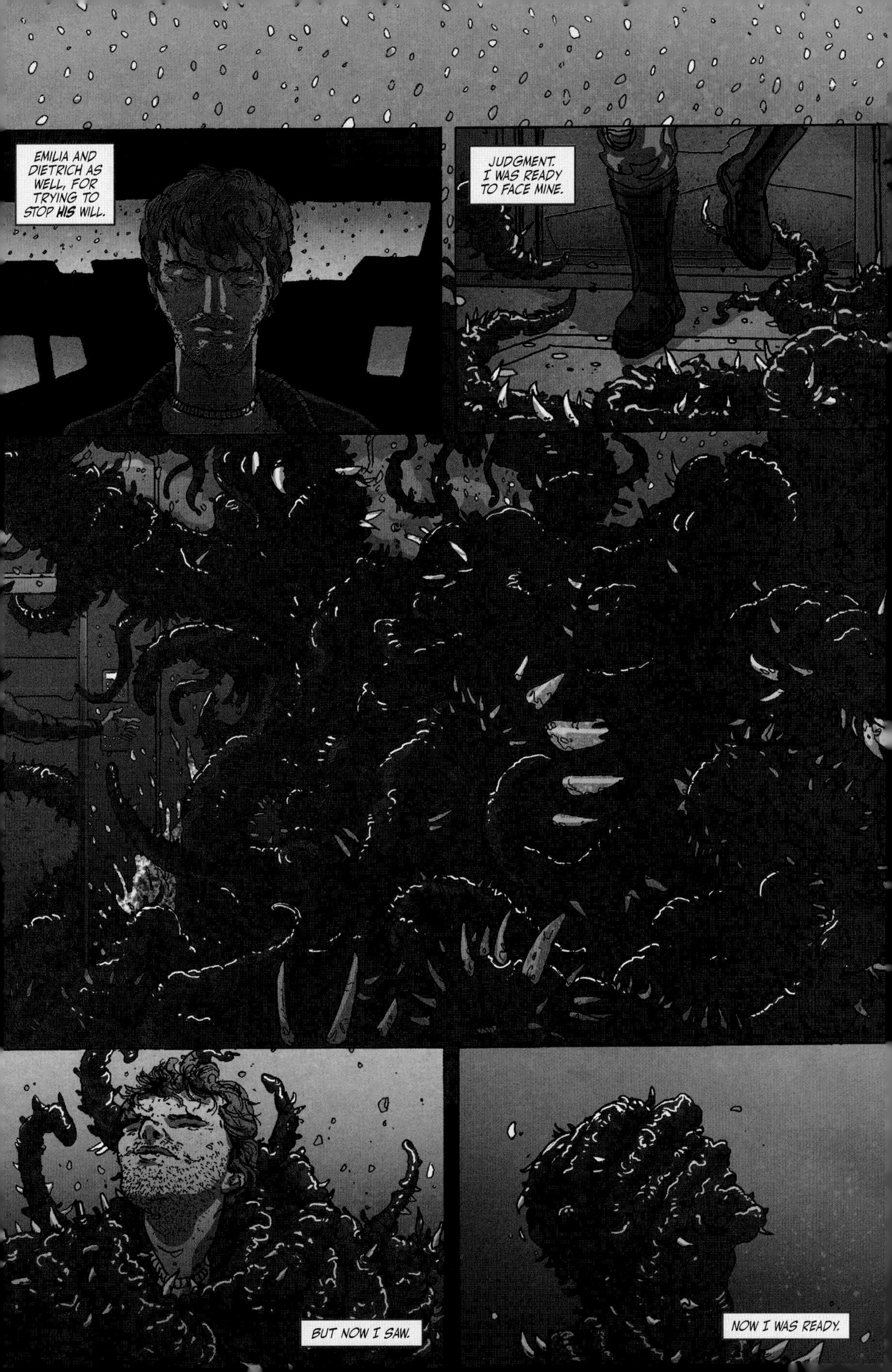
EMILIA AND DIETRICH AS WELL, FOR TRYING TO STOP HIS WILL.
JUDGMENT. I WAS READY TO FACE MINE.
BUT NOW I SAW.
NOW I WAS READY.

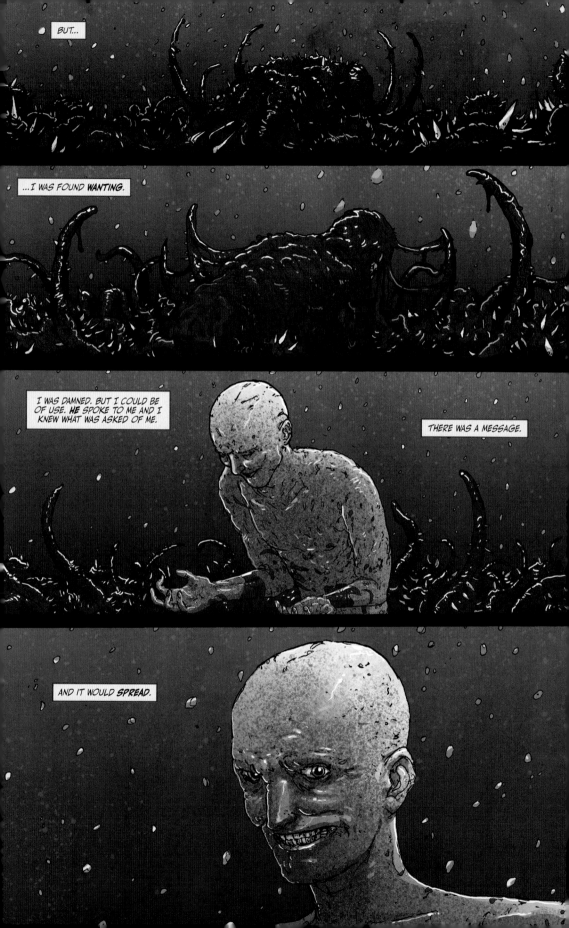

BUT...

...I WAS FOUND **WANTING.**

I WAS DAMNED. BUT I COULD BE OF USE. **HE** SPOKE TO ME AND I KNEW WHAT WAS ASKED OF ME.

THERE WAS A MESSAGE.

AND IT WOULD **SPREAD.**

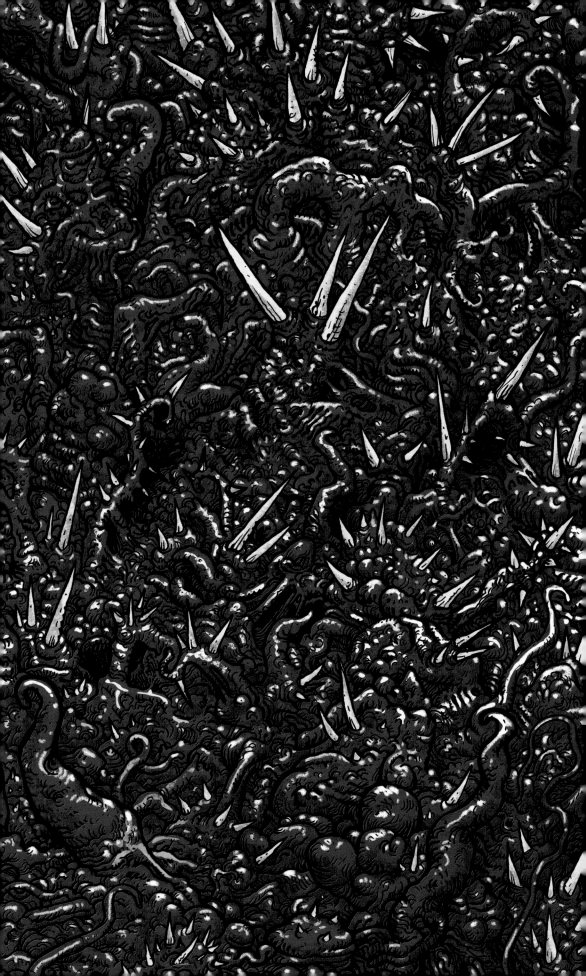

CHAPTER TWO

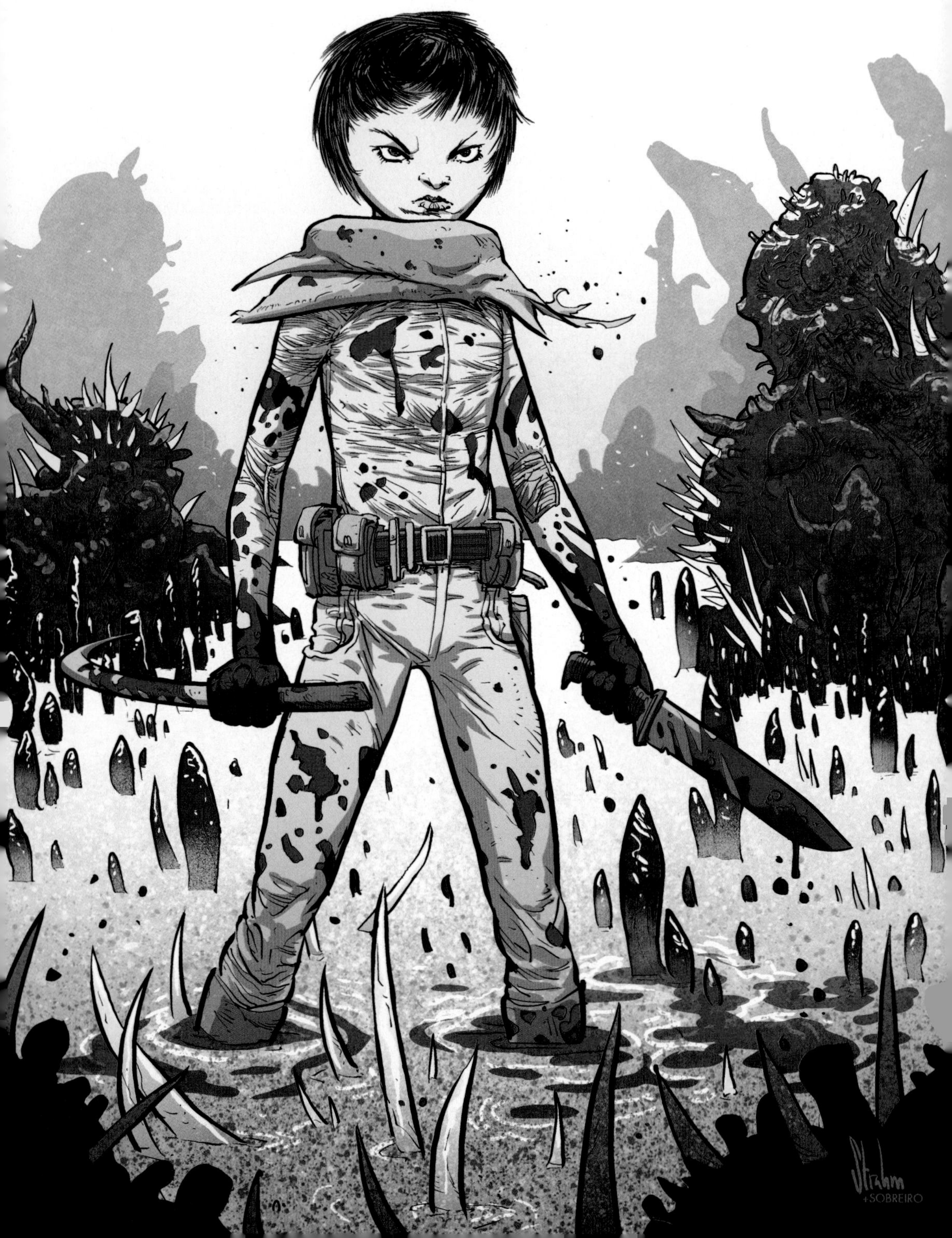

+SOBREIRO

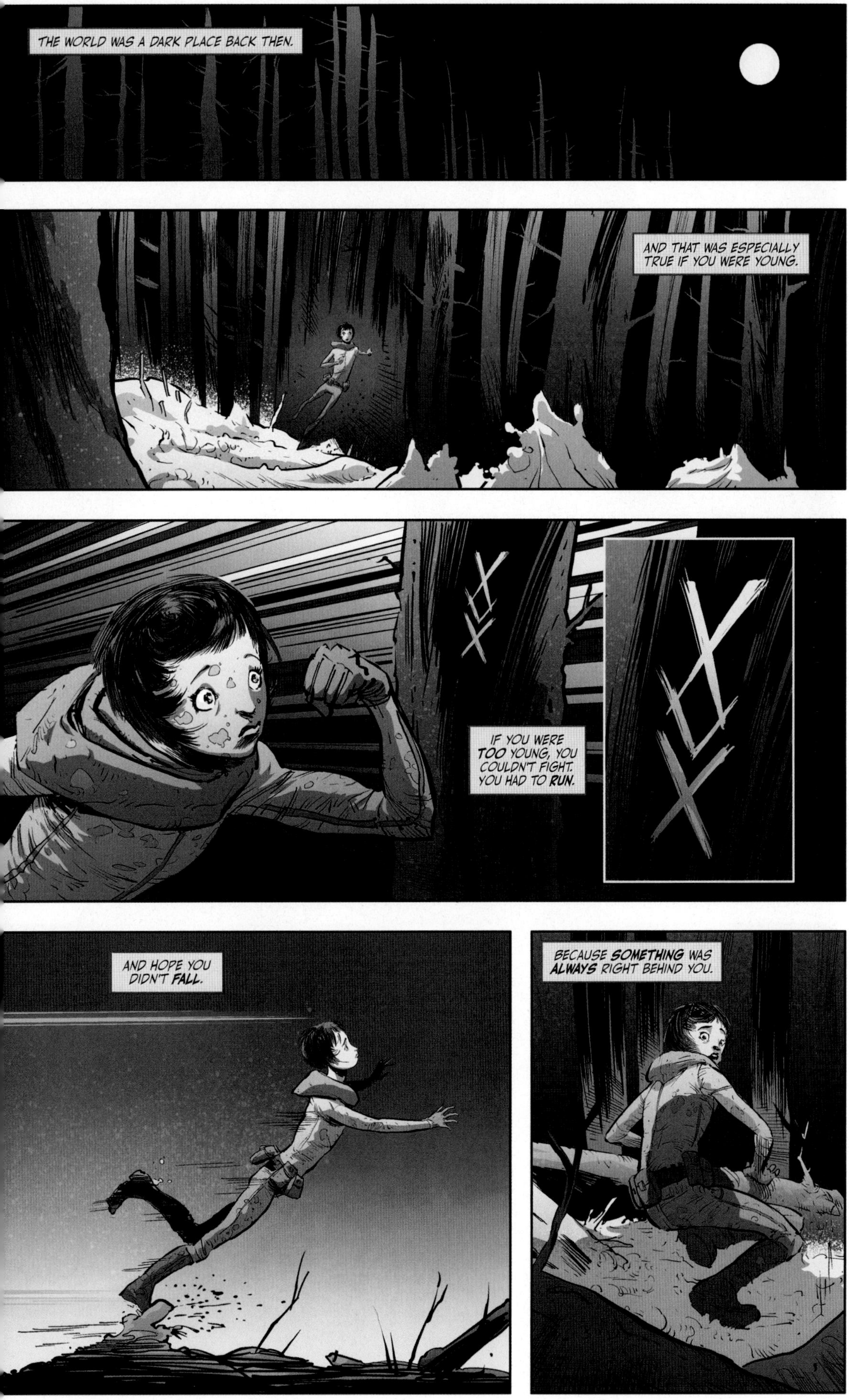
THE WORLD WAS A DARK PLACE BACK THEN.
AND THAT WAS ESPECIALLY TRUE IF YOU WERE YOUNG.
IF YOU WERE TOO YOUNG, YOU COULDN'T FIGHT. YOU HAD TO RUN.
AND HOPE YOU DIDN'T FALL.
BECAUSE SOMETHING WAS ALWAYS RIGHT BEHIND YOU.

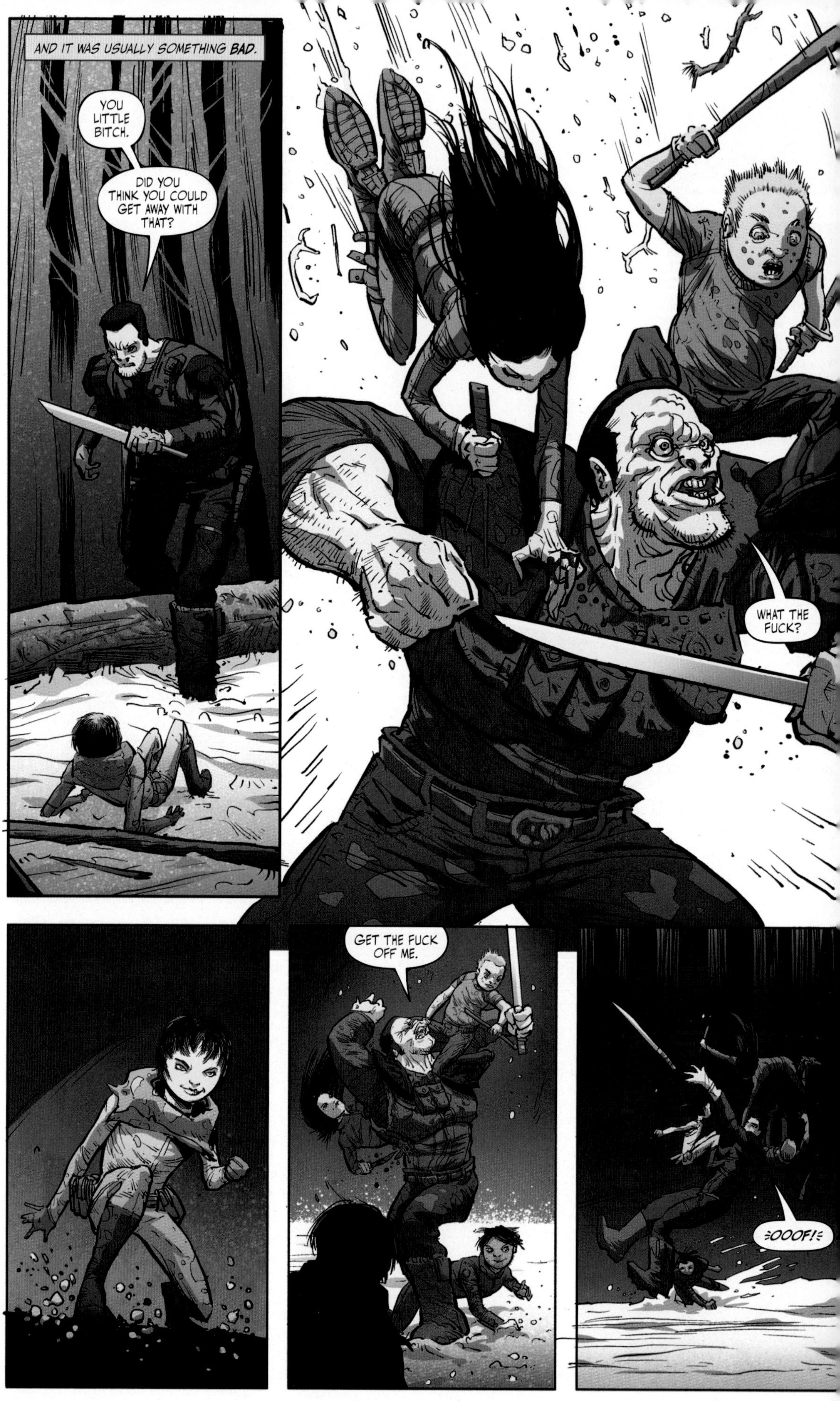

AND IT WAS USUALLY SOMETHING BAD.
YOU LITTLE BITCH.
DID YOU THINK YOU COULD GET AWAY WITH THAT?
WHAT THE FUCK?
GET THE FUCK OFF ME.
OOOF!

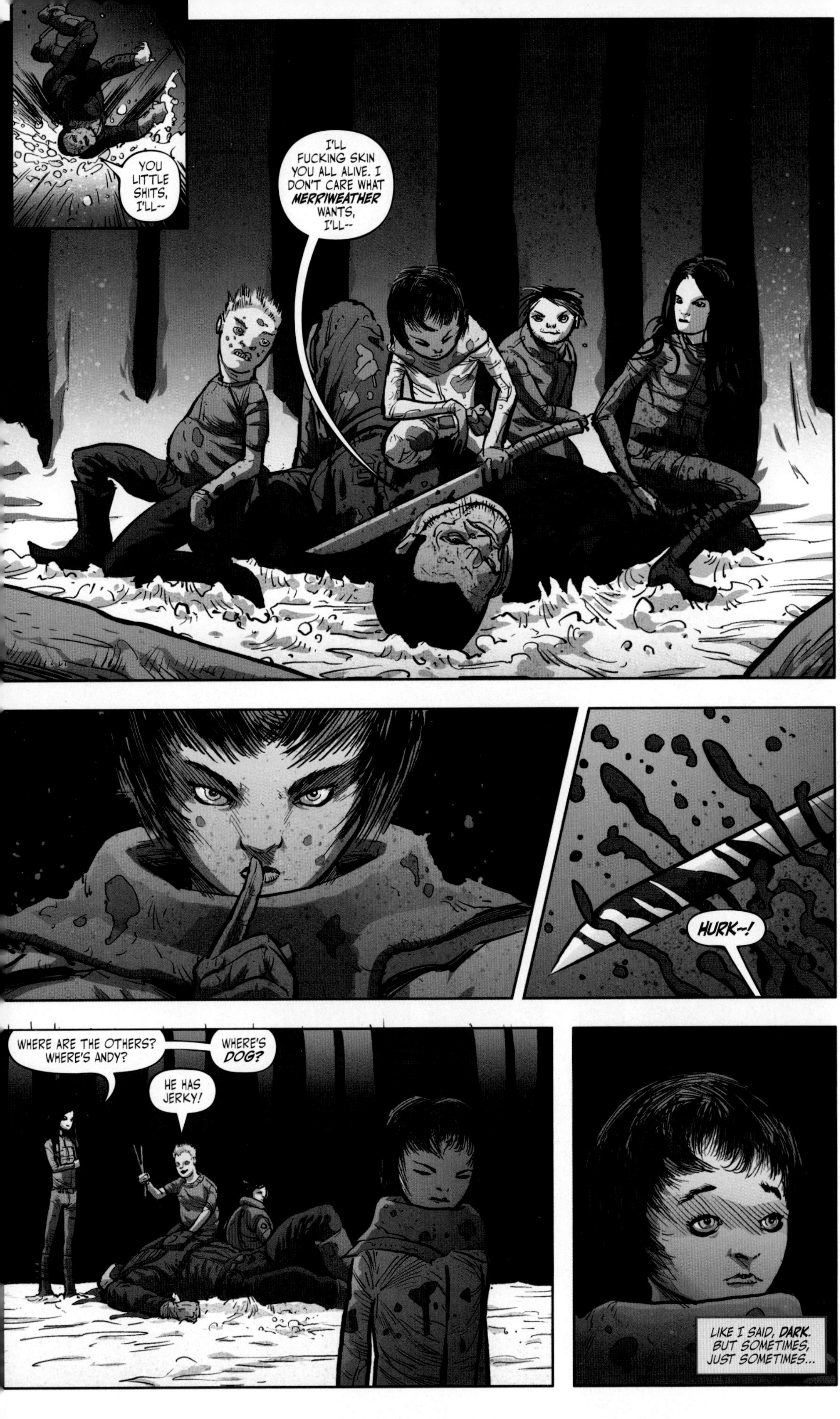
YOU LITTLE SHITS, I'LL--
I'LL FUCKING SKIN YOU ALL ALIVE. I DON'T CARE WHAT MERRIWEATHER WANTS, I'LL--
HURK--!
WHERE ARE THE OTHERS? WHERE'S ANDY?
WHERE'S DOG?
HE HAS JERKY!
LIKE I SAID, DARK. BUT SOMETIMES, JUST SOMETIMES...

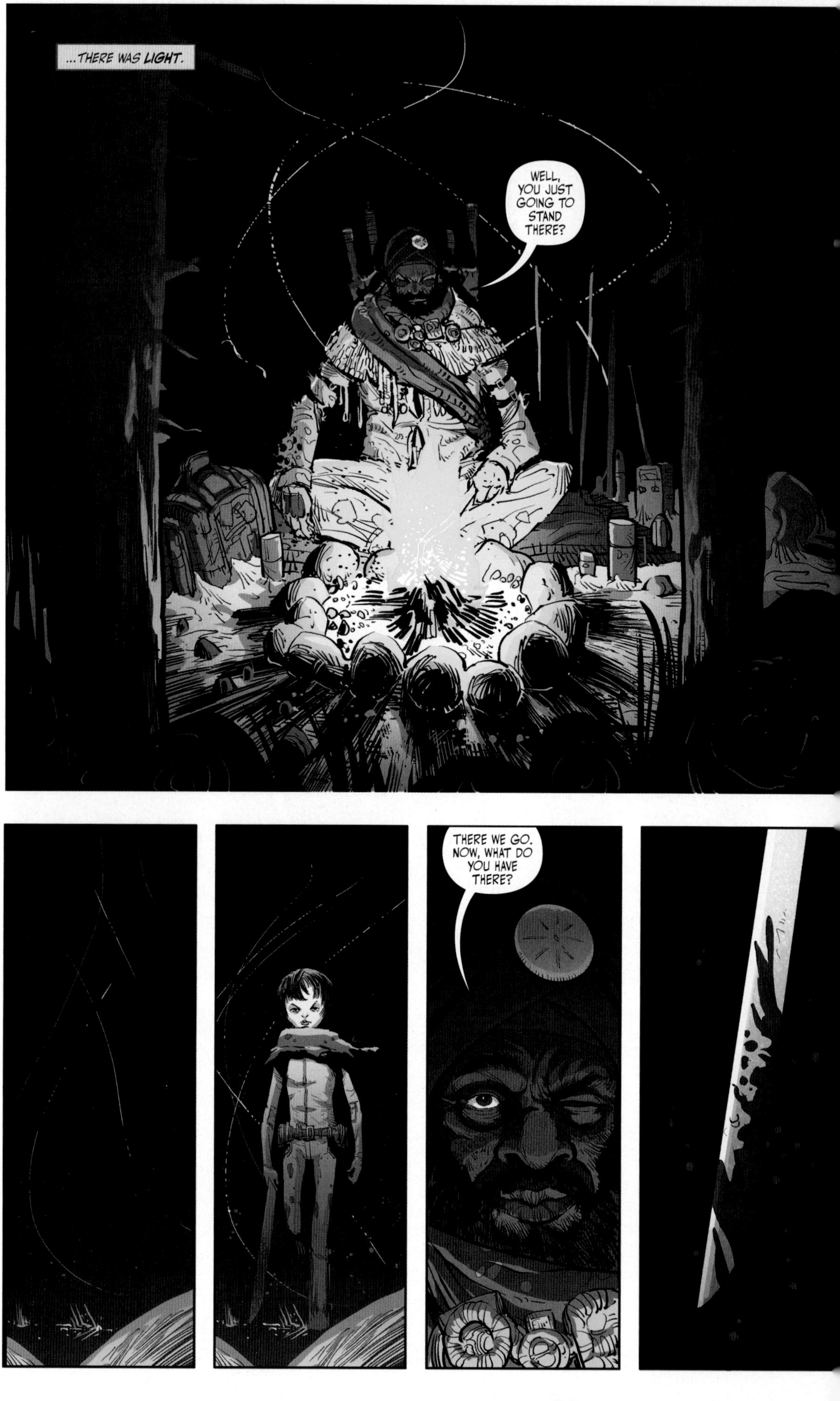
...THERE WAS LIGHT.
WELL, YOU JUST GOING TO STAND THERE?
THERE WE GO. NOW, WHAT DO YOU HAVE THERE?

I SEE.

THIS IS A FINE QUALITY BLADE, VOX.

YOU DID VERY WELL.

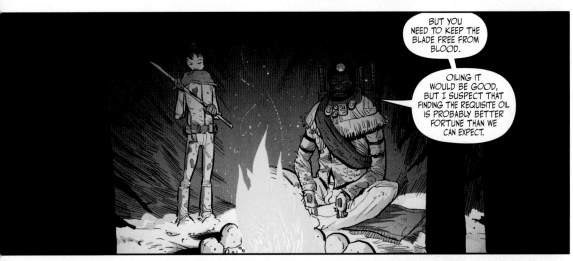

BUT YOU NEED TO KEEP THE BLADE FREE FROM BLOOD.

OILING IT WOULD BE GOOD, BUT I SUSPECT THAT FINDING THE REQUISITE OIL IS PROBABLY BETTER FORTUNE THAN WE CAN EXPECT.

NOW WHAT IS WRONG, CHILD?

WHERE ARE THE OTHERS?

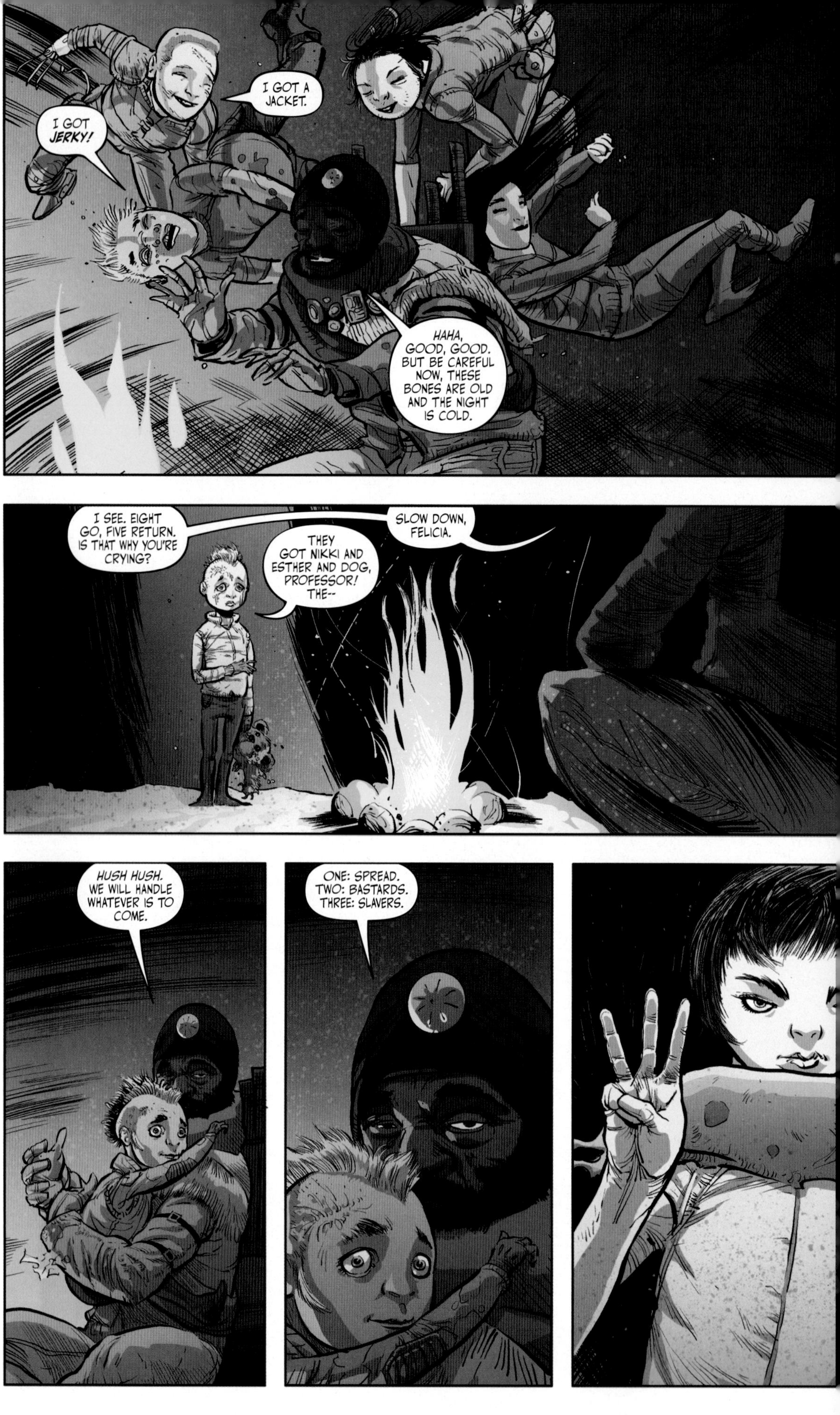
I GOT *JERKY!*
I GOT A JACKET.
HAHA, GOOD, GOOD. BUT BE CAREFUL NOW, THESE BONES ARE OLD AND THE NIGHT IS COLD.
I SEE. EIGHT GO, FIVE RETURN. IS THAT WHY YOU'RE CRYING?
THEY GOT NIKKI AND ESTHER AND DOG, PROFESSOR! THE--
SLOW DOWN, FELICIA.
HUSH HUSH. WE WILL HANDLE WHATEVER IS TO COME.
ONE: SPREAD. TWO: BASTARDS. THREE: SLAVERS.

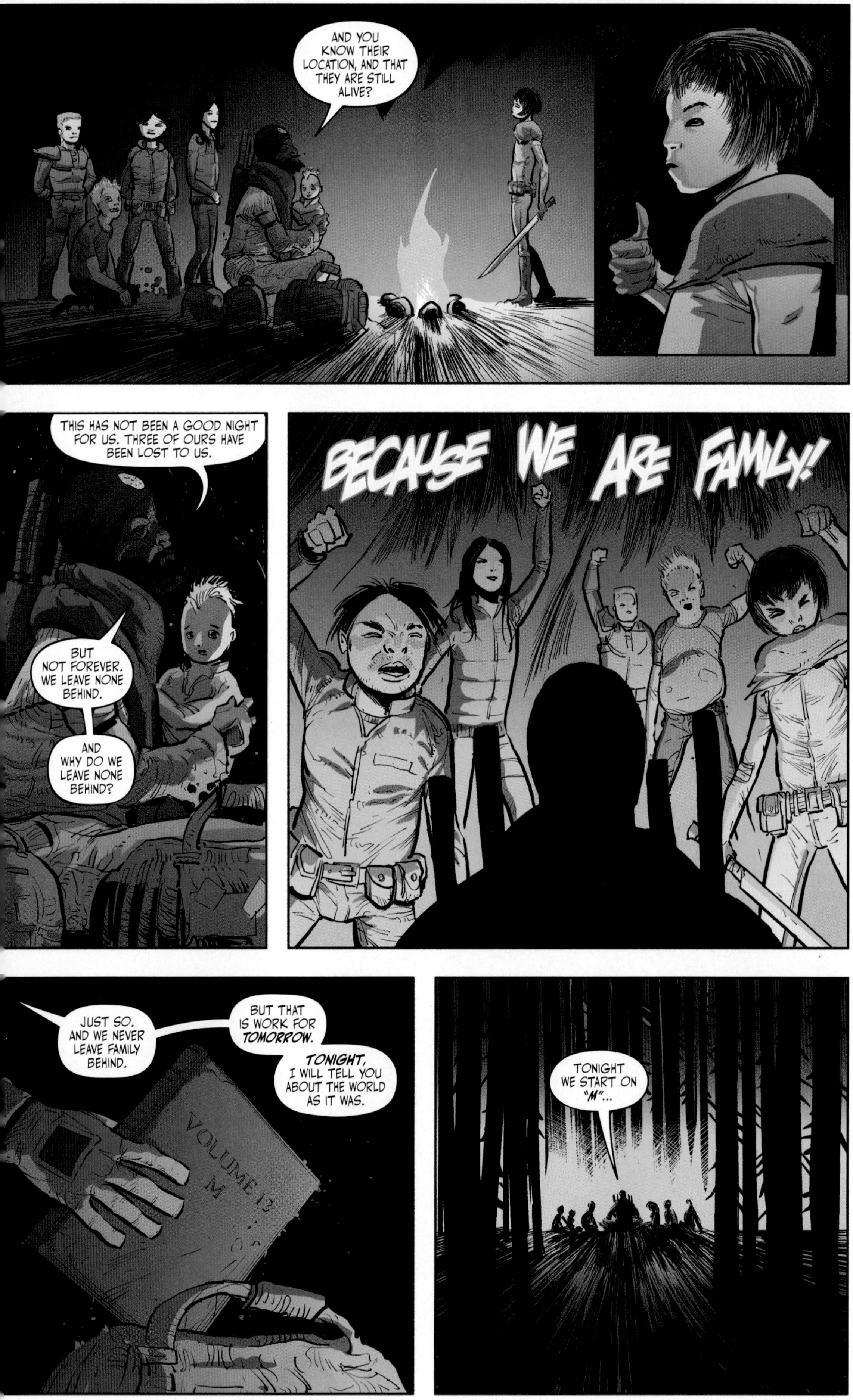
AND YOU KNOW THEIR LOCATION, AND THAT THEY ARE STILL ALIVE?
THIS HAS NOT BEEN A GOOD NIGHT FOR US. THREE OF OURS HAVE BEEN LOST TO US.
BUT NOT FOREVER. WE LEAVE NONE BEHIND.
AND WHY DO WE LEAVE NONE BEHIND?
BECAUSE WE ARE FAMILY!
JUST SO. AND WE NEVER LEAVE FAMILY BEHIND.
BUT THAT IS WORK FOR TOMORROW.
TONIGHT, I WILL TELL YOU ABOUT THE WORLD AS IT WAS.
VOLUME 13 M
TONIGHT WE START ON "M"...

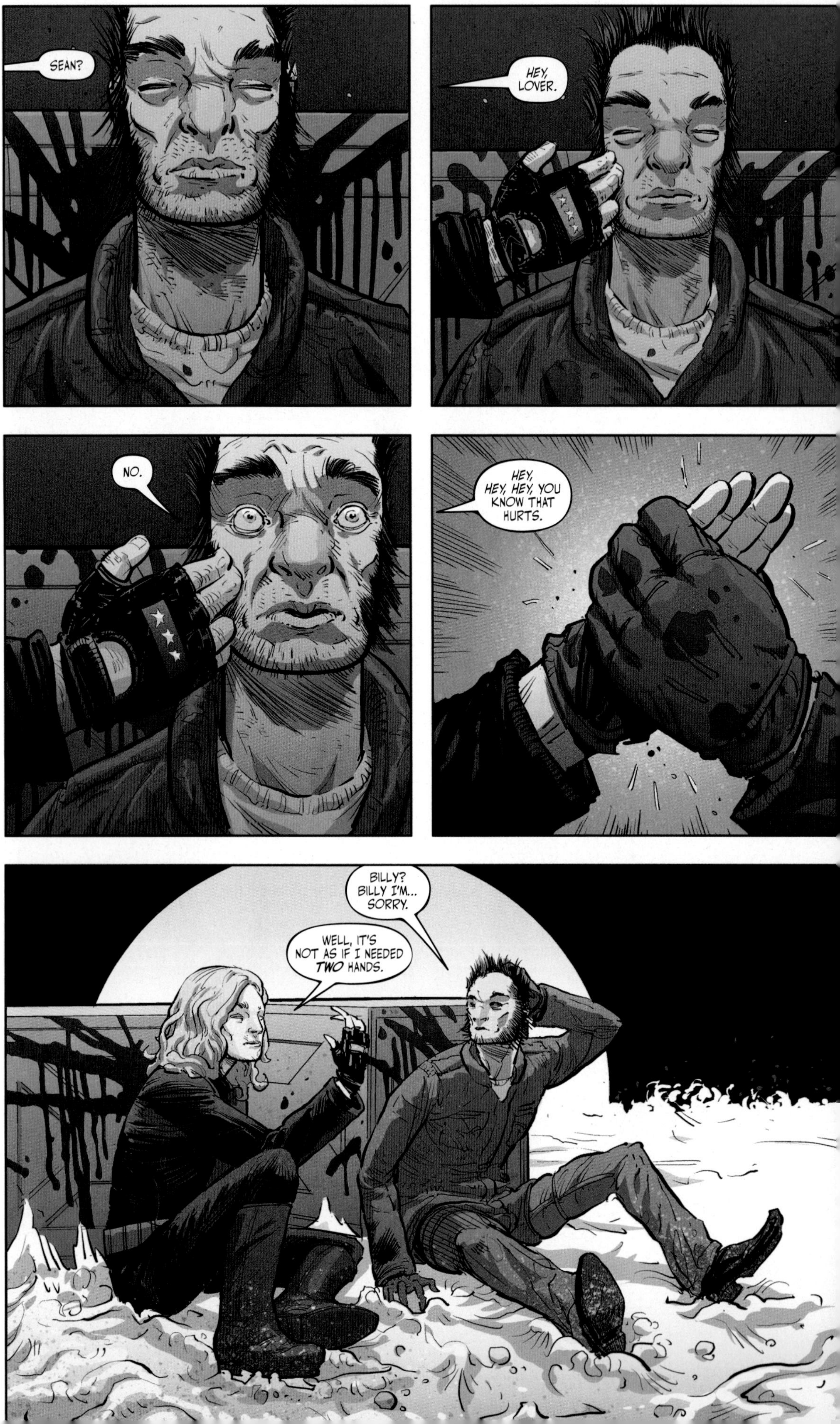
SEAN?
HEY, LOVER.
NO.
HEY, HEY, HEY, YOU KNOW THAT HURTS.
BILLY? BILLY I'M... SORRY.
WELL, IT'S NOT AS IF I NEEDED *TWO* HANDS.

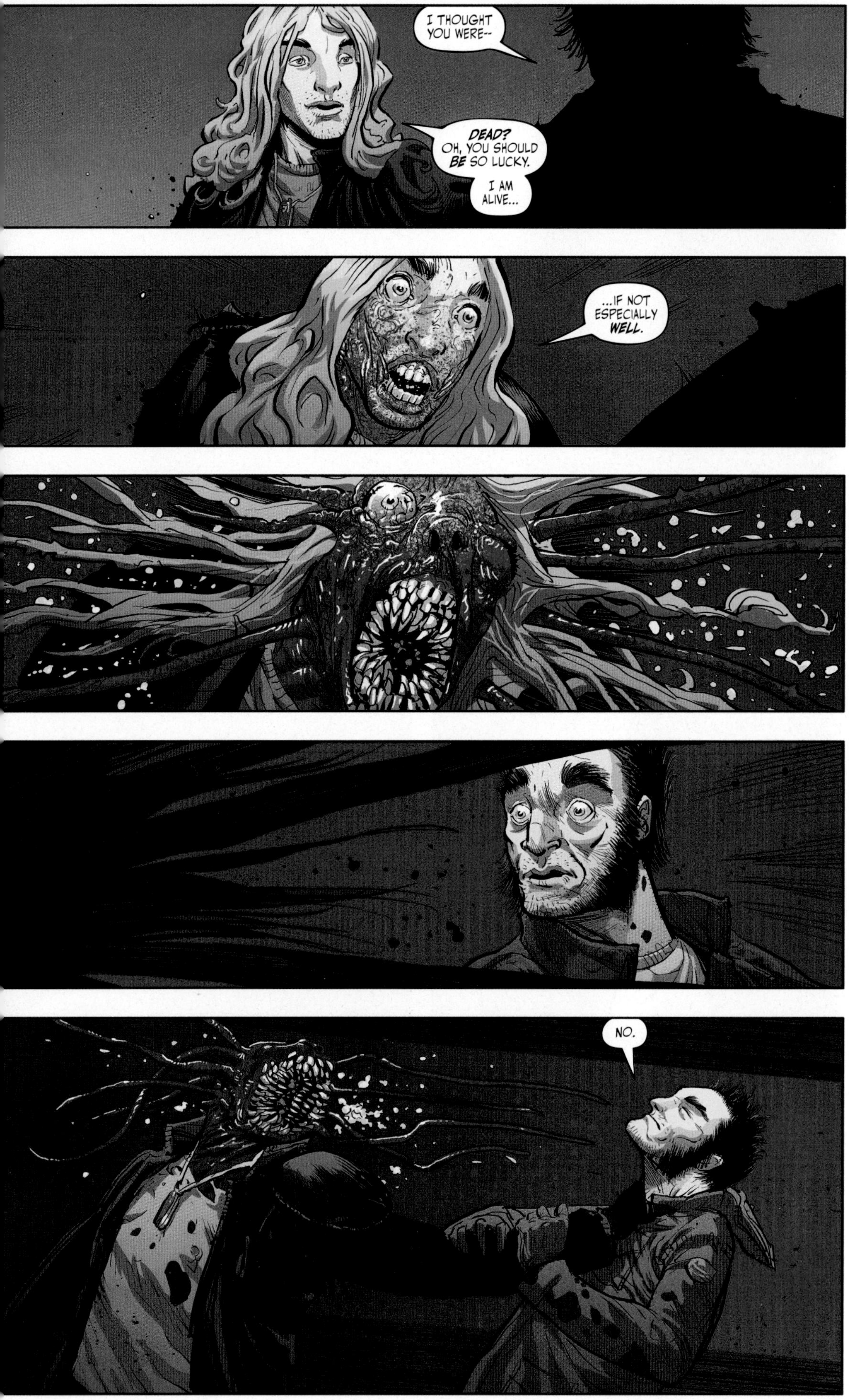
I THOUGHT YOU WERE--
DEAD? OH, YOU SHOULD BE SO LUCKY.
I AM ALIVE...
...IF NOT ESPECIALLY WELL.
NO.

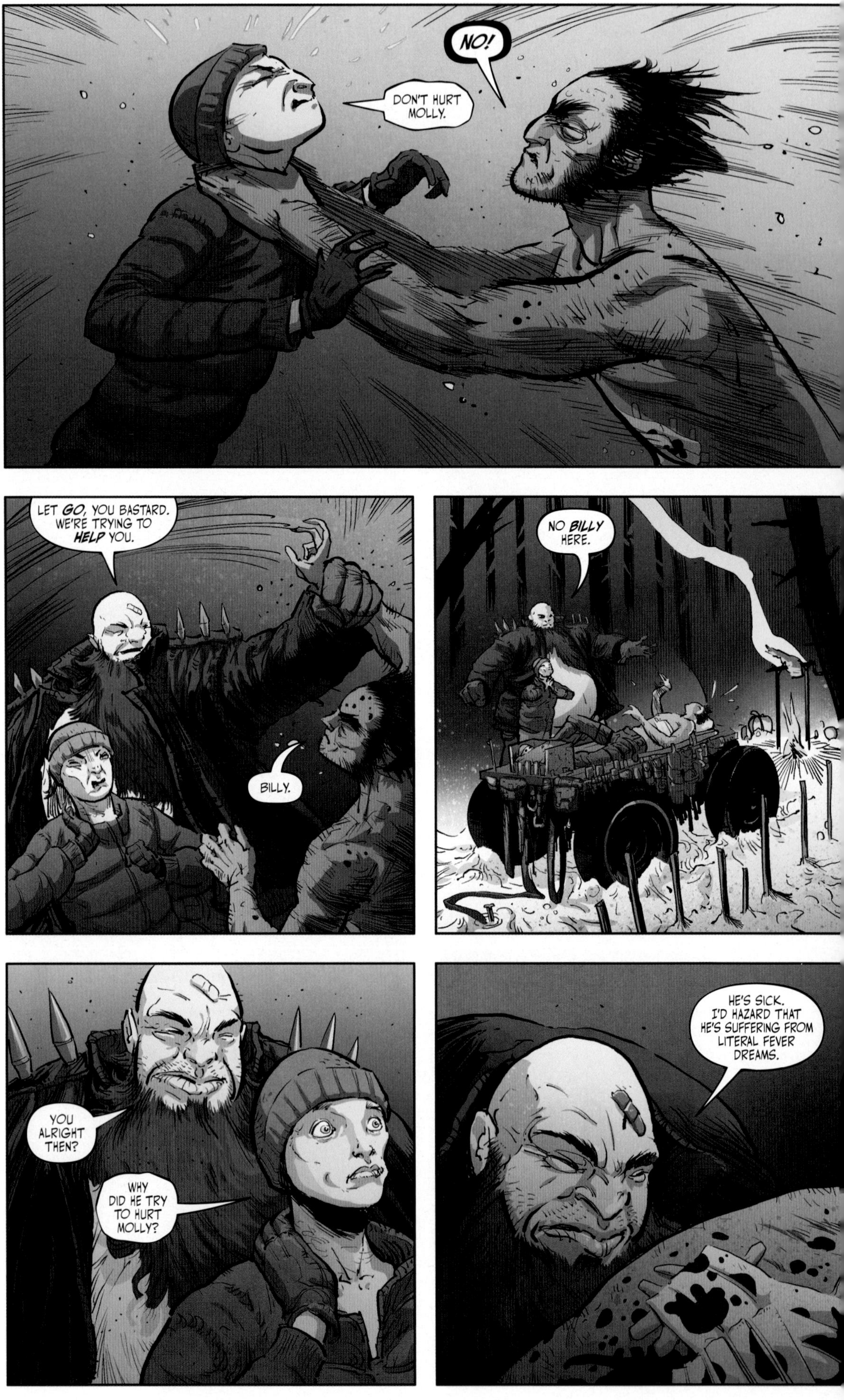

DON'T HURT MOLLY.
NO!
LET GO, YOU BASTARD. WE'RE TRYING TO HELP YOU.
BILLY.
NO BILLY HERE.
YOU ALRIGHT THEN?
WHY DID HE TRY TO HURT MOLLY?
HE'S SICK. I'D HAZARD THAT HE'S SUFFERING FROM LITERAL FEVER DREAMS.

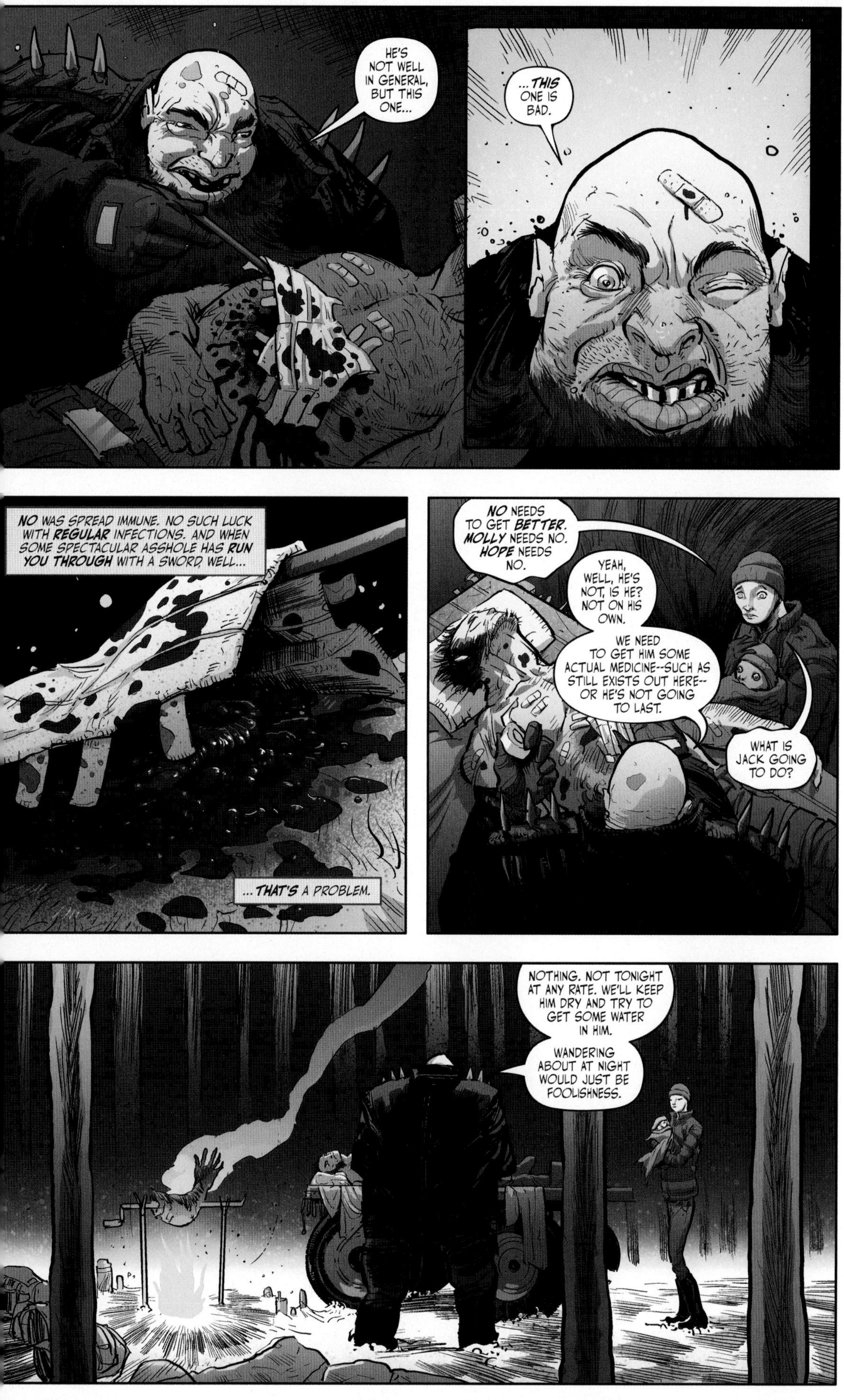

HE'S NOT WELL IN GENERAL, BUT THIS ONE...
...THIS ONE IS BAD.
NO WAS SPREAD IMMUNE. NO SUCH LUCK WITH REGULAR INFECTIONS. AND WHEN SOME SPECTACULAR ASSHOLE HAS RUN YOU THROUGH WITH A SWORD, WELL...
...THAT'S A PROBLEM.
NO NEEDS TO GET BETTER. MOLLY NEEDS NO. HOPE NEEDS NO.
YEAH, WELL, HE'S NOT, IS HE? NOT ON HIS OWN.
WE NEED TO GET HIM SOME ACTUAL MEDICINE--SUCH AS STILL EXISTS OUT HERE--OR HE'S NOT GOING TO LAST.
WHAT IS JACK GOING TO DO?
NOTHING. NOT TONIGHT AT ANY RATE. WE'LL KEEP HIM DRY AND TRY TO GET SOME WATER IN HIM.
WANDERING ABOUT AT NIGHT WOULD JUST BE FOOLISHNESS.

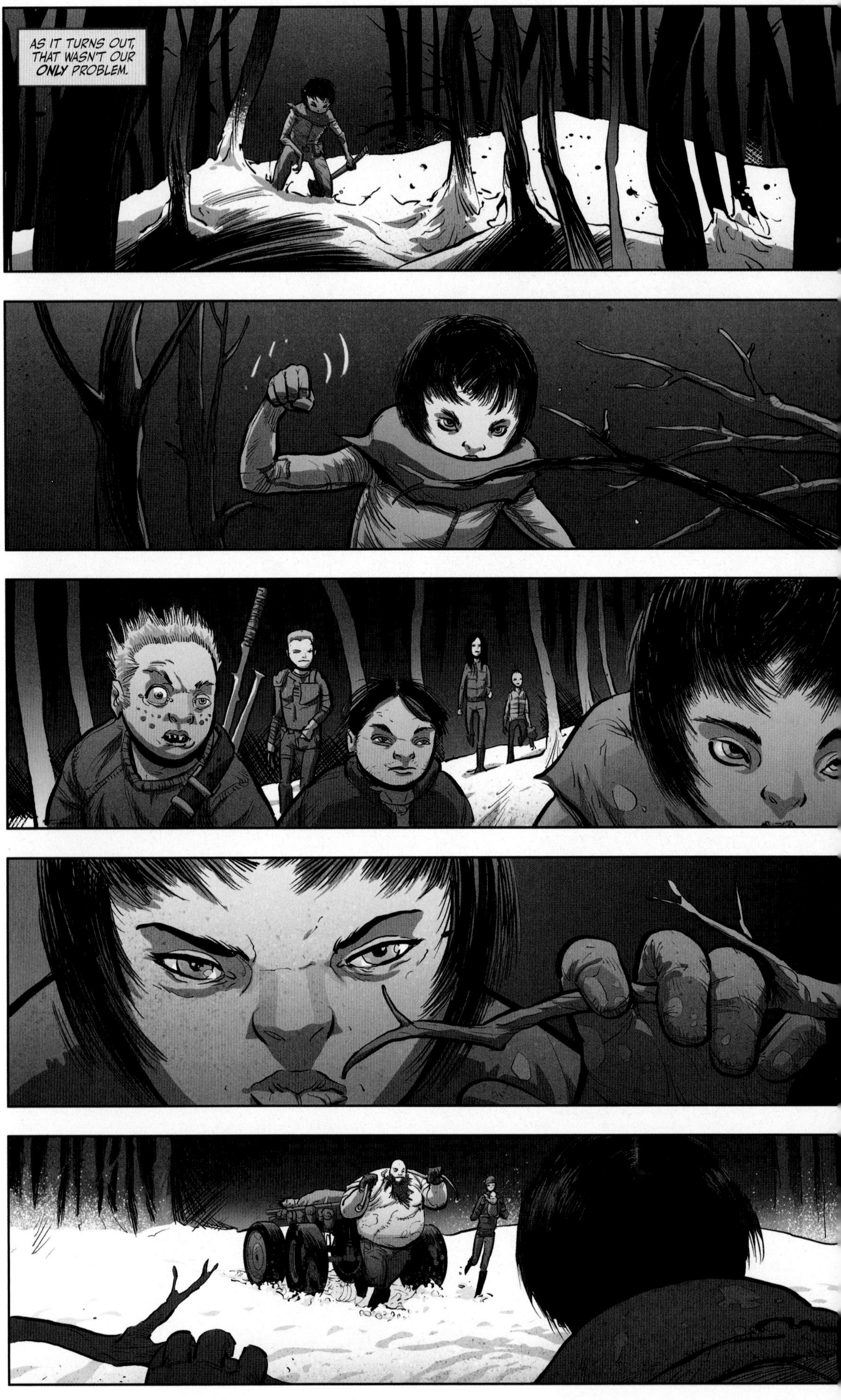
AS IT TURNS OUT, THAT WASN'T OUR ONLY PROBLEM.

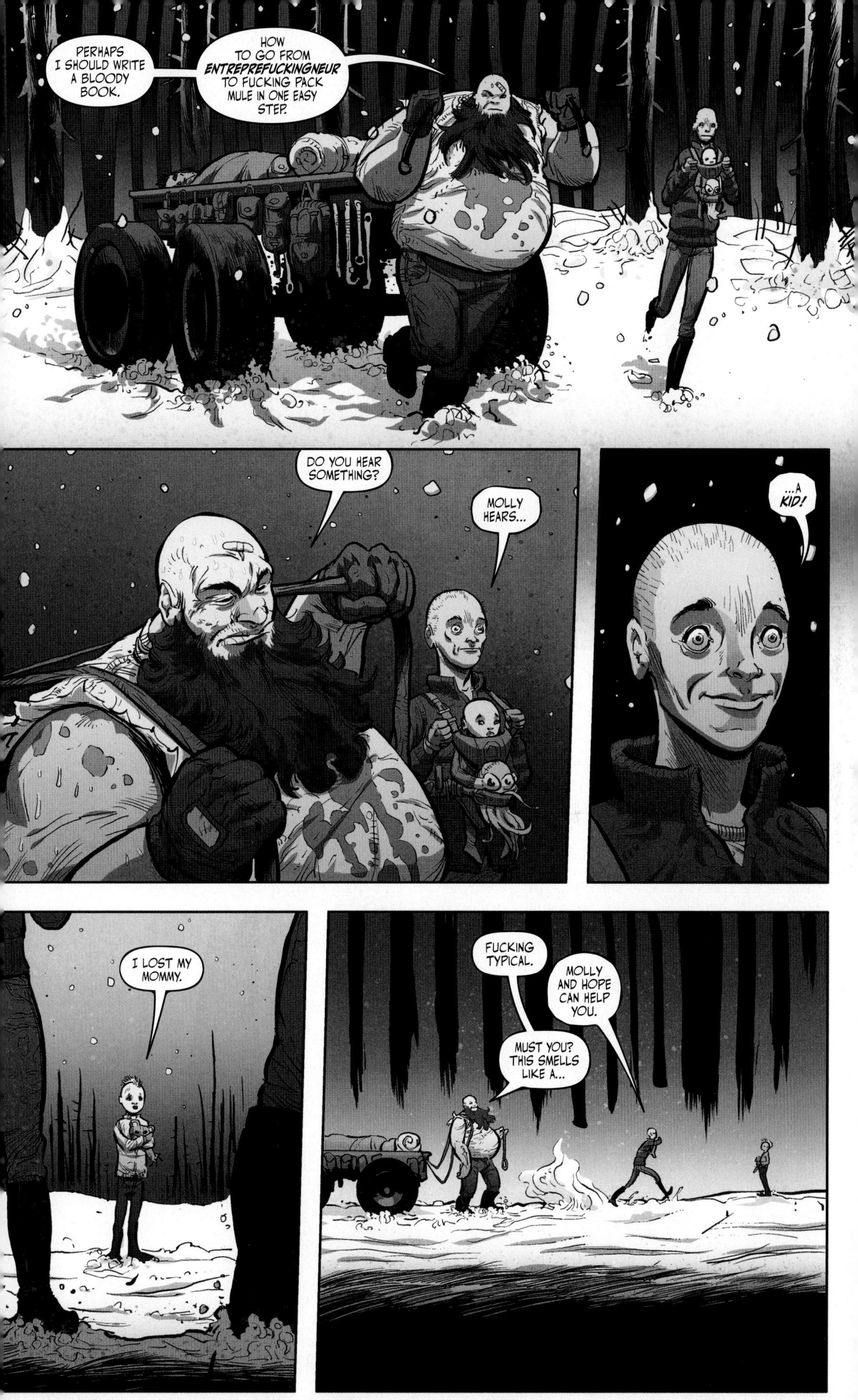

PERHAPS I SHOULD WRITE A BLOODY BOOK.
HOW TO GO FROM ENTREPREFUCKINGNEUR TO FUCKING PACK MULE IN ONE EASY STEP.
DO YOU HEAR SOMETHING?
MOLLY HEARS...
...A KID!
I LOST MY MOMMY.
FUCKING TYPICAL.
MOLLY AND HOPE CAN HELP YOU.
MUST YOU? THIS SMELLS LIKE A...

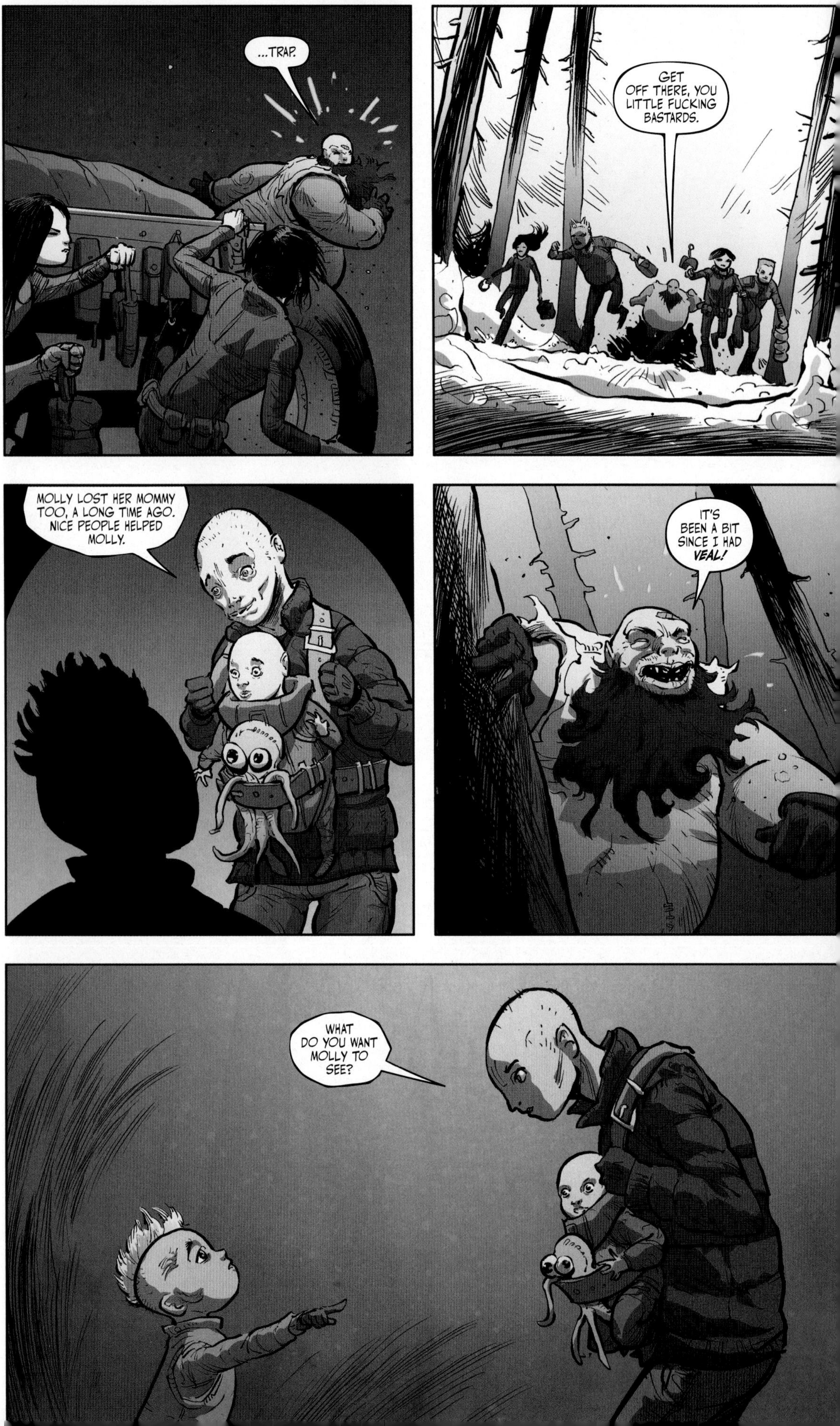
...TRAP.
GET OFF THERE, YOU LITTLE FUCKING BASTARDS.
MOLLY LOST HER MOMMY TOO, A LONG TIME AGO. NICE PEOPLE HELPED MOLLY.
IT'S BEEN A BIT SINCE I HAD VEAL!
WHAT DO YOU WANT MOLLY TO SEE?

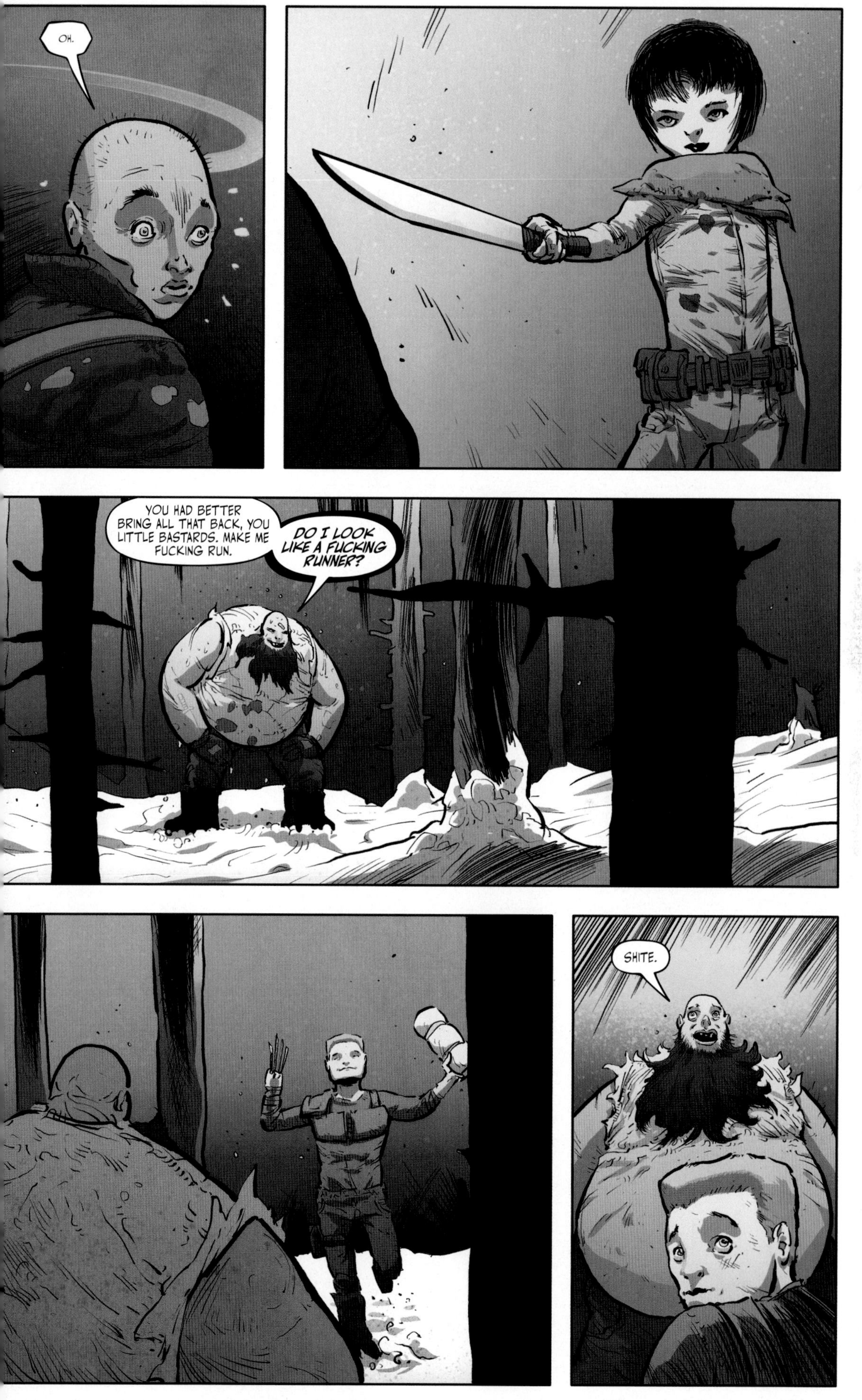
OH.
YOU HAD BETTER BRING ALL THAT BACK, YOU LITTLE BASTARDS. MAKE ME FUCKING RUN.
DO I LOOK LIKE A FUCKING RUNNER?
SHITE.

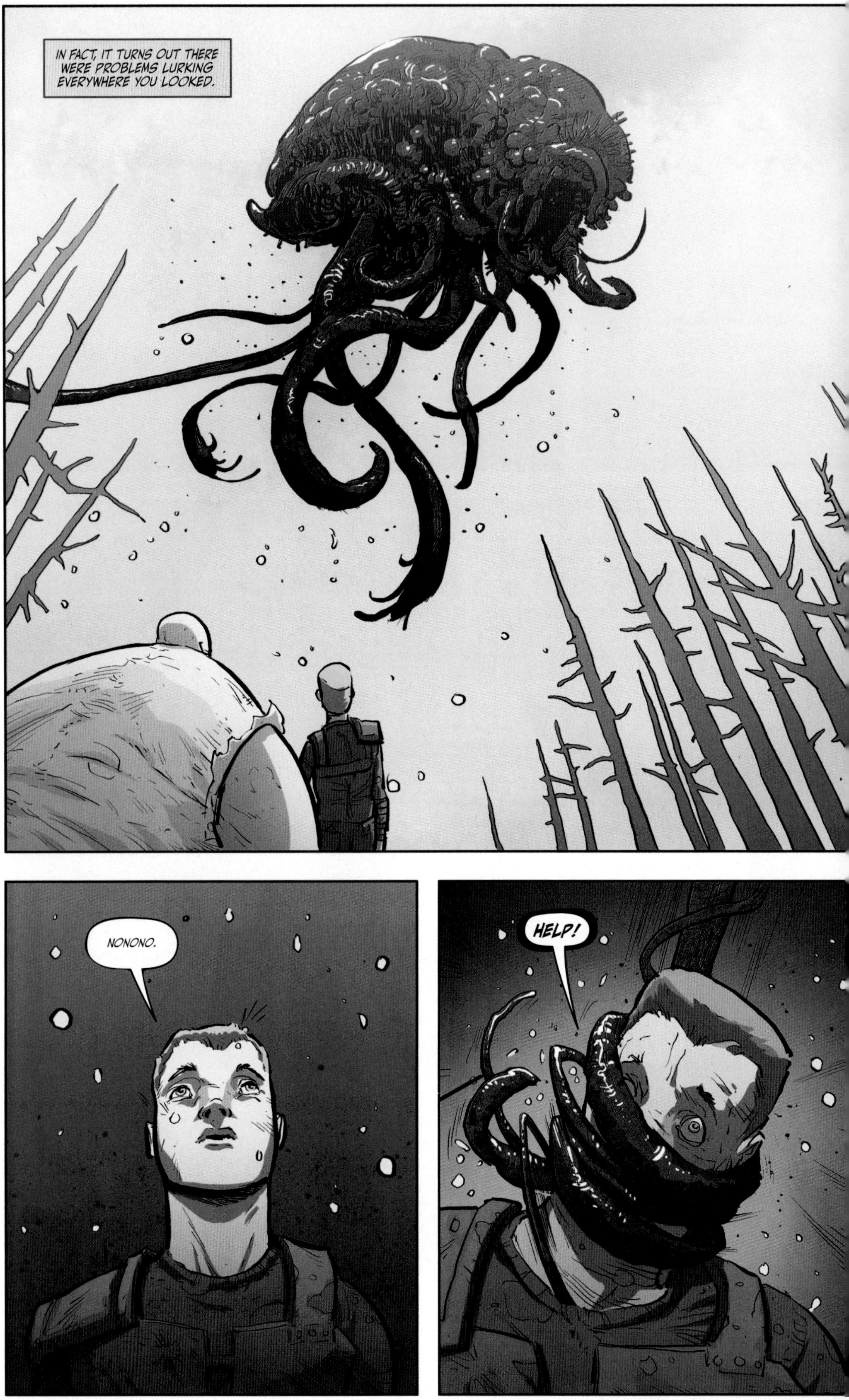
IN FACT, IT TURNS OUT THERE WERE PROBLEMS LURKING EVERYWHERE YOU LOOKED.
NONONO.
HELP!

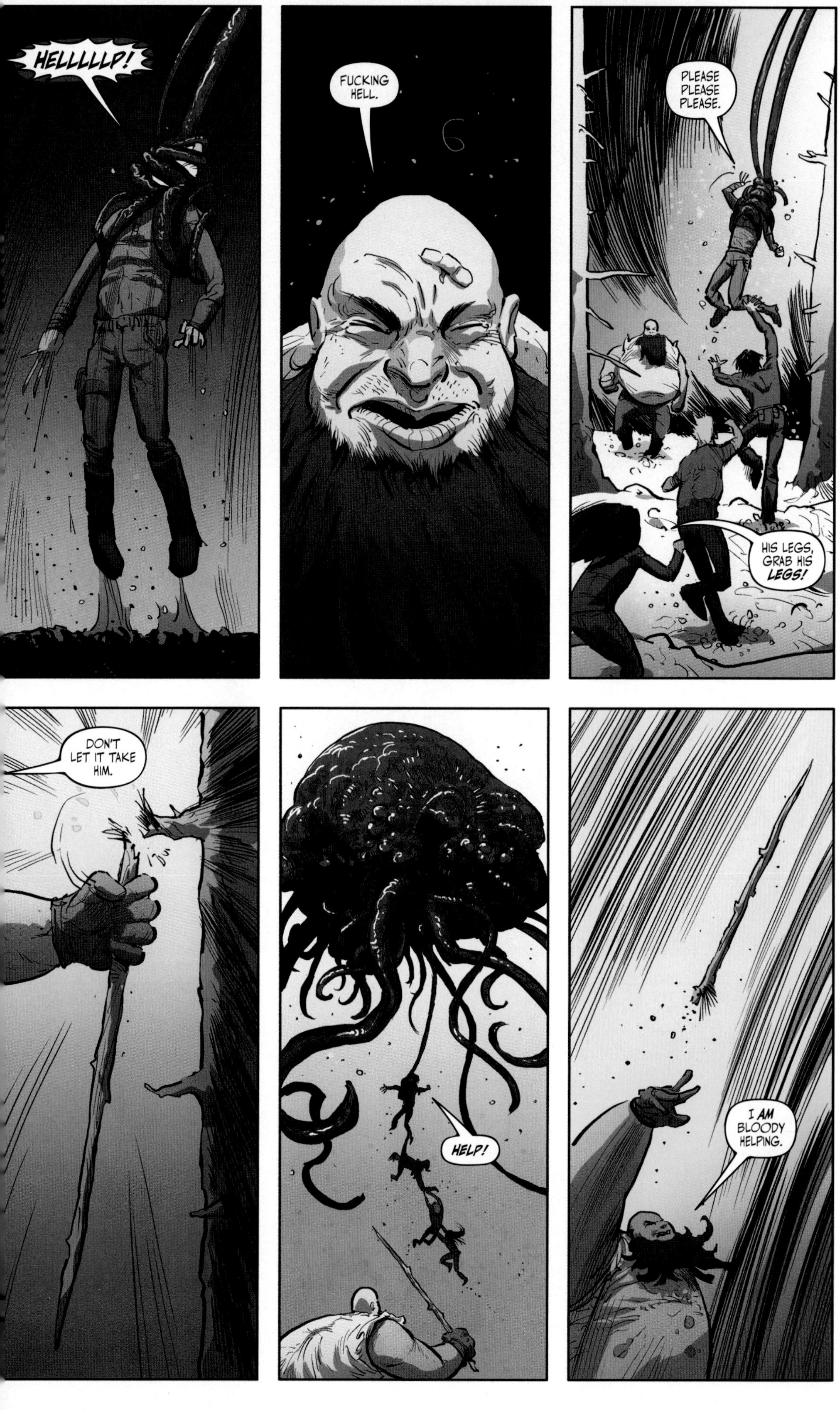
HELLLLLLP!
FUCKING HELL.
PLEASE PLEASE PLEASE.
HIS LEGS, GRAB HIS LEGS!
DON'T LET IT TAKE HIM.
HELP!
I AM BLOODY HELPING.

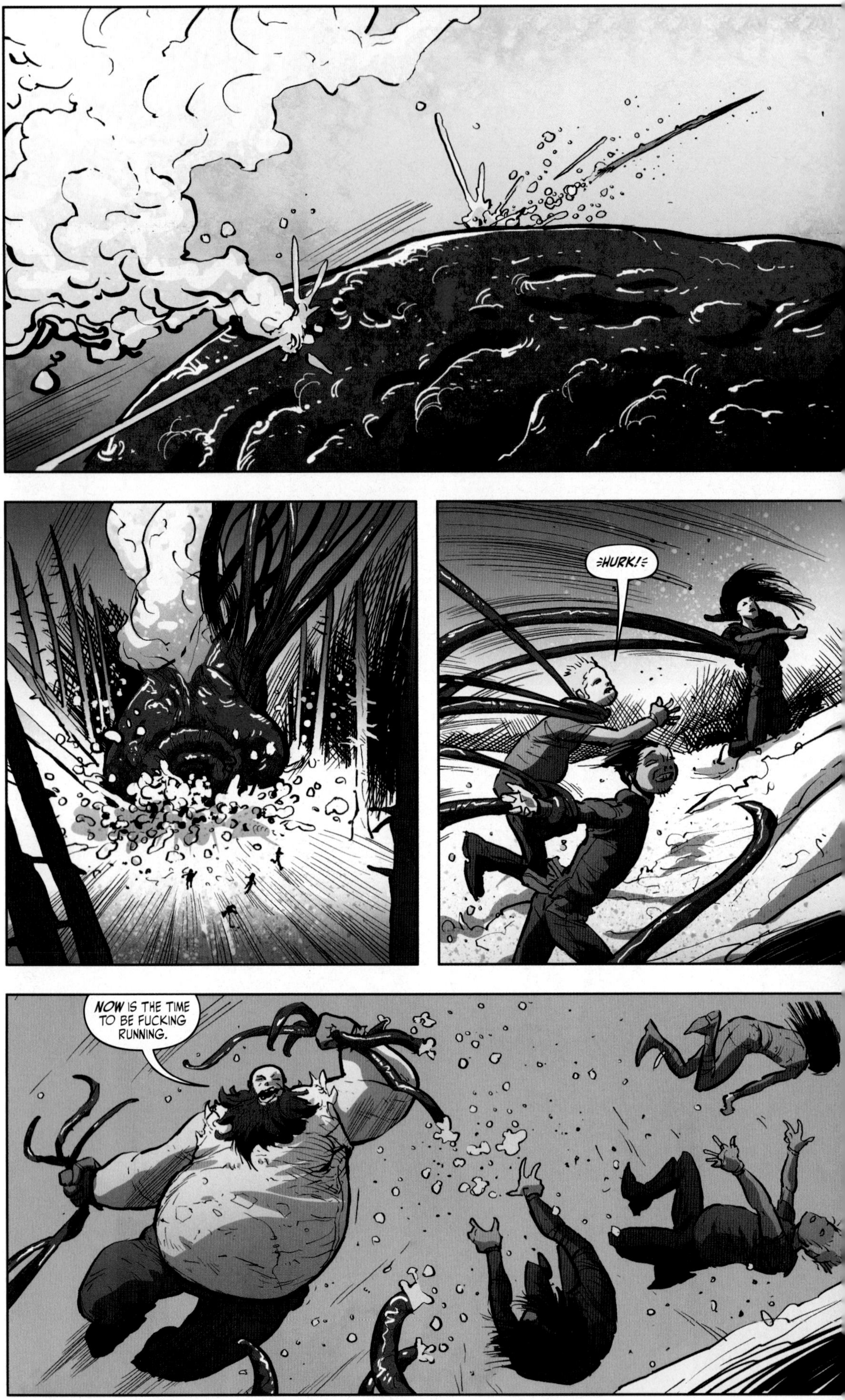
HURK!
NOW IS THE TIME TO BE FUCKING RUNNING.

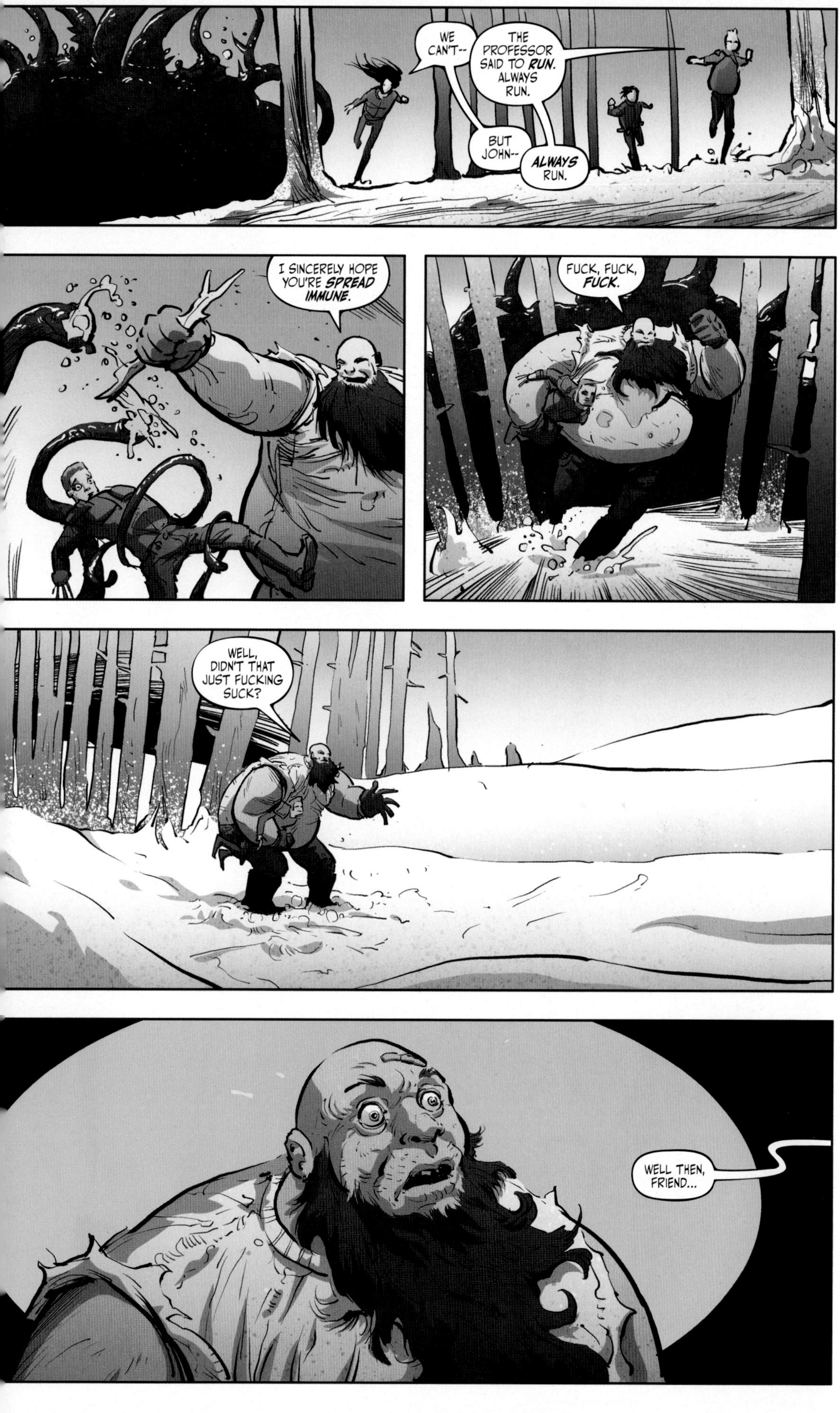

WE CAN'T--
THE PROFESSOR SAID TO RUN. ALWAYS RUN.
BUT JOHN--
ALWAYS RUN.
I SINCERELY HOPE YOU'RE SPREAD IMMUNE.
FUCK, FUCK, FUCK.
WELL, DIDN'T THAT JUST FUCKING SUCK?
WELL THEN, FRIEND...

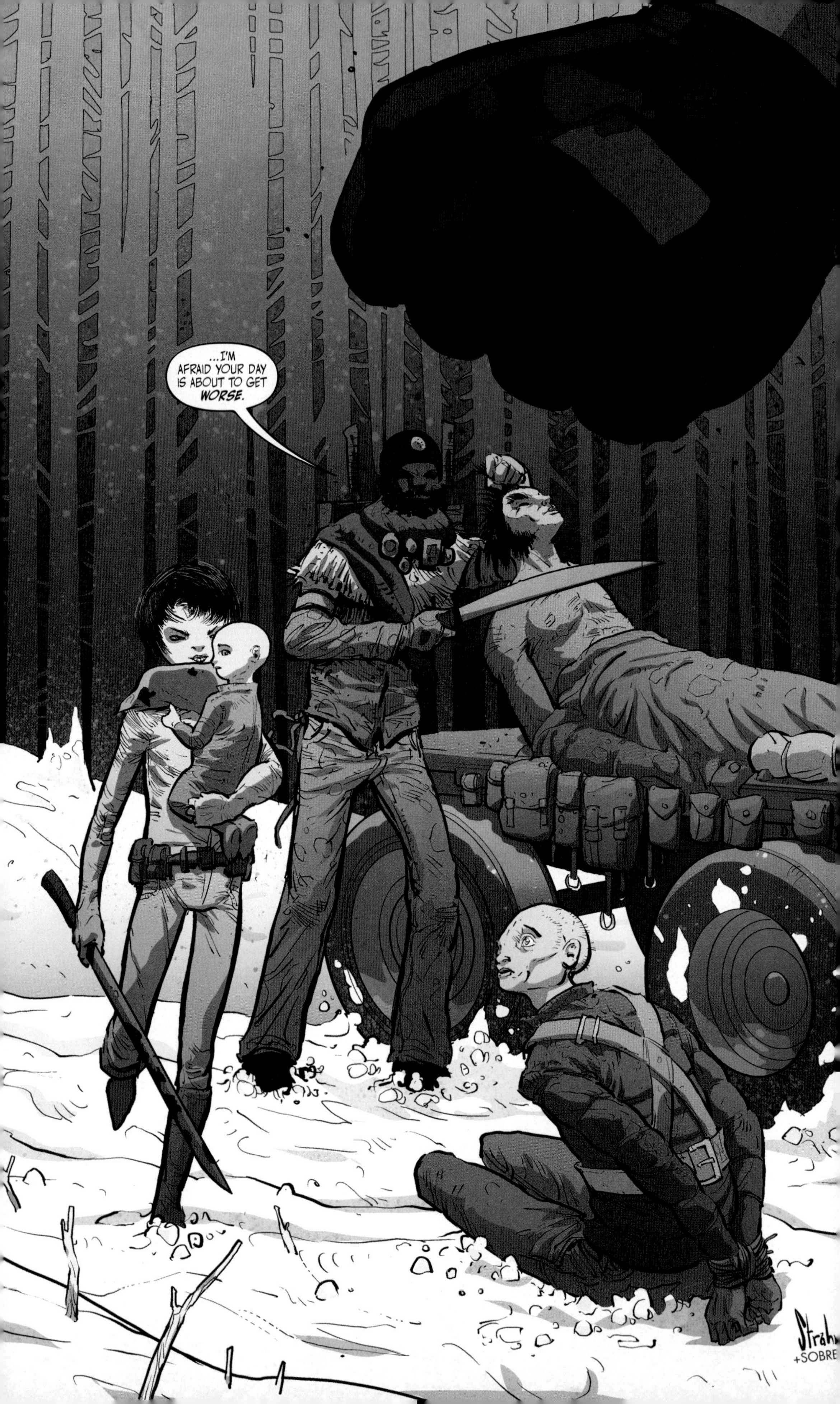

...I'M AFRAID YOUR DAY IS ABOUT TO GET WORSE.

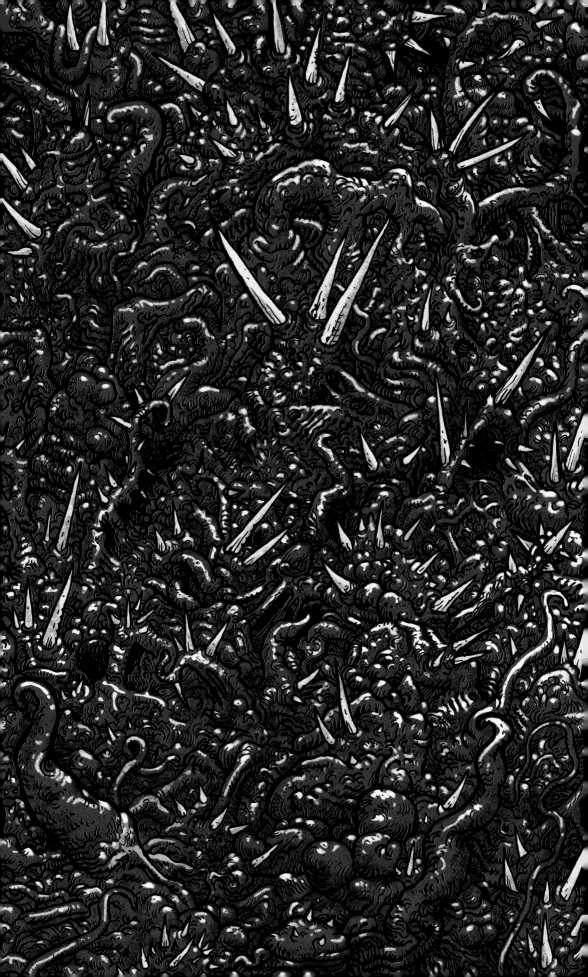

CHAPTER THREE

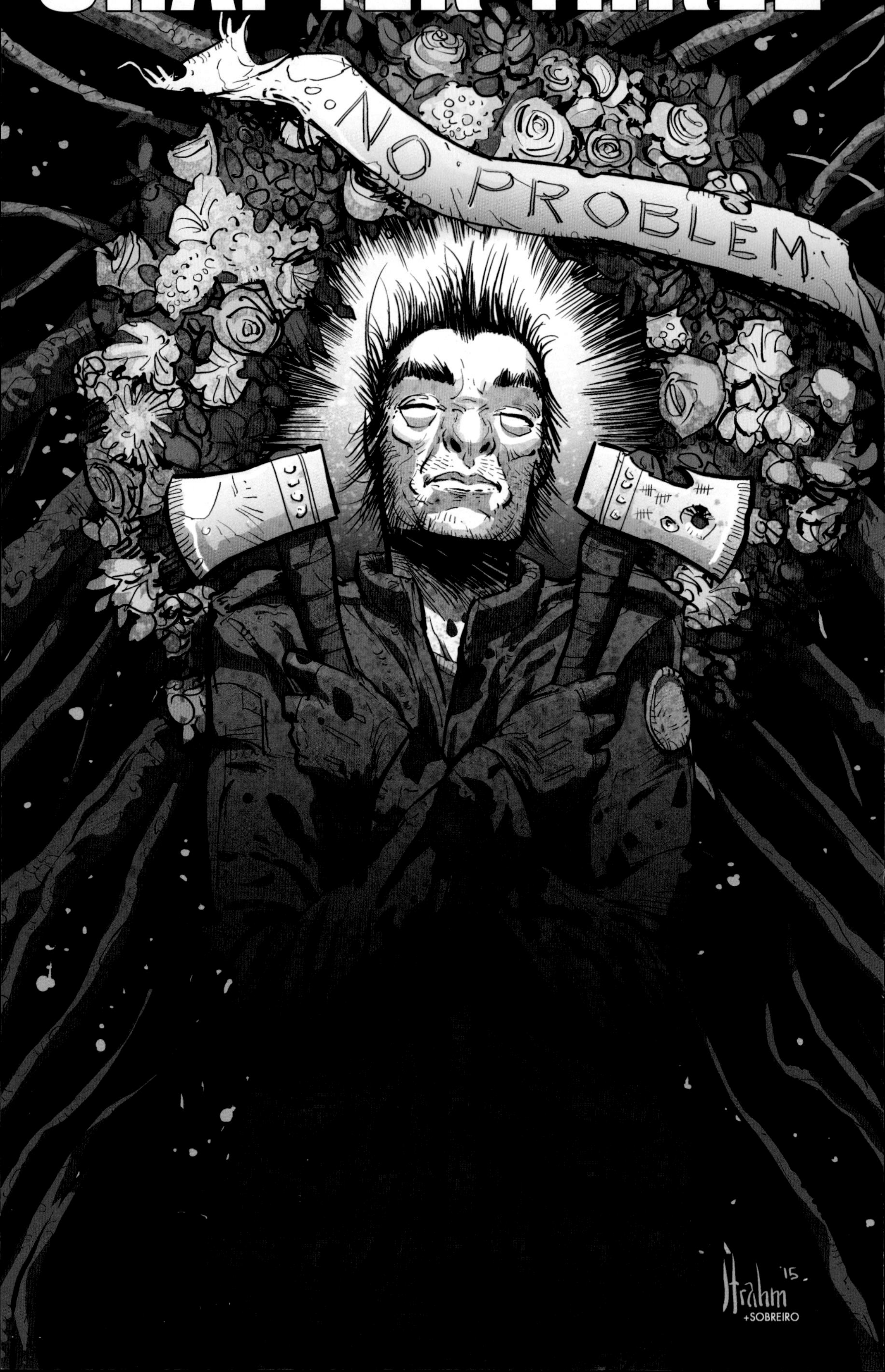
NO PROBLEM
Strahm '15
+SOBREIRO

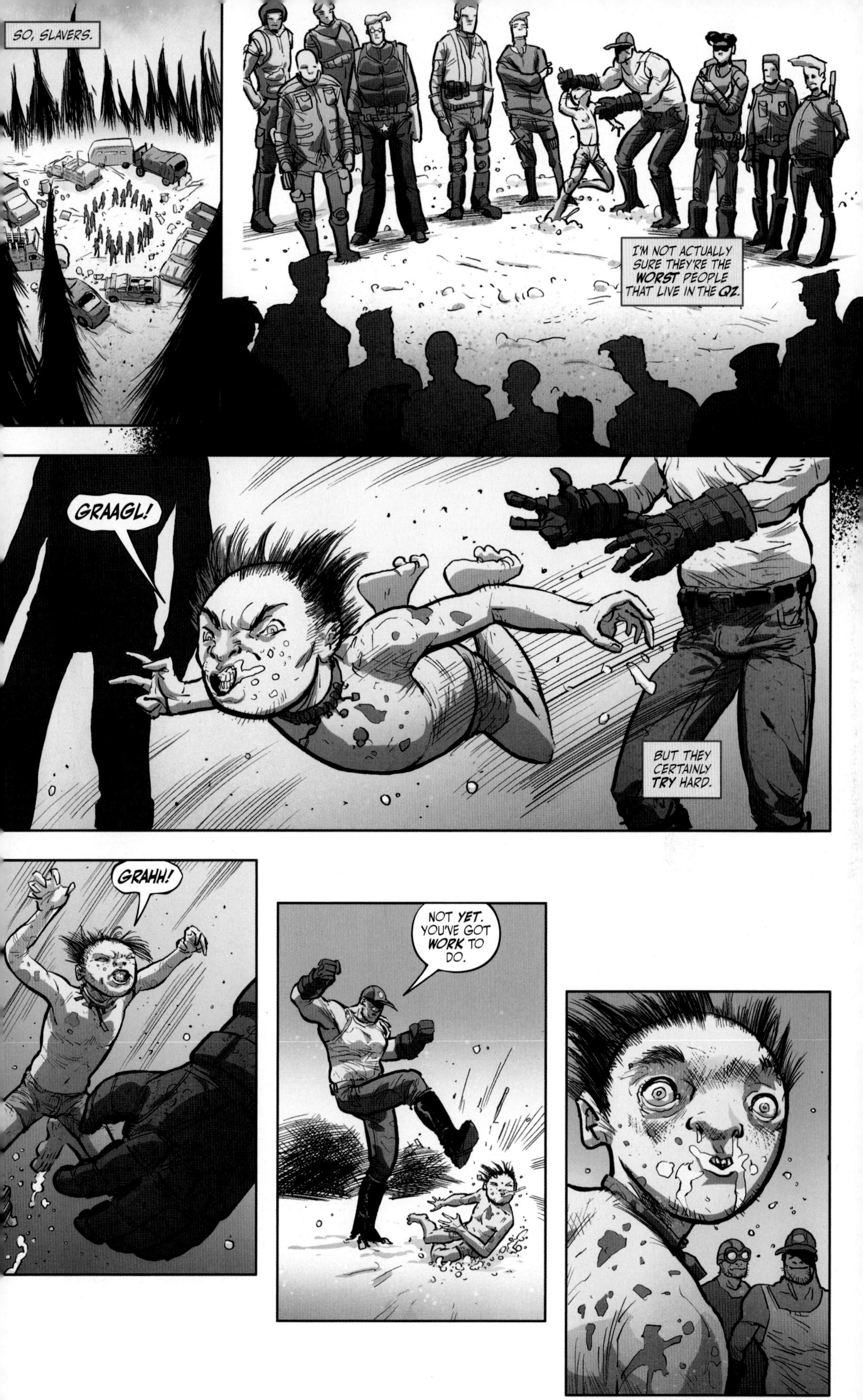
SO, SLAVERS.
I'M NOT ACTUALLY SURE THEY'RE THE WORST PEOPLE THAT LIVE IN THE QZ.
GRAAGL!
BUT THEY CERTAINLY TRY HARD.
GRAHH!
NOT YET. YOU'VE GOT WORK TO DO.

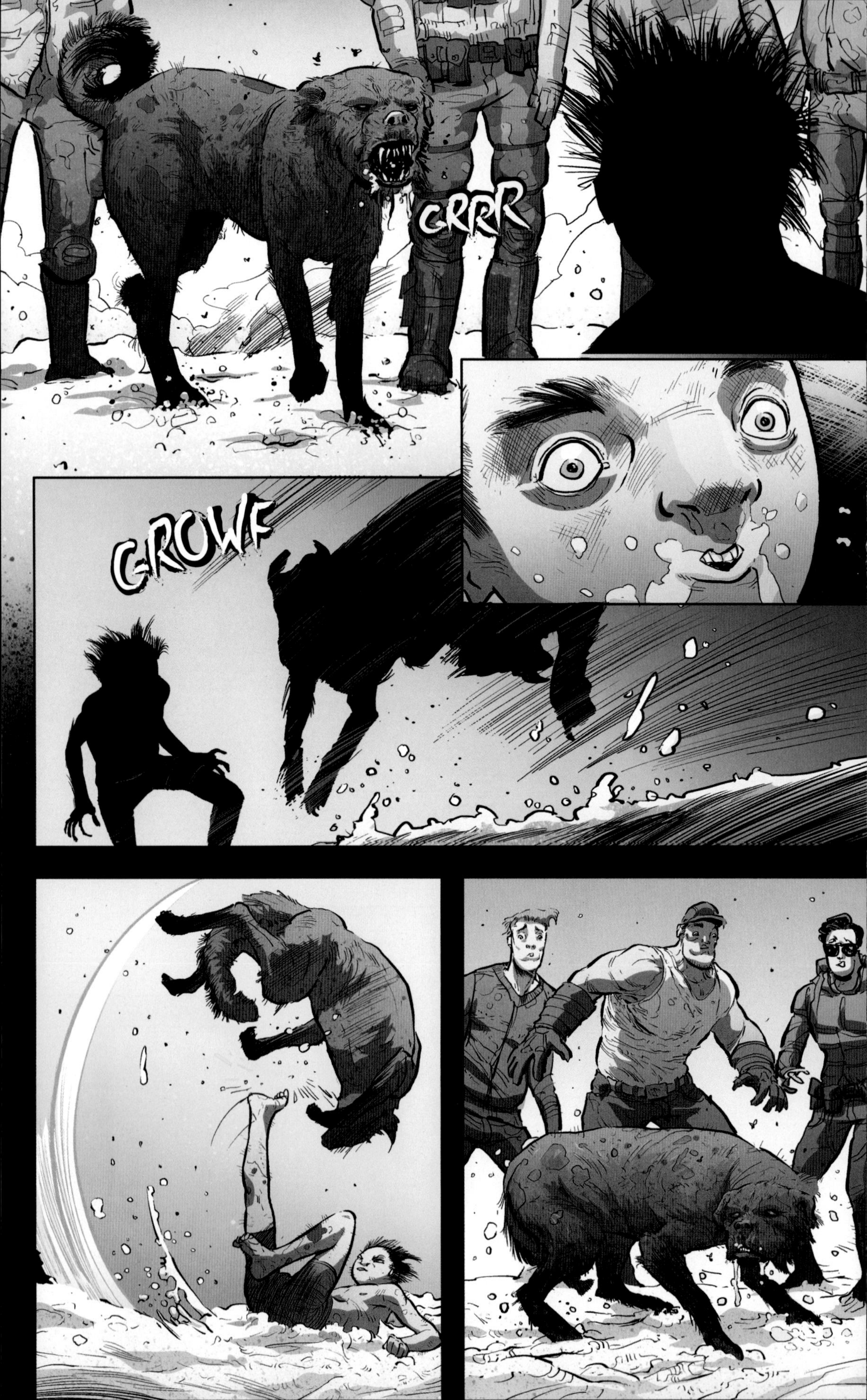
CRRR
GROWF

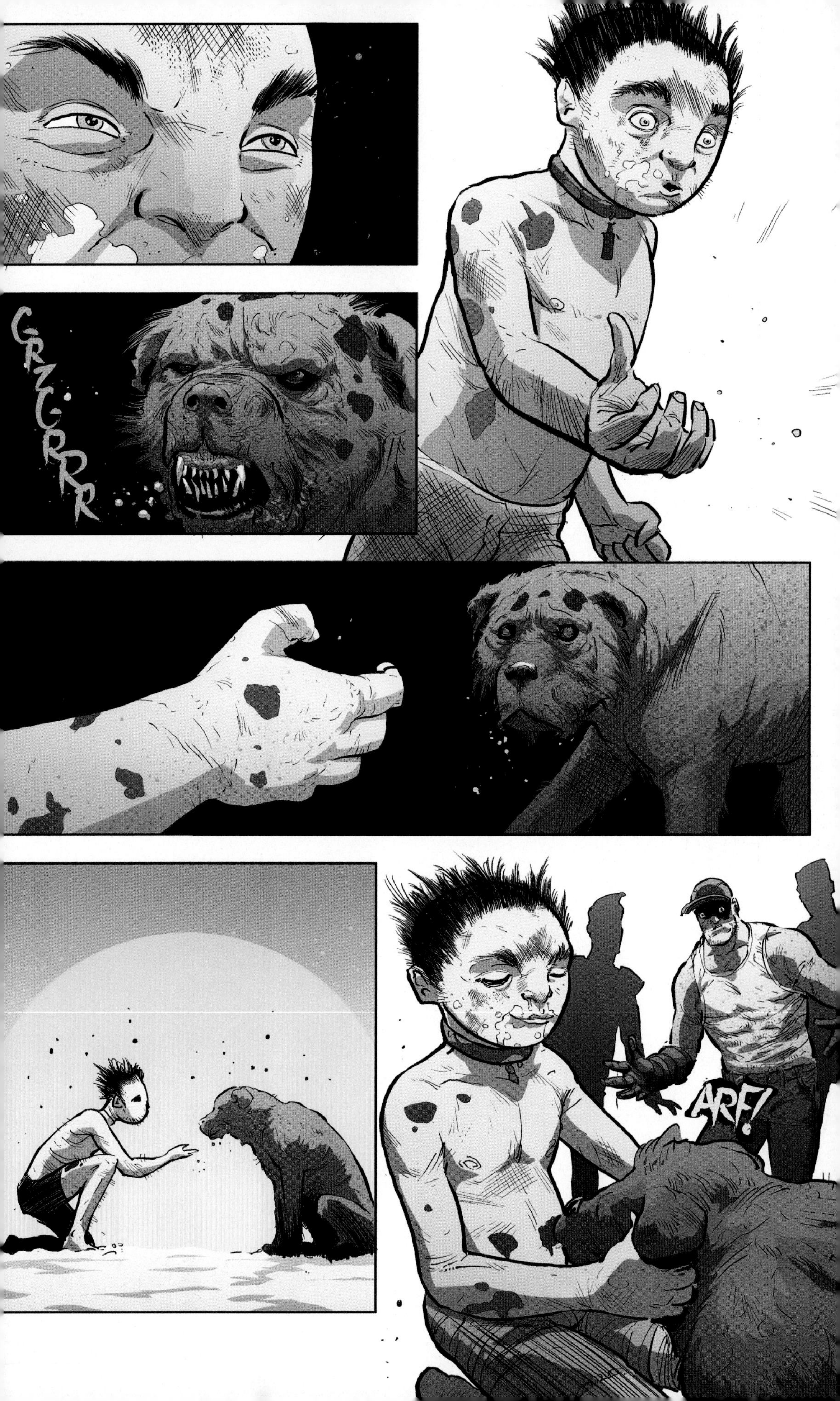
GRZGRRR
ARF!

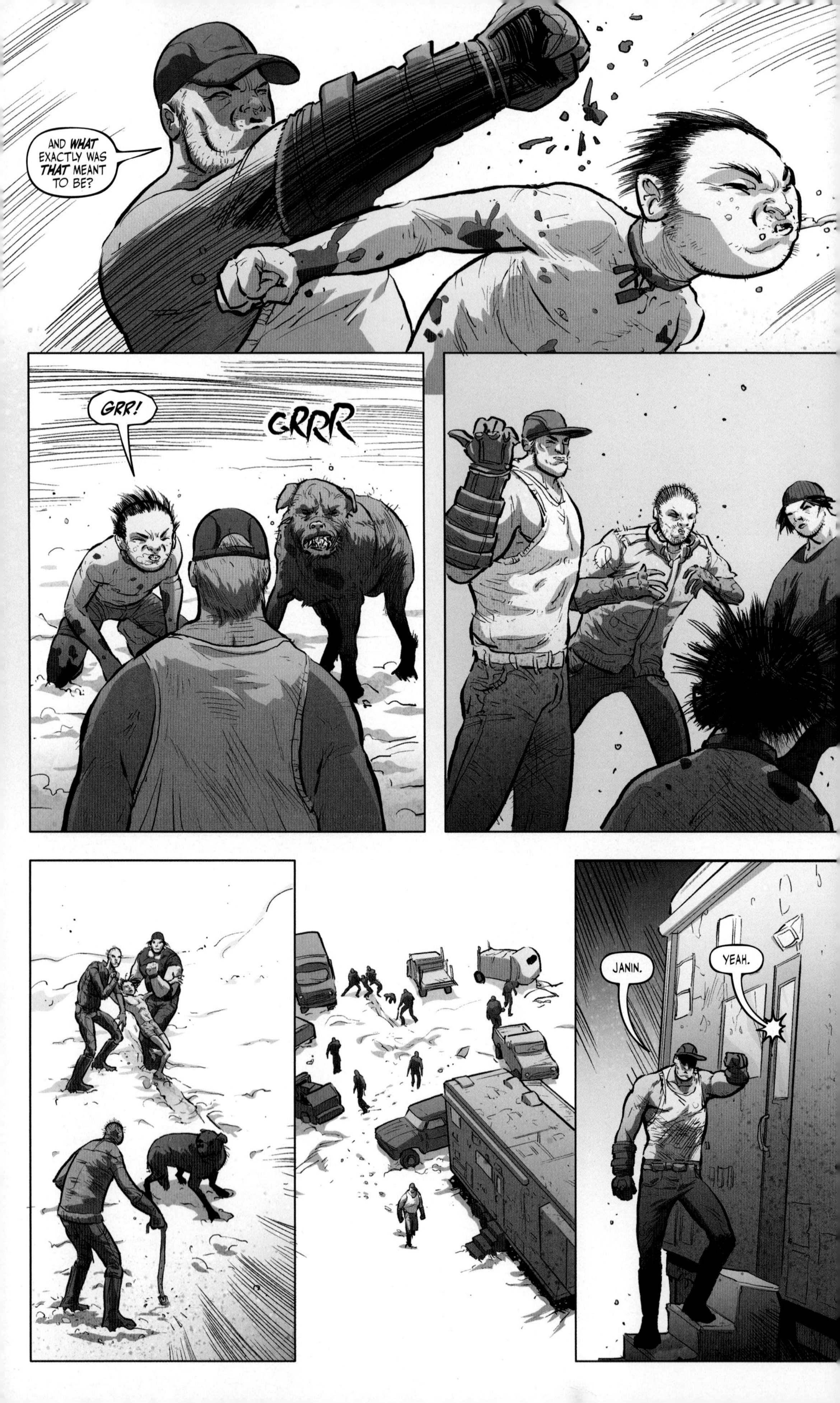

AND WHAT EXACTLY WAS THAT MEANT TO BE?
GRR!
GRRR
JANIN.
YEAH.

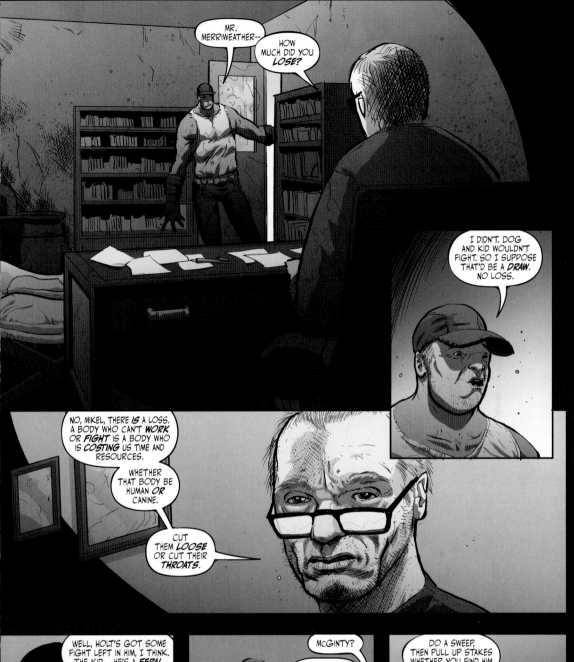

MR. MERRIWEATHER--

HOW MUCH DID YOU *LOSE?*

I DIDN'T. DOG AND KID WOULDN'T FIGHT. SO I SUPPOSE THAT'D BE A *DRAW.* NO LOSS.

NO, MIKEL, THERE *IS* A LOSS. A BODY WHO CAN'T *WORK* OR *FIGHT* IS A BODY WHO IS *COSTING* US TIME AND RESOURCES.

WHETHER THAT BODY BE HUMAN *OR* CANINE.

CUT THEM *LOOSE* OR CUT THEIR *THROATS.*

WELL, HOLT'S GOT SOME FIGHT LEFT IN HIM, I THINK. THE KID... HE'S A *FERAL.* HE'LL FIGHT.

IF THEY COST *ME*, THEY COST *YOU*. UNDERSTOOD?

YEAH, I--

I DON'T CARE.

McGINTY?

NO SIGN. HE NEVER CAME BACK AFTER THE KIDS SCATTERED.

DO A SWEEP, THEN PULL UP STAKES WHETHER YOU FIND HIM OR NOT.

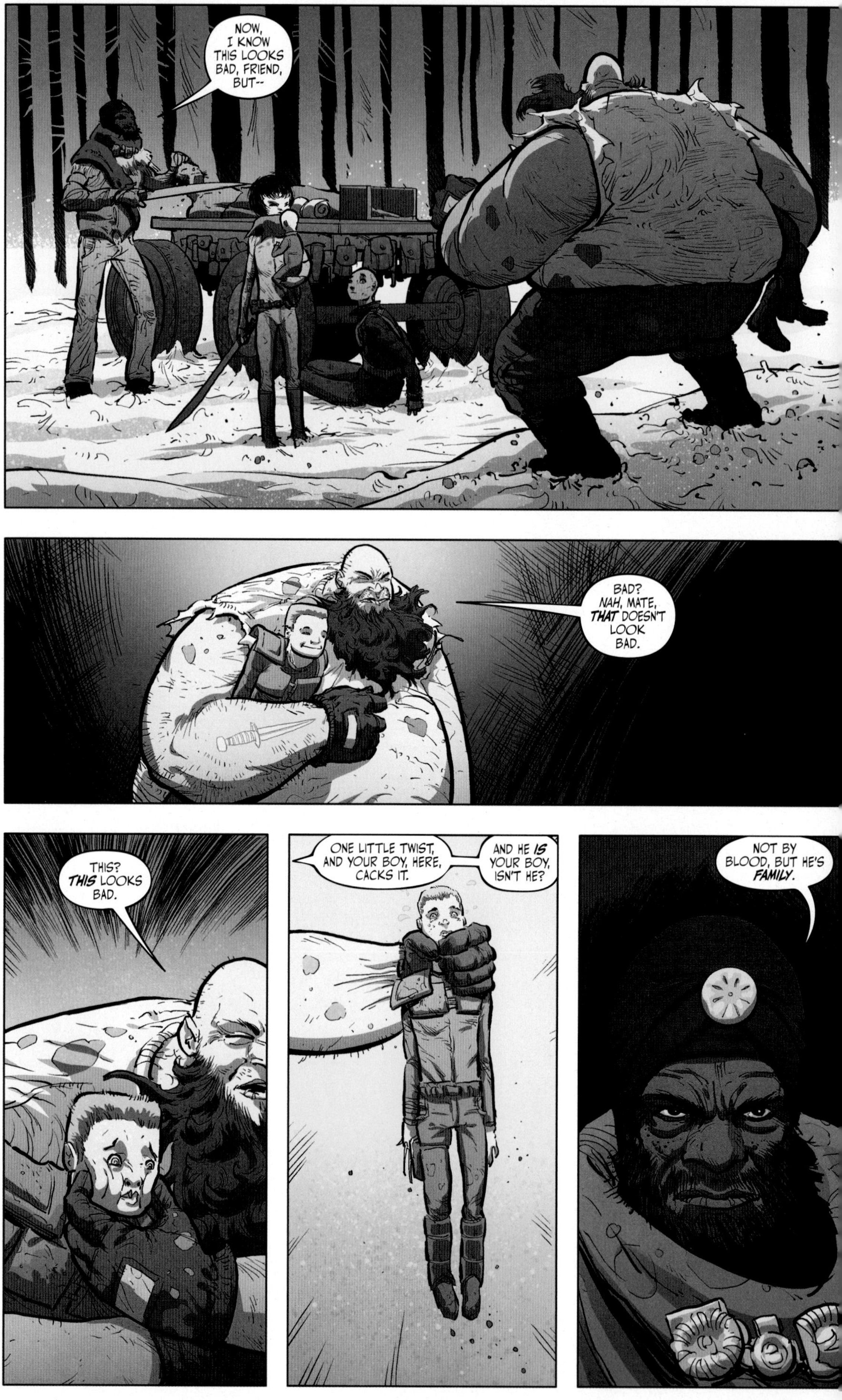
NOW, I KNOW THIS LOOKS BAD, FRIEND, BUT--
BAD? NAH, MATE, THAT DOESN'T LOOK BAD.
THIS? THIS LOOKS BAD.
ONE LITTLE TWIST, AND YOUR BOY, HERE, CACKS IT.
AND HE IS YOUR BOY, ISN'T HE?
NOT BY BLOOD, BUT HE'S FAMILY.

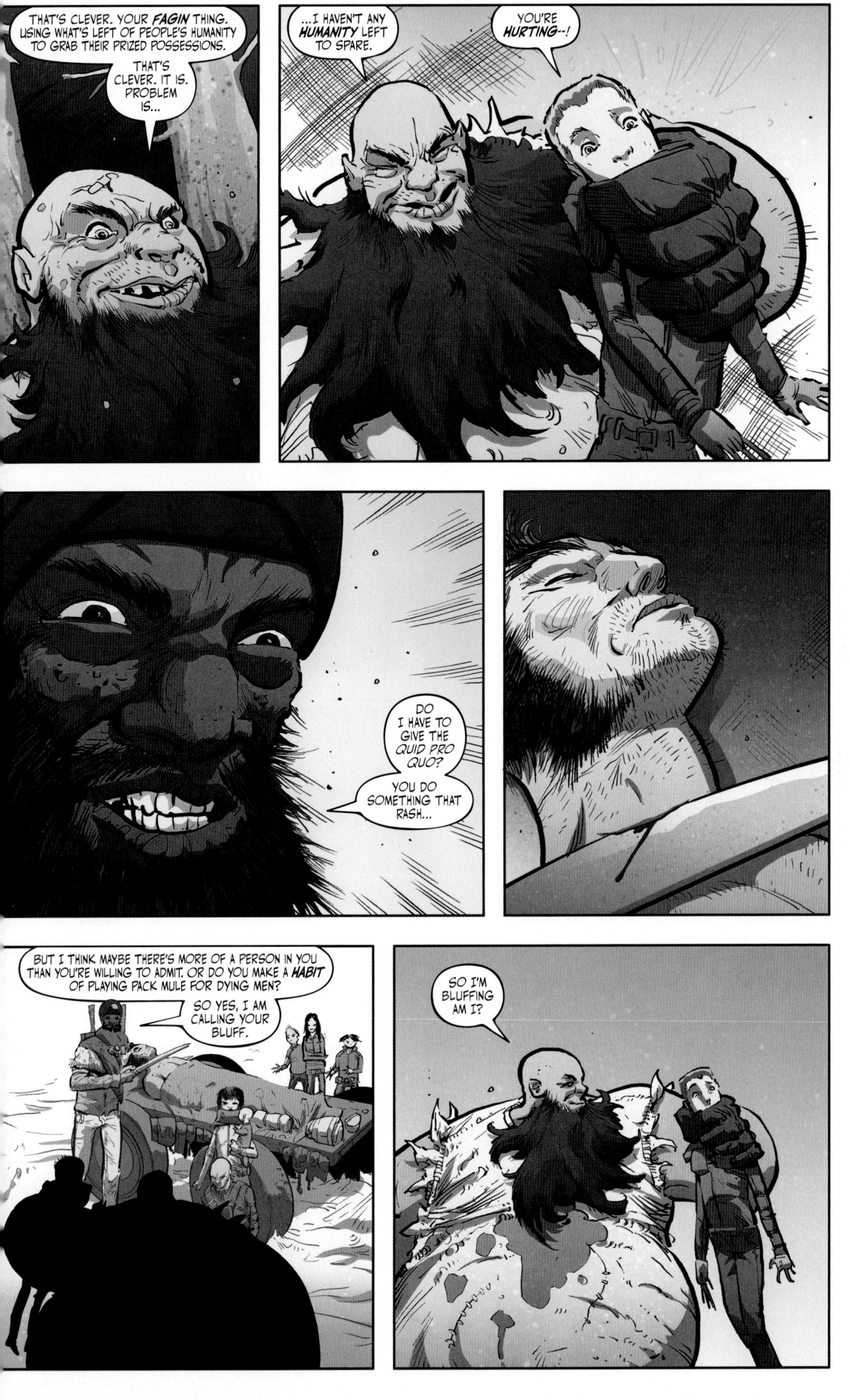

THAT'S CLEVER. YOUR *FAGIN* THING. USING WHAT'S LEFT OF PEOPLE'S HUMANITY TO GRAB THEIR PRIZED POSSESSIONS.
THAT'S CLEVER. IT IS. PROBLEM IS...
...I HAVEN'T ANY *HUMANITY* LEFT TO SPARE.
YOU'RE *HURTING*--!
DO I HAVE TO GIVE THE *QUID PRO QUO*?
YOU DO SOMETHING THAT RASH...
BUT I THINK MAYBE THERE'S MORE OF A PERSON IN YOU THAN YOU'RE WILLING TO ADMIT. OR DO YOU MAKE A *HABIT* OF PLAYING PACK MULE FOR DYING MEN?
SO YES, I AM CALLING YOUR BLUFF.
SO I'M BLUFFING AM I?

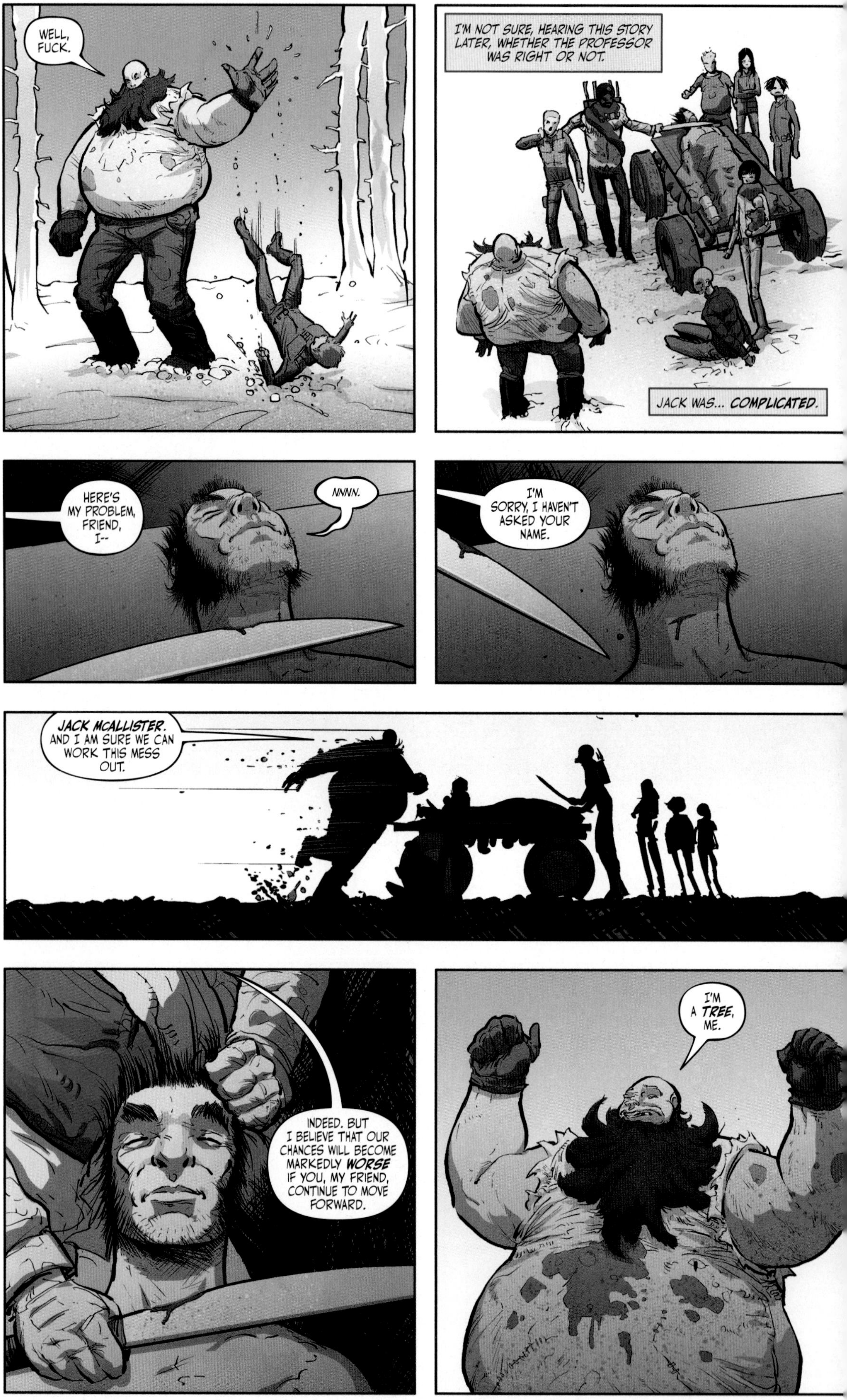

WELL, FUCK.
I'M NOT SURE, HEARING THIS STORY LATER, WHETHER THE PROFESSOR WAS RIGHT OR NOT.
JACK WAS... COMPLICATED.
HERE'S MY PROBLEM, FRIEND, I--
NNNN.
I'M SORRY, I HAVEN'T ASKED YOUR NAME.
JACK MCALLISTER. AND I AM SURE WE CAN WORK THIS MESS OUT.
INDEED. BUT I BELIEVE THAT OUR CHANCES WILL BECOME MARKEDLY WORSE IF YOU, MY FRIEND, CONTINUE TO MOVE FORWARD.
I'M A TREE, ME.

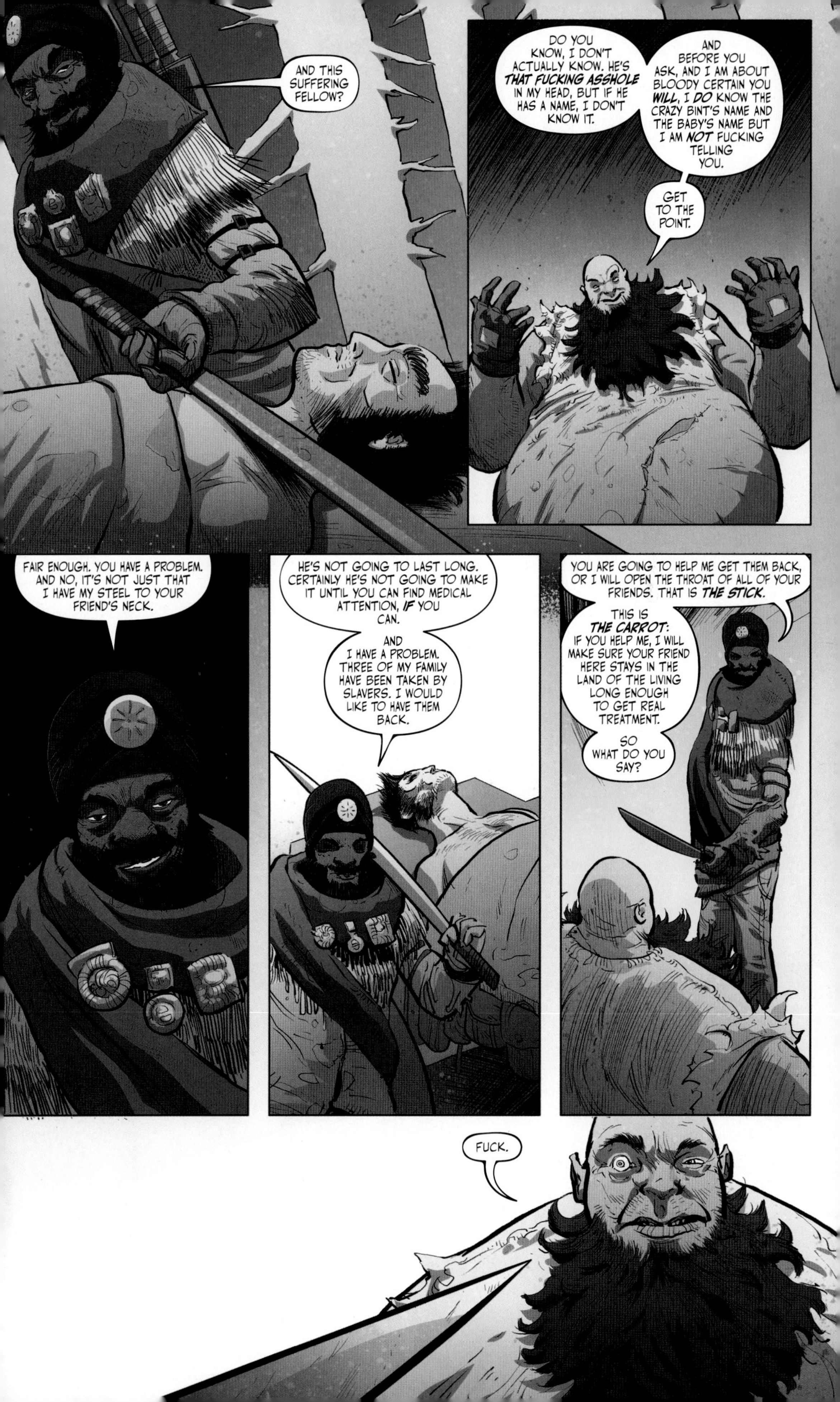
AND THIS SUFFERING FELLOW?
DO YOU KNOW, I DON'T ACTUALLY KNOW. HE'S THAT FUCKING ASSHOLE IN MY HEAD, BUT IF HE HAS A NAME, I DON'T KNOW IT.
AND BEFORE YOU ASK, AND I AM ABOUT BLOODY CERTAIN YOU WILL, I DO KNOW THE CRAZY BINT'S NAME AND THE BABY'S NAME BUT I AM NOT FUCKING TELLING YOU.
GET TO THE POINT.
FAIR ENOUGH. YOU HAVE A PROBLEM. AND NO, IT'S NOT JUST THAT I HAVE MY STEEL TO YOUR FRIEND'S NECK.
HE'S NOT GOING TO LAST LONG. CERTAINLY HE'S NOT GOING TO MAKE IT UNTIL YOU CAN FIND MEDICAL ATTENTION, IF YOU CAN.
AND I HAVE A PROBLEM. THREE OF MY FAMILY HAVE BEEN TAKEN BY SLAVERS. I WOULD LIKE TO HAVE THEM BACK.
YOU ARE GOING TO HELP ME GET THEM BACK, OR I WILL OPEN THE THROAT OF ALL OF YOUR FRIENDS. THAT IS THE STICK.
THIS IS THE CARROT: IF YOU HELP ME, I WILL MAKE SURE YOUR FRIEND HERE STAYS IN THE LAND OF THE LIVING LONG ENOUGH TO GET REAL TREATMENT.
SO WHAT DO YOU SAY?
FUCK.

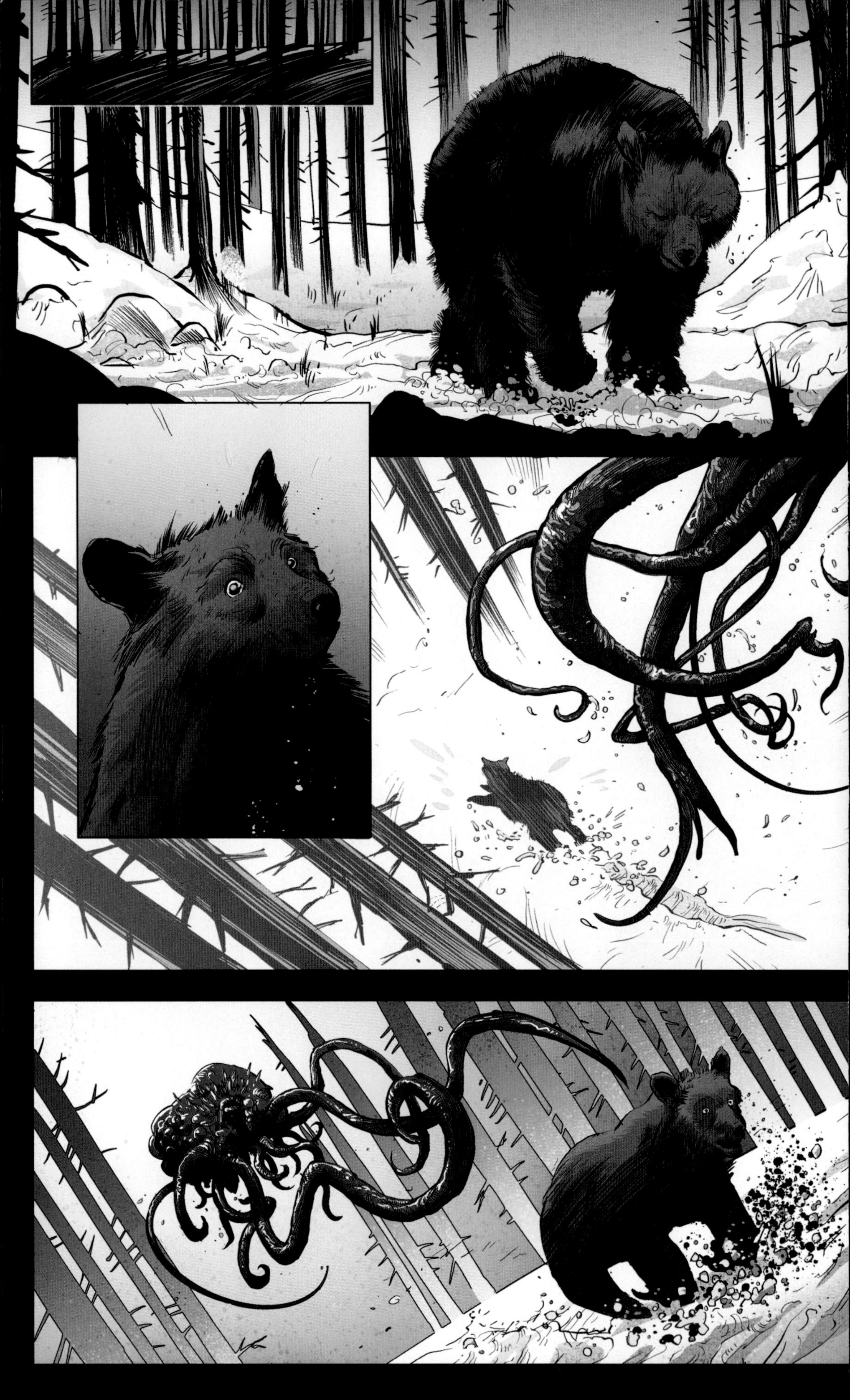

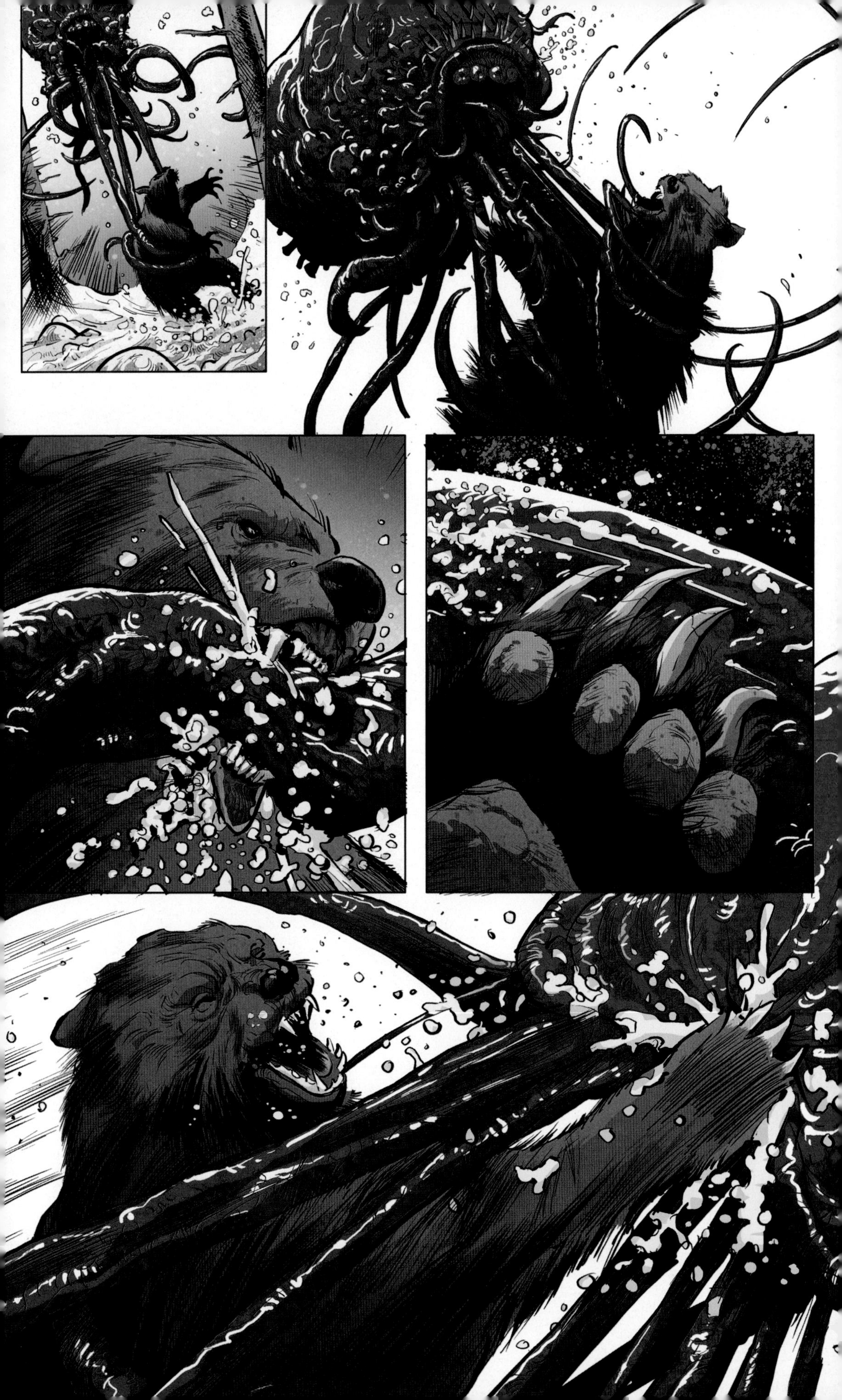

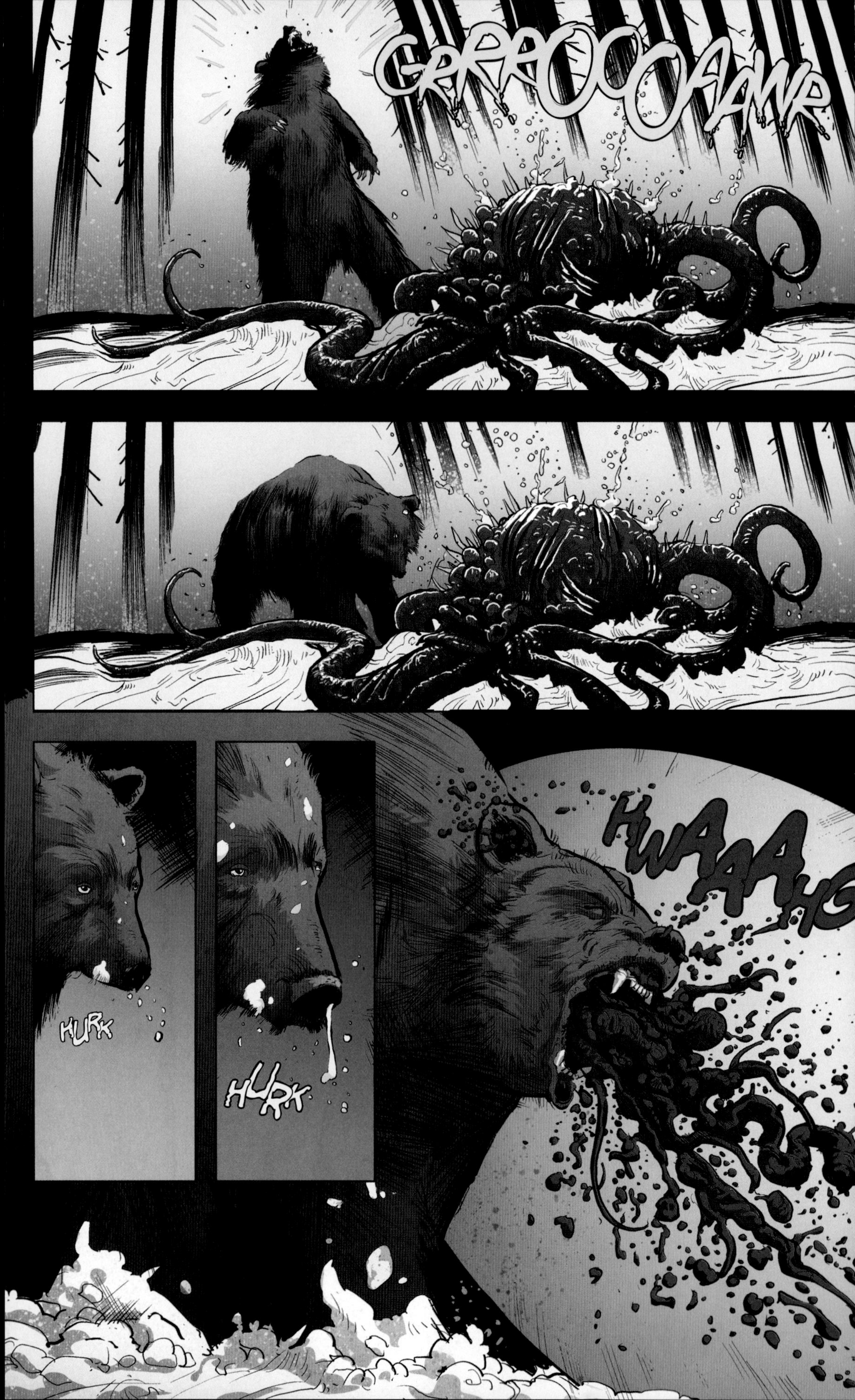
GRRROOOAAWR
HURK
HURK
HWAAAHG

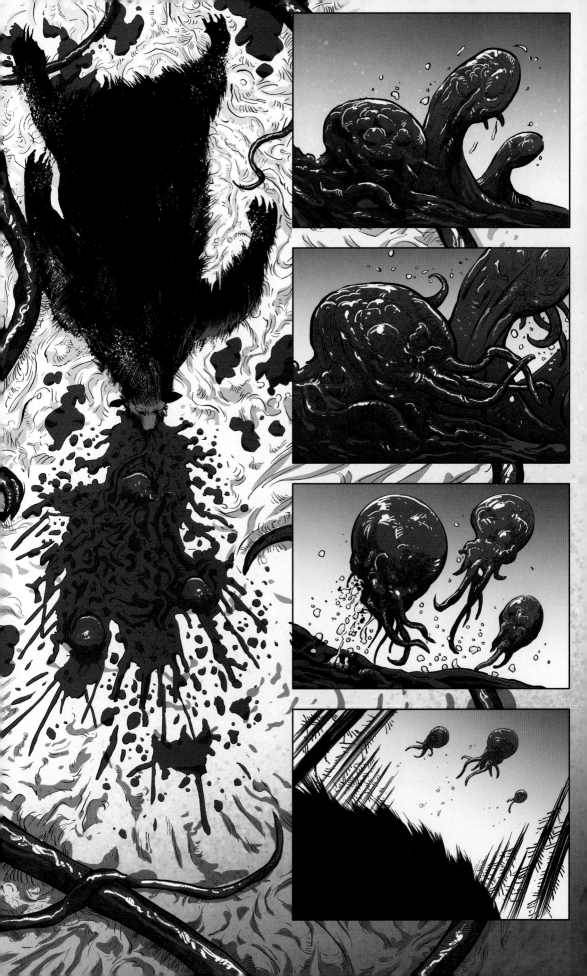

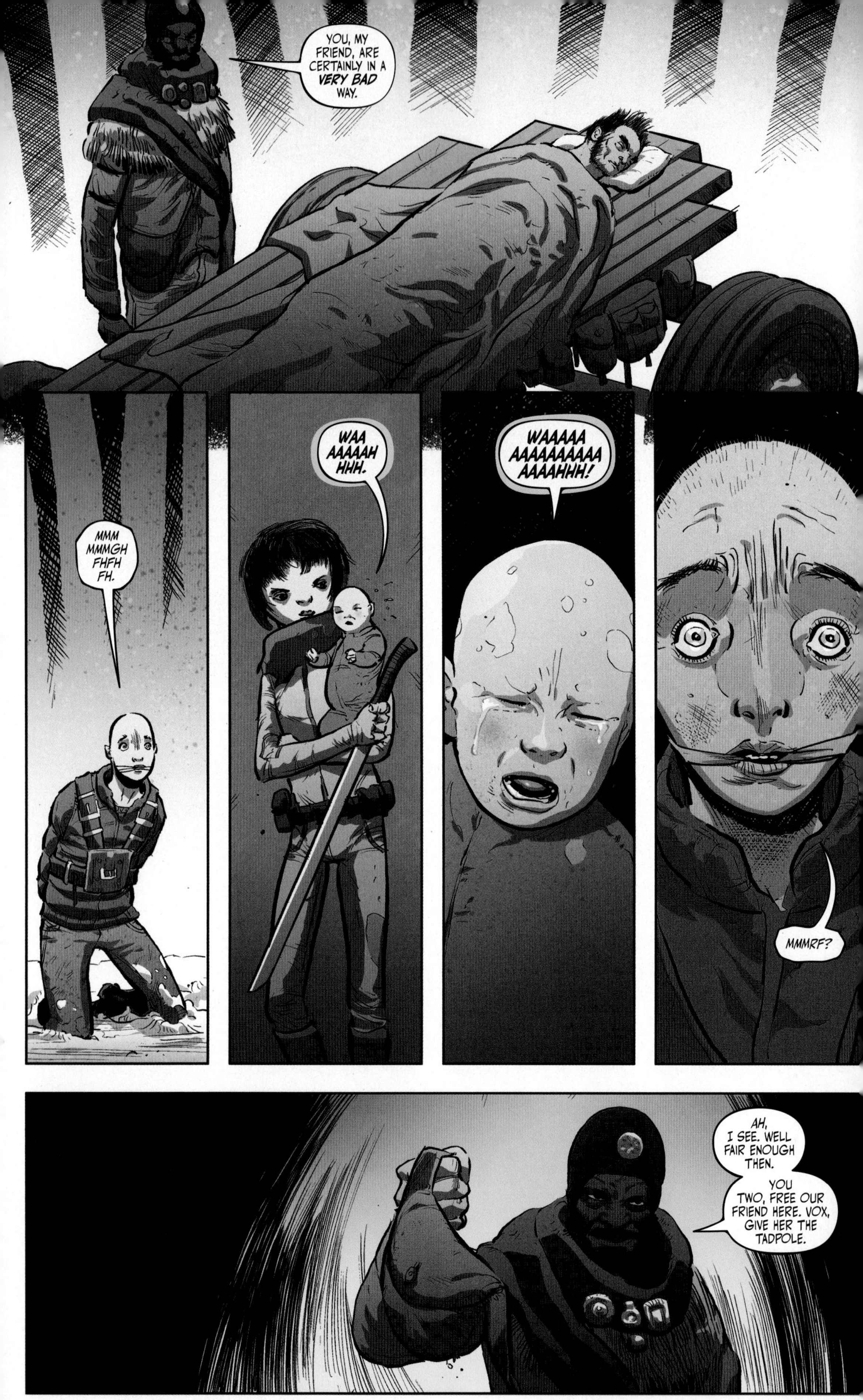

YOU, MY FRIEND, ARE CERTAINLY IN A VERY BAD WAY.
MMM MMMGH FHFH FH.
WAA AAAAAH HHH.
WAAAAA AAAAAAAAAA AAAAHHH!
MMMRF?
AH, I SEE. WELL FAIR ENOUGH THEN.
YOU TWO, FREE OUR FRIEND HERE. VOX, GIVE HER THE TADPOLE.

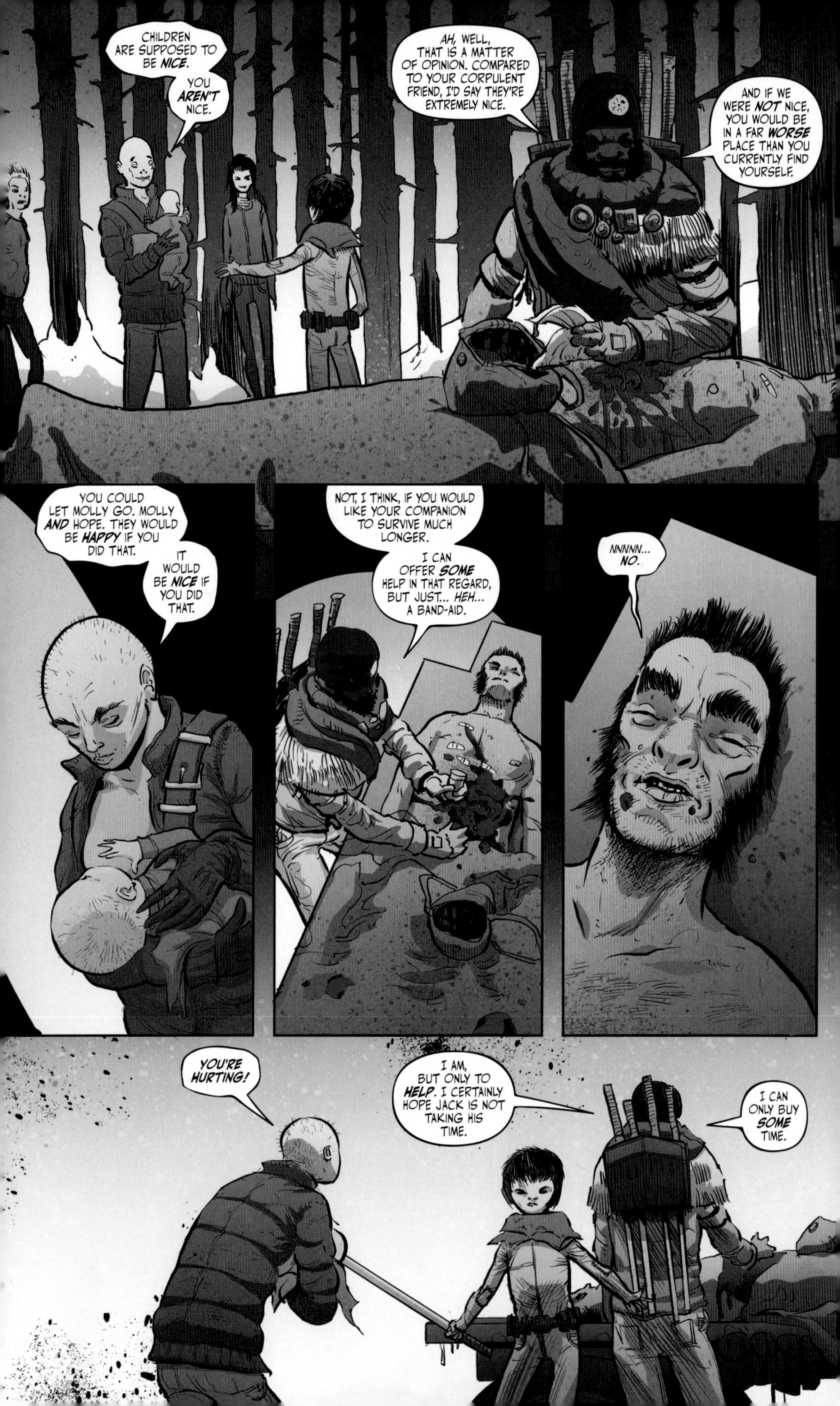

CHILDREN ARE SUPPOSED TO BE *NICE*.
YOU *AREN'T* NICE.
AH, WELL, THAT IS A MATTER OF OPINION. COMPARED TO YOUR CORPULENT FRIEND, I'D SAY THEY'RE EXTREMELY NICE.
AND IF WE WERE *NOT* NICE, YOU WOULD BE IN A FAR *WORSE* PLACE THAN YOU CURRENTLY FIND YOURSELF.
YOU COULD LET MOLLY GO. MOLLY *AND* HOPE. THEY WOULD BE *HAPPY* IF YOU DID THAT.
IT WOULD BE *NICE* IF YOU DID THAT.
NOT, I THINK, IF YOU WOULD LIKE YOUR COMPANION TO SURVIVE MUCH LONGER.
I CAN OFFER *SOME* HELP IN THAT REGARD, BUT JUST... *HEH*... A BAND-AID.
NNNNN... NO.
YOU'RE HURTING!
I AM, BUT ONLY TO *HELP*. I CERTAINLY HOPE JACK IS NOT TAKING HIS TIME.
I CAN ONLY BUY *SOME* TIME.

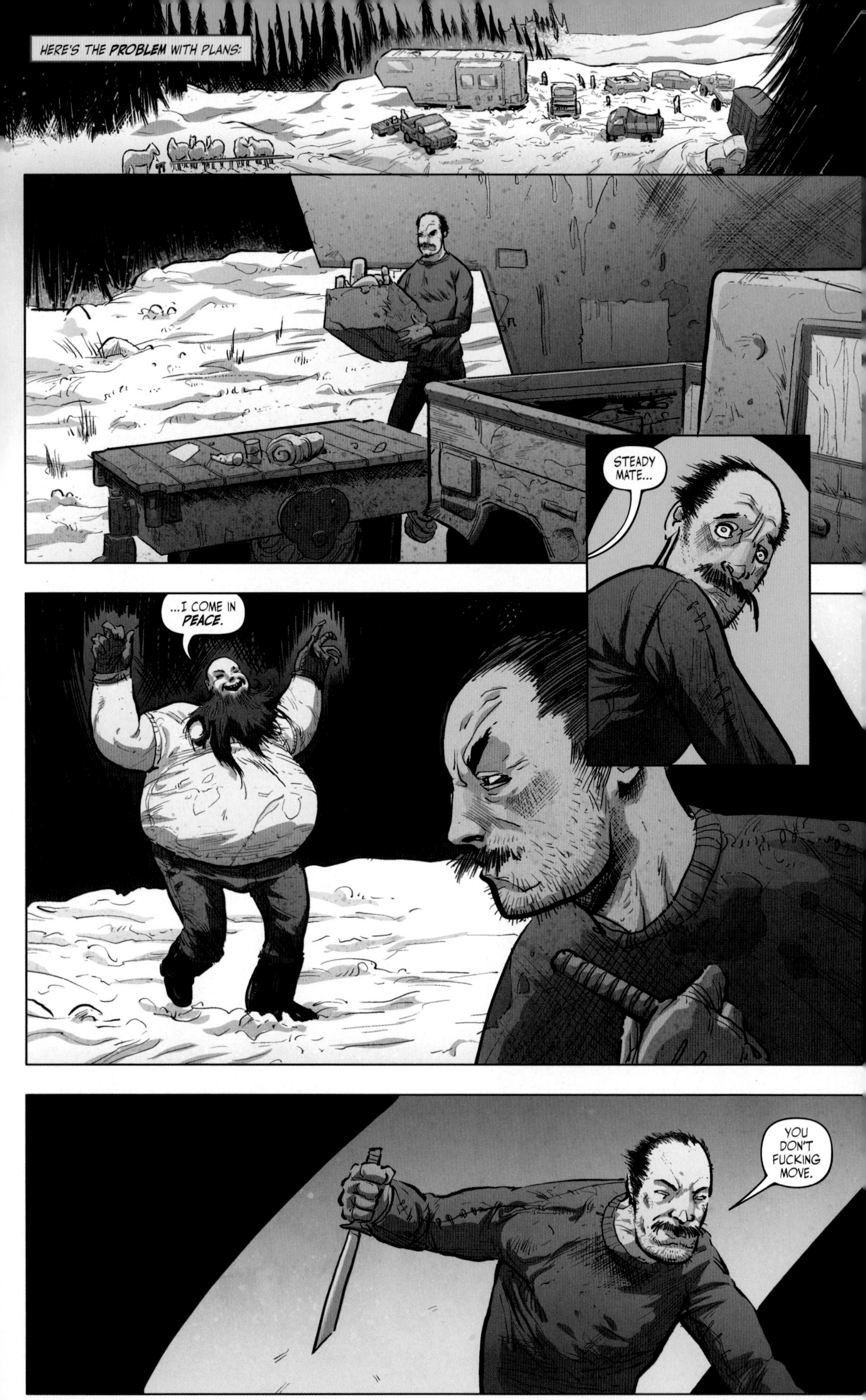
HERE'S THE PROBLEM WITH PLANS:
STEADY MATE...
...I COME IN PEACE.
YOU DON'T FUCKING MOVE.

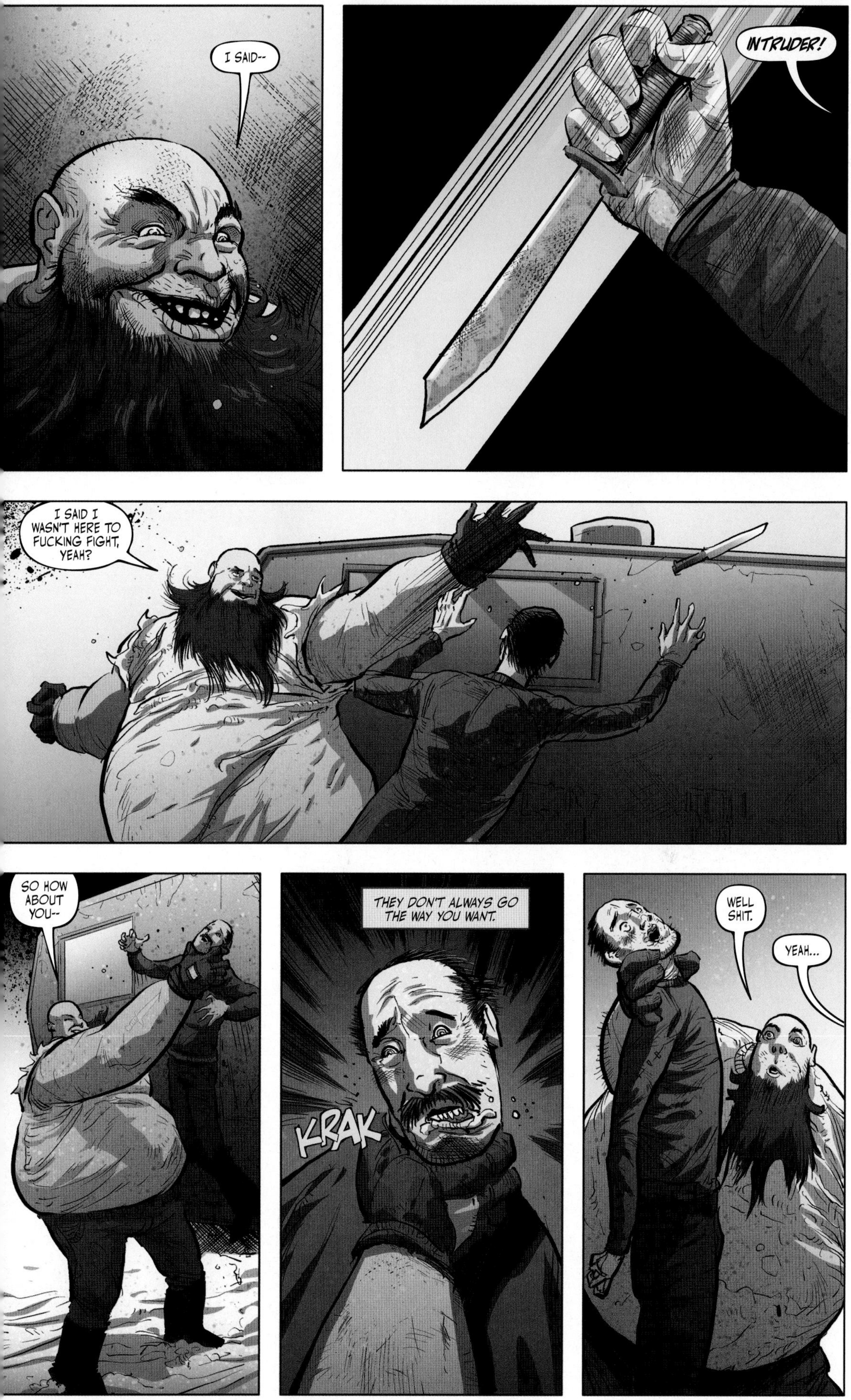
I SAID--
INTRUDER!
I SAID I WASN'T HERE TO FUCKING FIGHT, YEAH?
SO HOW ABOUT YOU--
THEY DON'T ALWAYS GO THE WAY YOU WANT.
KRAK
WELL SHIT.
YEAH...

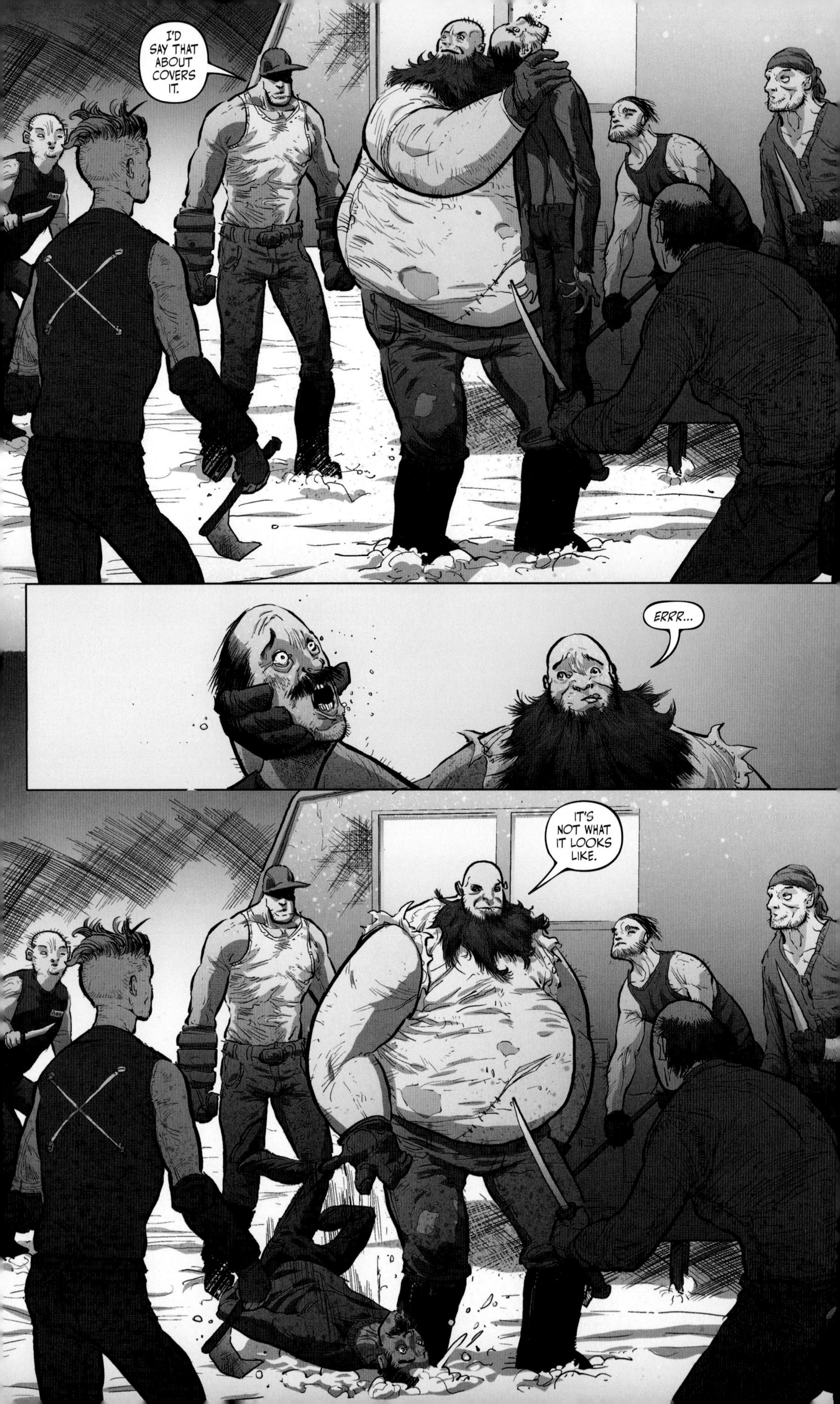
I'D SAY THAT ABOUT COVERS IT.
ERRR...
IT'S NOT WHAT IT LOOKS LIKE.

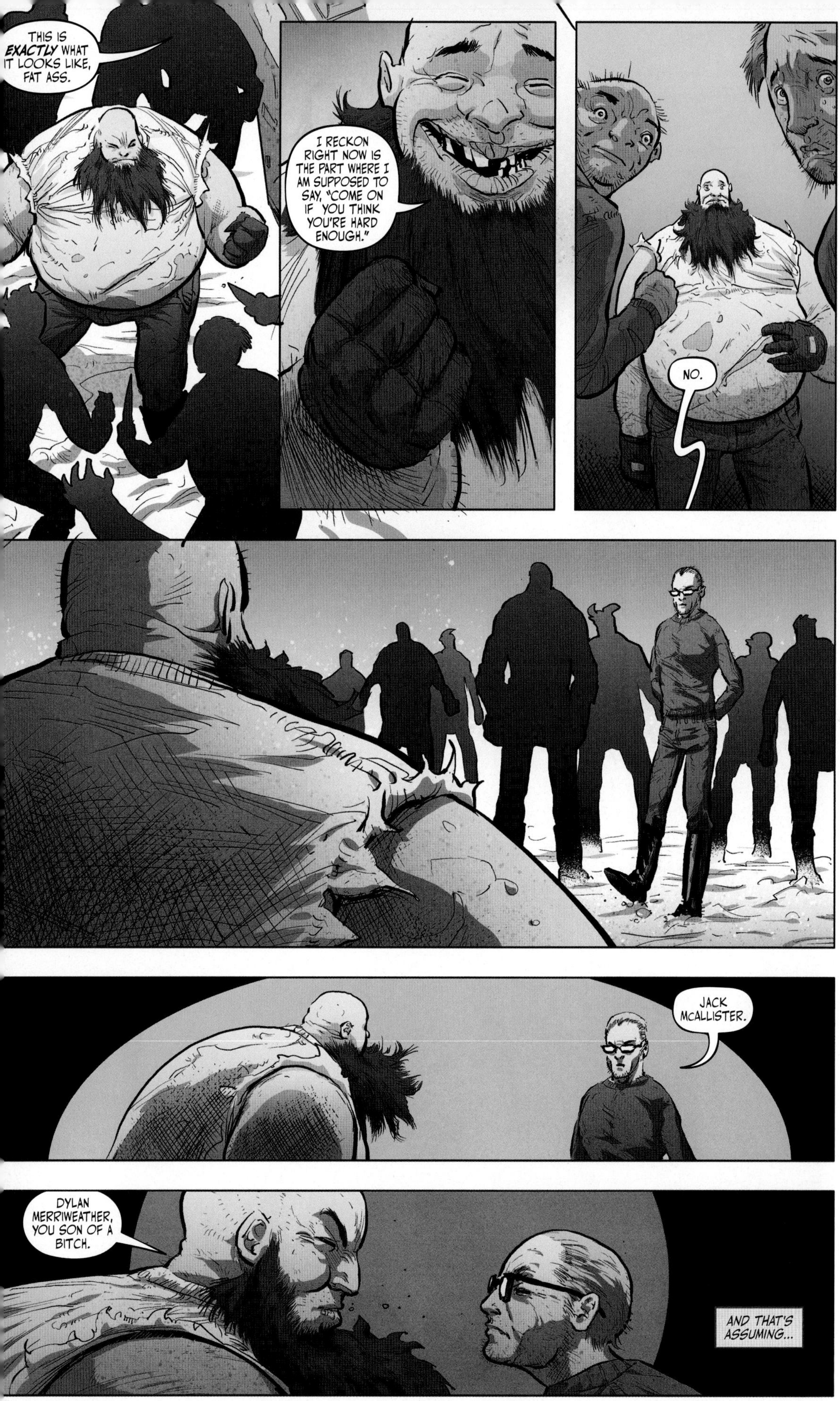
THIS IS EXACTLY WHAT IT LOOKS LIKE, FAT ASS.
I RECKON RIGHT NOW IS THE PART WHERE I AM SUPPOSED TO SAY, "COME ON IF YOU THINK YOU'RE HARD ENOUGH."
NO.
JACK MCALLISTER.
DYLAN MERRIWEATHER, YOU SON OF A BITCH.
AND THAT'S ASSUMING...

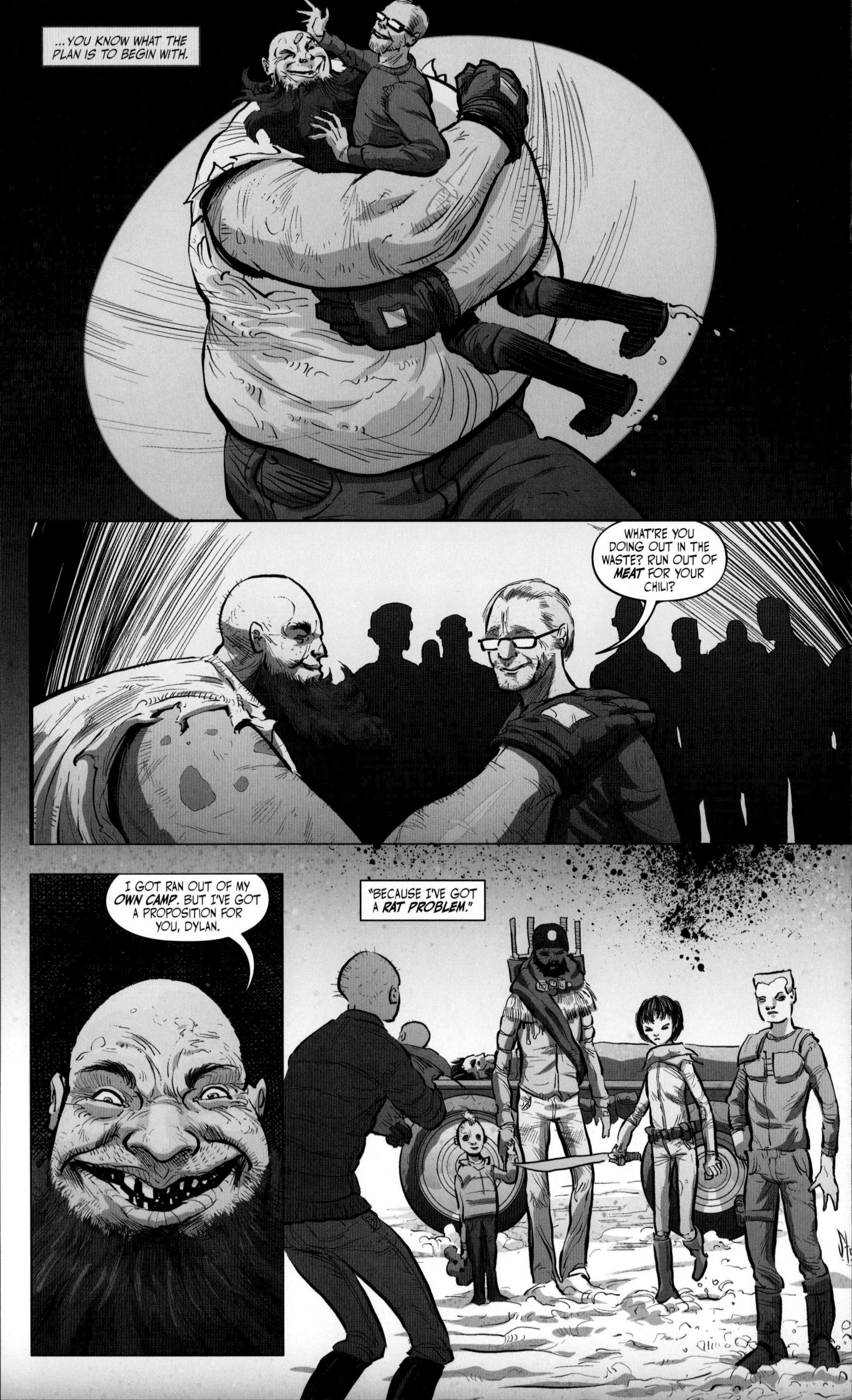
...YOU KNOW WHAT THE PLAN IS TO BEGIN WITH.
WHAT'RE YOU DOING OUT IN THE WASTE? RUN OUT OF **MEAT** FOR YOUR CHILI?
I GOT RAN OUT OF MY **OWN CAMP**. BUT I'VE GOT A PROPOSITION FOR YOU, DYLAN.
"BECAUSE I'VE GOT A **RAT PROBLEM**."

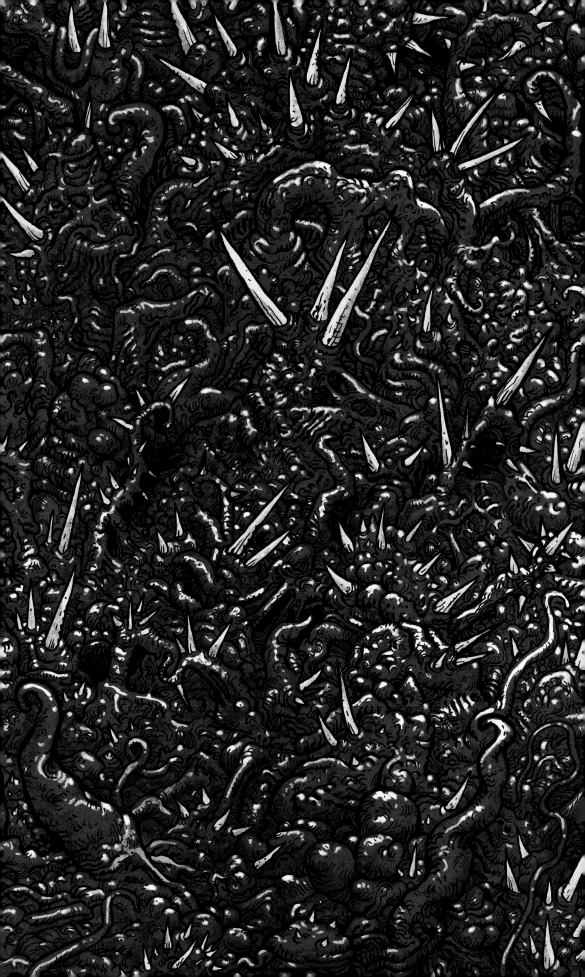

CHAPTER FOUR

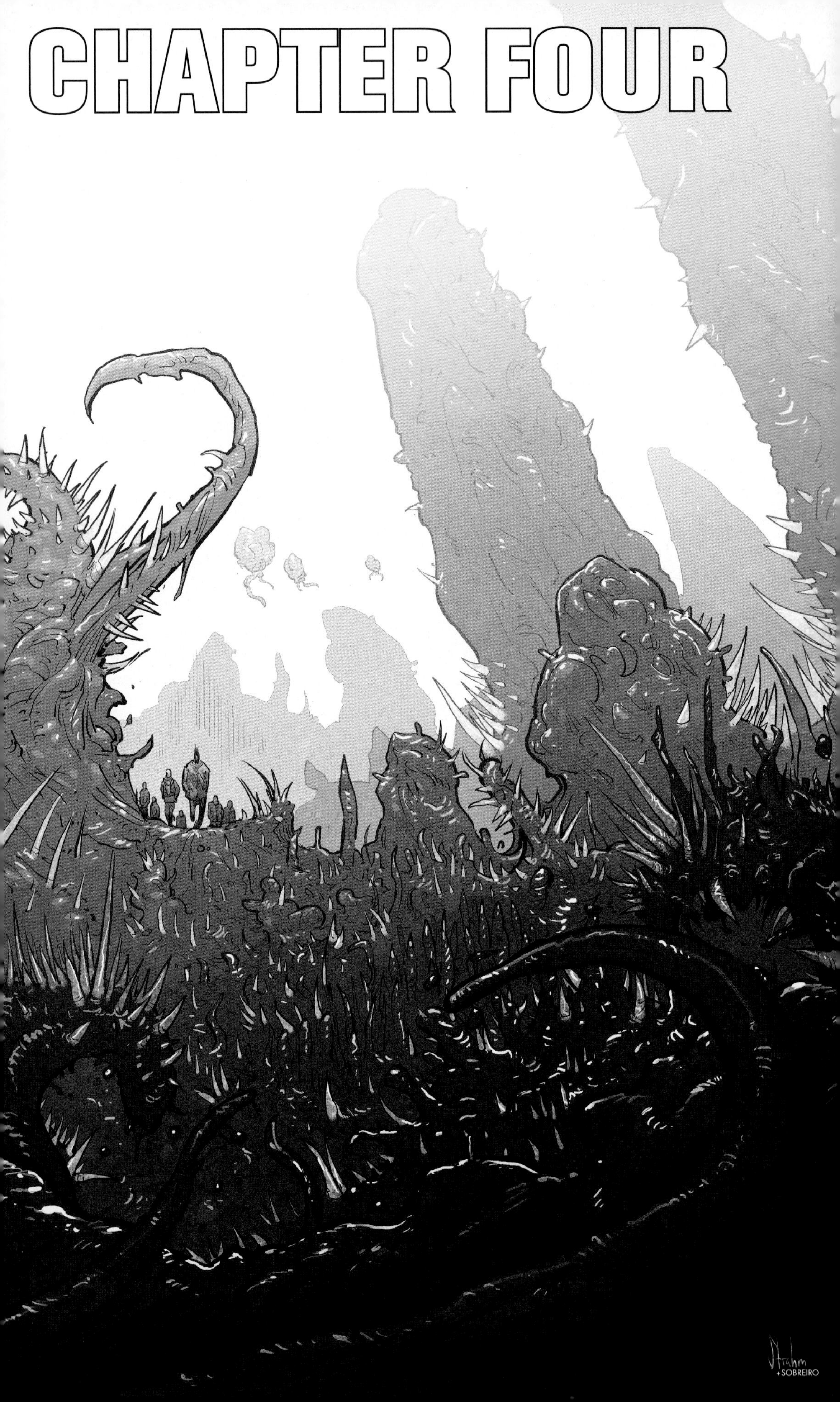

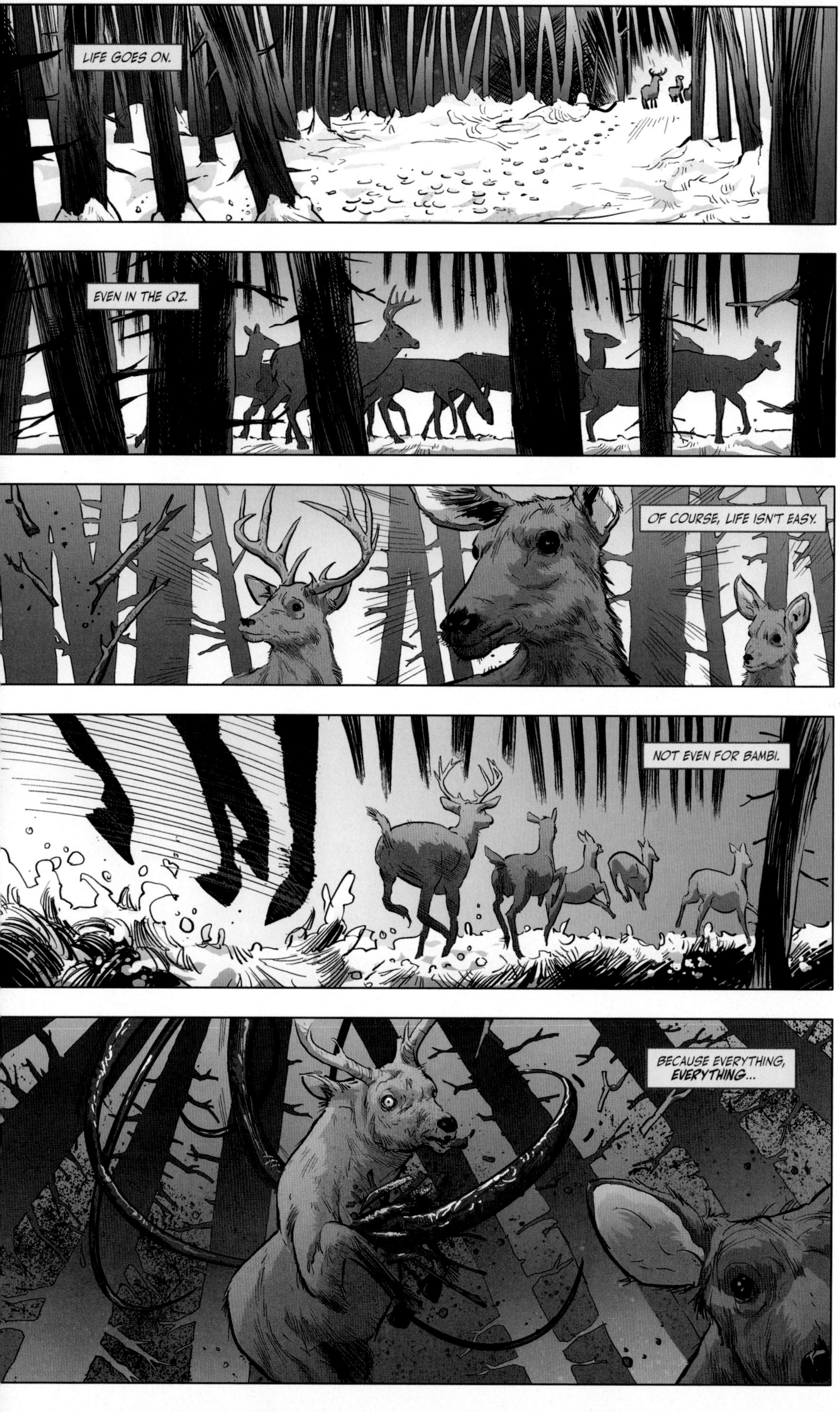
LIFE GOES ON.
EVEN IN THE QZ.
OF COURSE, LIFE ISN'T EASY.
NOT EVEN FOR BAMBI.
BECAUSE EVERYTHING, EVERYTHING...

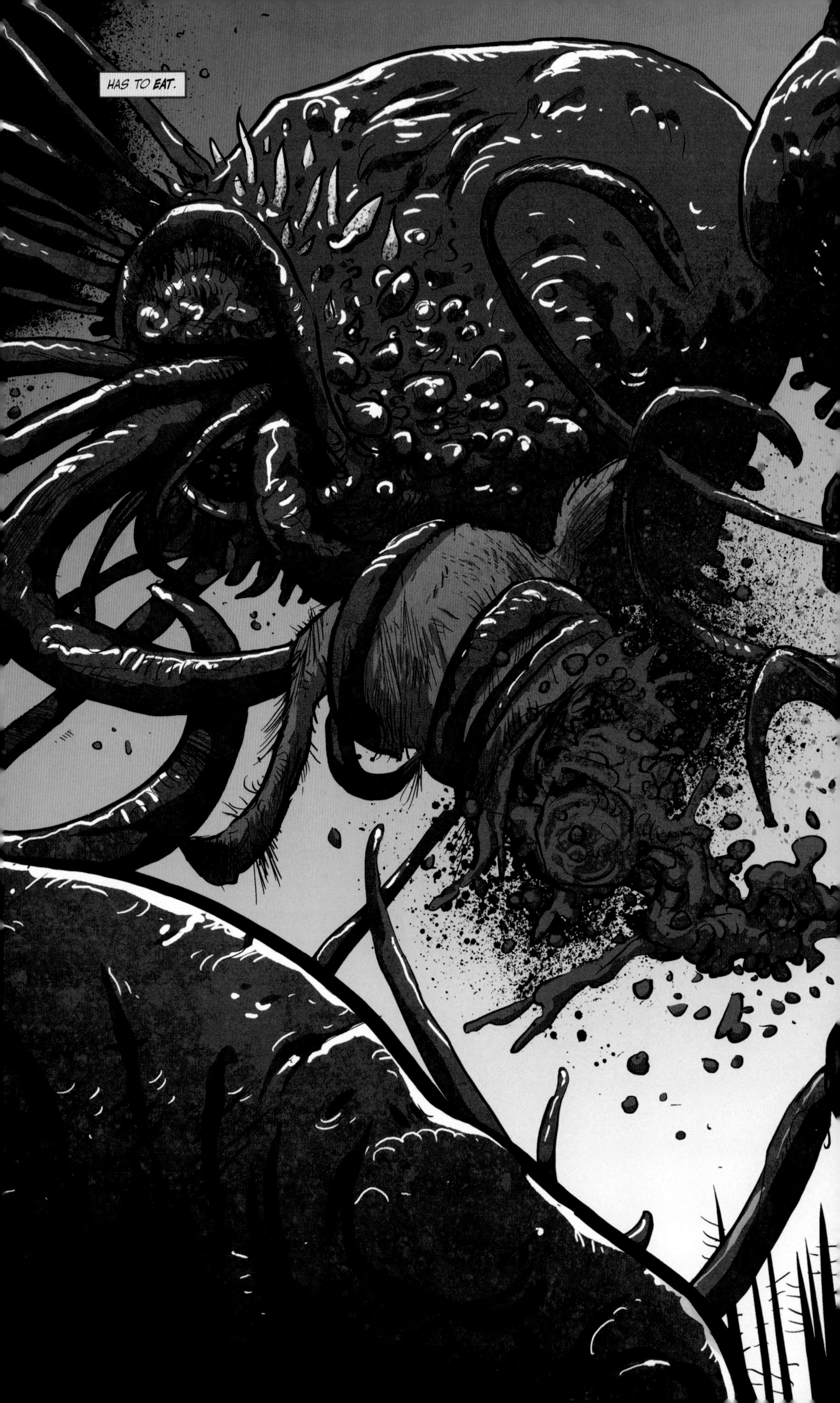
HAS TO EAT.

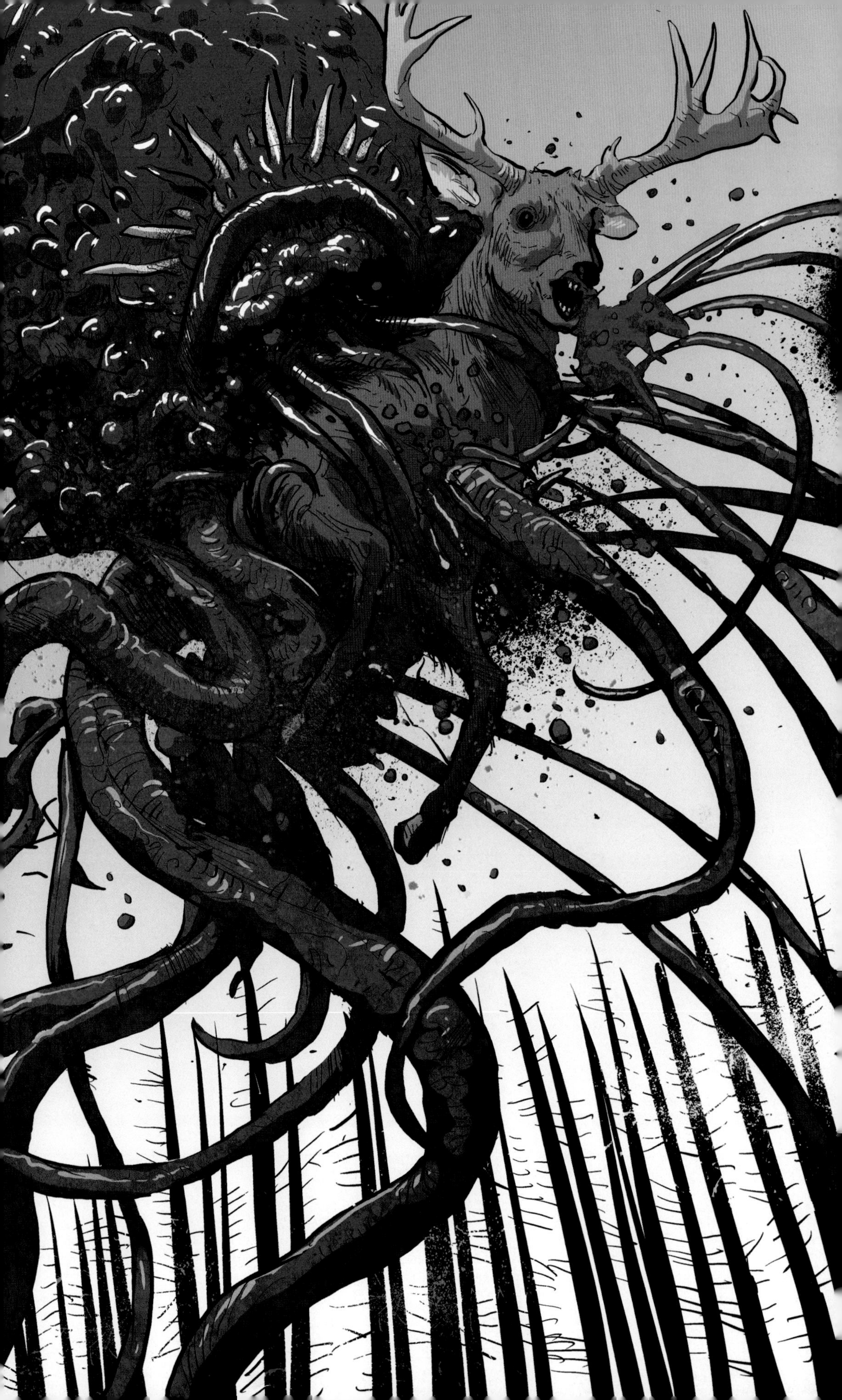

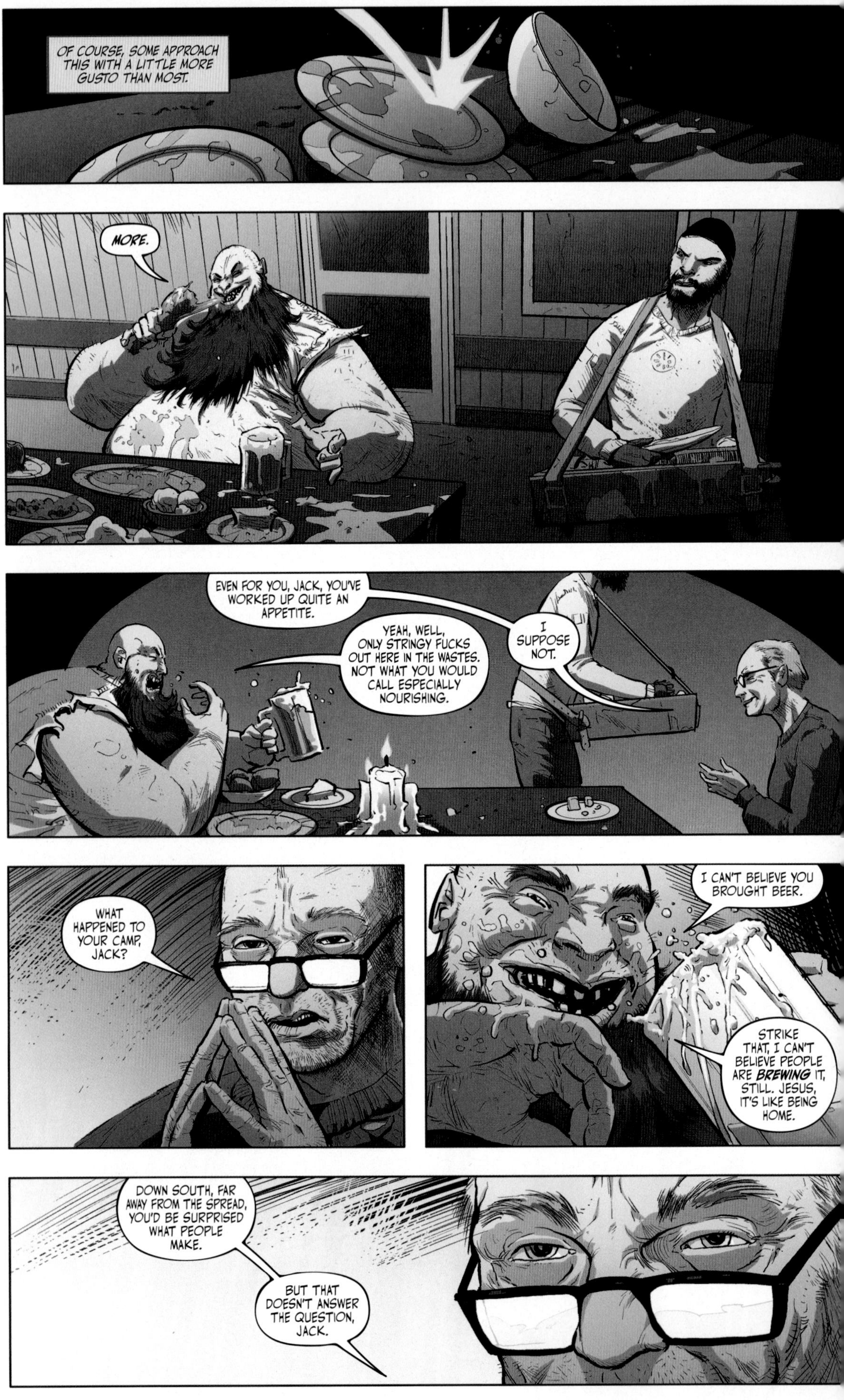
OF COURSE, SOME APPROACH THIS WITH A LITTLE MORE GUSTO THAN MOST.
MORE.
EVEN FOR YOU, JACK, YOU'VE WORKED UP QUITE AN APPETITE.
YEAH, WELL, ONLY STRINGY FUCKS OUT HERE IN THE WASTES. NOT WHAT YOU WOULD CALL ESPECIALLY NOURISHING.
I SUPPOSE NOT.
WHAT HAPPENED TO YOUR CAMP, JACK?
I CAN'T BELIEVE YOU BROUGHT BEER.
STRIKE THAT, I CAN'T BELIEVE PEOPLE ARE BREWING IT, STILL. JESUS, IT'S LIKE BEING HOME.
DOWN SOUTH, FAR AWAY FROM THE SPREAD, YOU'D BE SURPRISED WHAT PEOPLE MAKE.
BUT THAT DOESN'T ANSWER THE QUESTION, JACK.

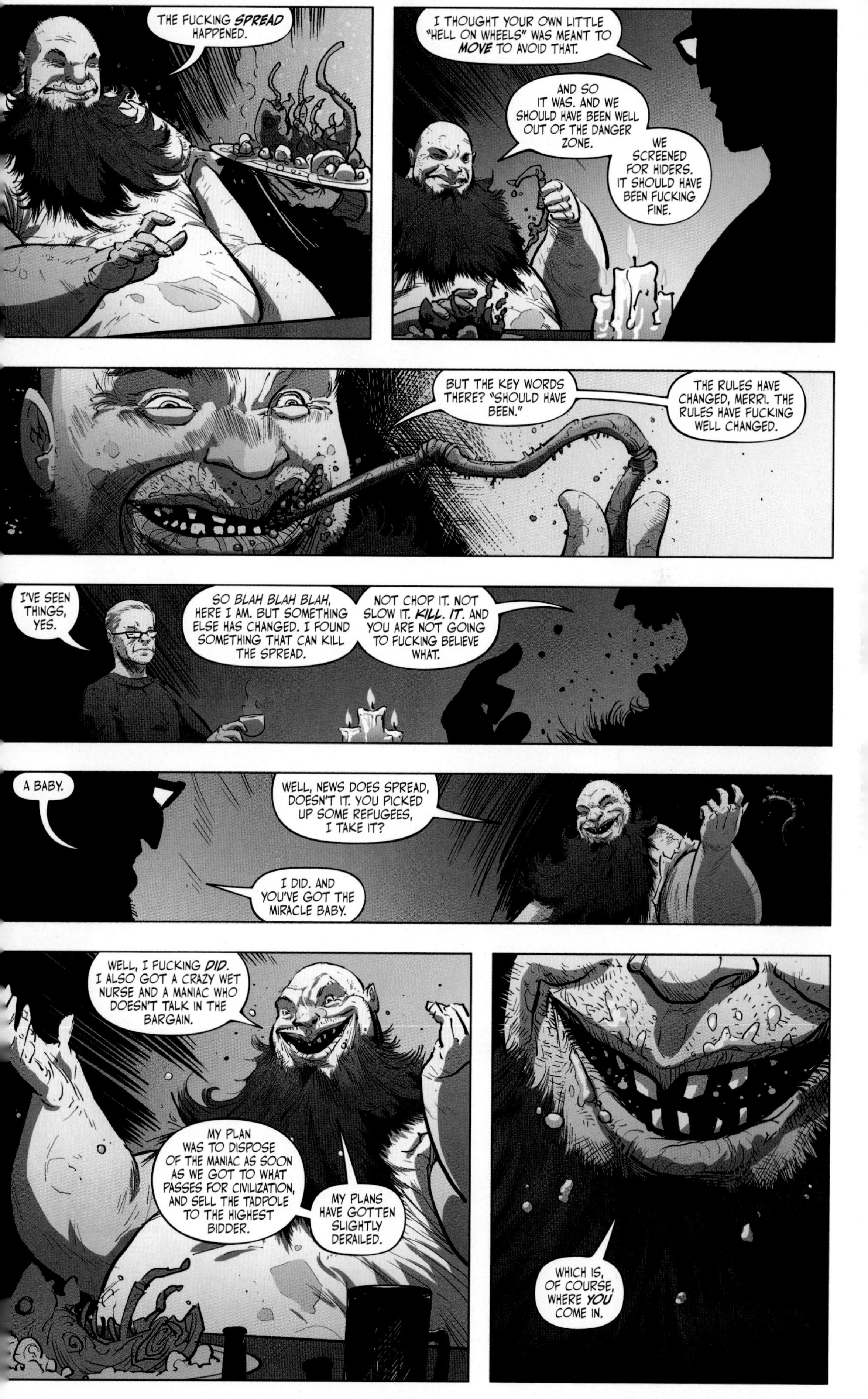
THE FUCKING SPREAD HAPPENED.
I THOUGHT YOUR OWN LITTLE "HELL ON WHEELS" WAS MEANT TO MOVE TO AVOID THAT.
AND SO IT WAS. AND WE SHOULD HAVE BEEN WELL OUT OF THE DANGER ZONE.
WE SCREENED FOR HIDERS. IT SHOULD HAVE BEEN FUCKING FINE.
BUT THE KEY WORDS THERE? "SHOULD HAVE BEEN."
THE RULES HAVE CHANGED, MERRI. THE RULES HAVE FUCKING WELL CHANGED.
I'VE SEEN THINGS, YES.
SO BLAH BLAH BLAH, HERE I AM. BUT SOMETHING ELSE HAS CHANGED. I FOUND SOMETHING THAT CAN KILL THE SPREAD.
NOT CHOP IT. NOT SLOW IT. KILL. IT. AND YOU ARE NOT GOING TO FUCKING BELIEVE WHAT.
A BABY.
WELL, NEWS DOES SPREAD, DOESN'T IT. YOU PICKED UP SOME REFUGEES, I TAKE IT?
I DID. AND YOU'VE GOT THE MIRACLE BABY.
WELL, I FUCKING DID. I ALSO GOT A CRAZY WET NURSE AND A MANIAC WHO DOESN'T TALK IN THE BARGAIN.
MY PLAN WAS TO DISPOSE OF THE MANIAC AS SOON AS WE GOT TO WHAT PASSES FOR CIVILIZATION, AND SELL THE TADPOLE TO THE HIGHEST BIDDER.
MY PLANS HAVE GOTTEN SLIGHTLY DERAILED.
WHICH IS, OF COURSE, WHERE YOU COME IN.

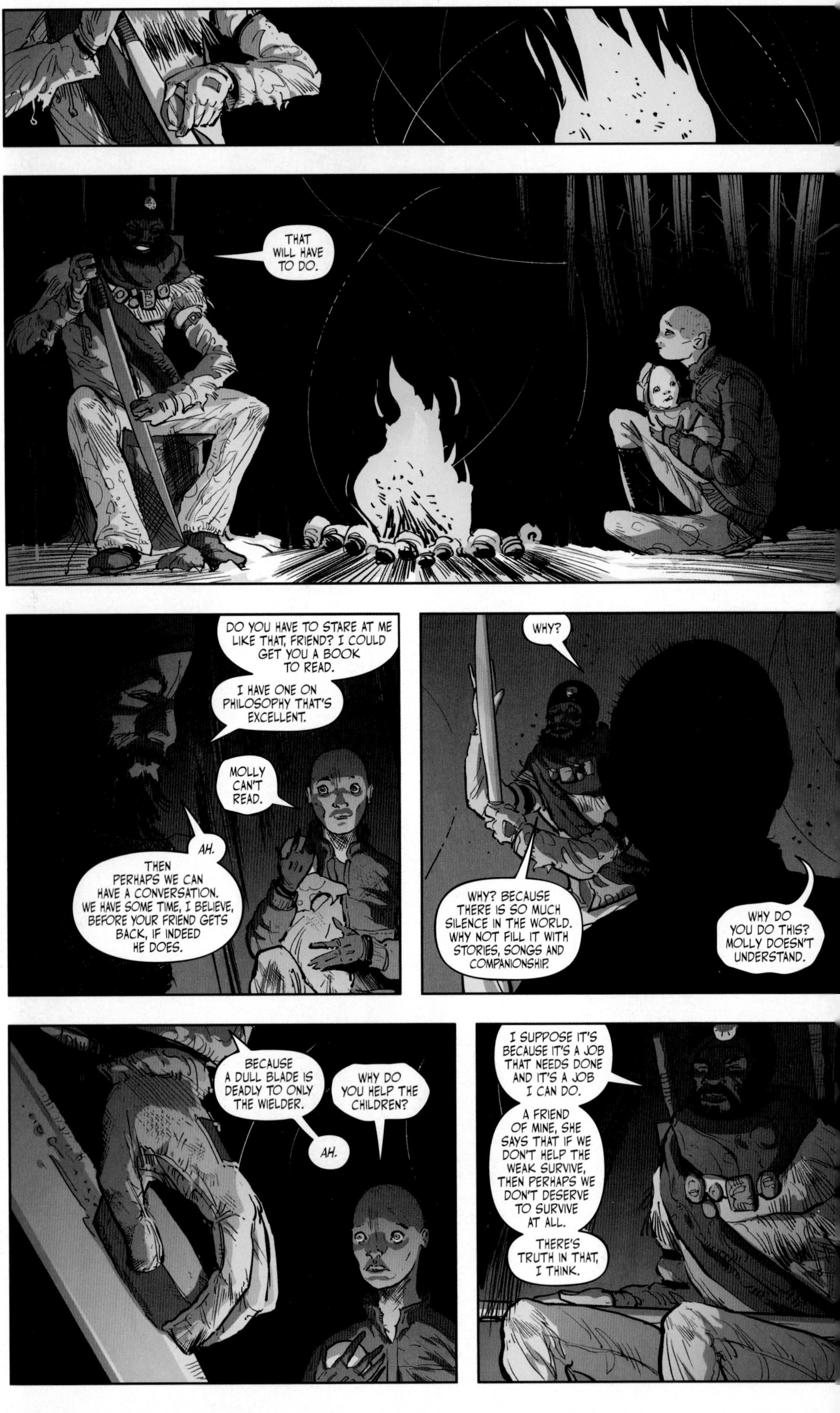

THAT WILL HAVE TO DO.
DO YOU HAVE TO STARE AT ME LIKE THAT, FRIEND? I COULD GET YOU A BOOK TO READ.
I HAVE ONE ON PHILOSOPHY THAT'S EXCELLENT.
MOLLY CAN'T READ.
AH.
THEN PERHAPS WE CAN HAVE A CONVERSATION. WE HAVE SOME TIME, I BELIEVE, BEFORE YOUR FRIEND GETS BACK, IF INDEED HE DOES.
WHY?
WHY? BECAUSE THERE IS SO MUCH SILENCE IN THE WORLD. WHY NOT FILL IT WITH STORIES, SONGS AND COMPANIONSHIP.
WHY DO YOU DO THIS? MOLLY DOESN'T UNDERSTAND.
BECAUSE A DULL BLADE IS DEADLY TO ONLY THE WIELDER.
AH.
WHY DO YOU HELP THE CHILDREN?
I SUPPOSE IT'S BECAUSE IT'S A JOB THAT NEEDS DONE AND IT'S A JOB I CAN DO.
A FRIEND OF MINE, SHE SAYS THAT IF WE DON'T HELP THE WEAK SURVIVE, THEN PERHAPS WE DON'T DESERVE TO SURVIVE AT ALL.
THERE'S TRUTH IN THAT, I THINK.

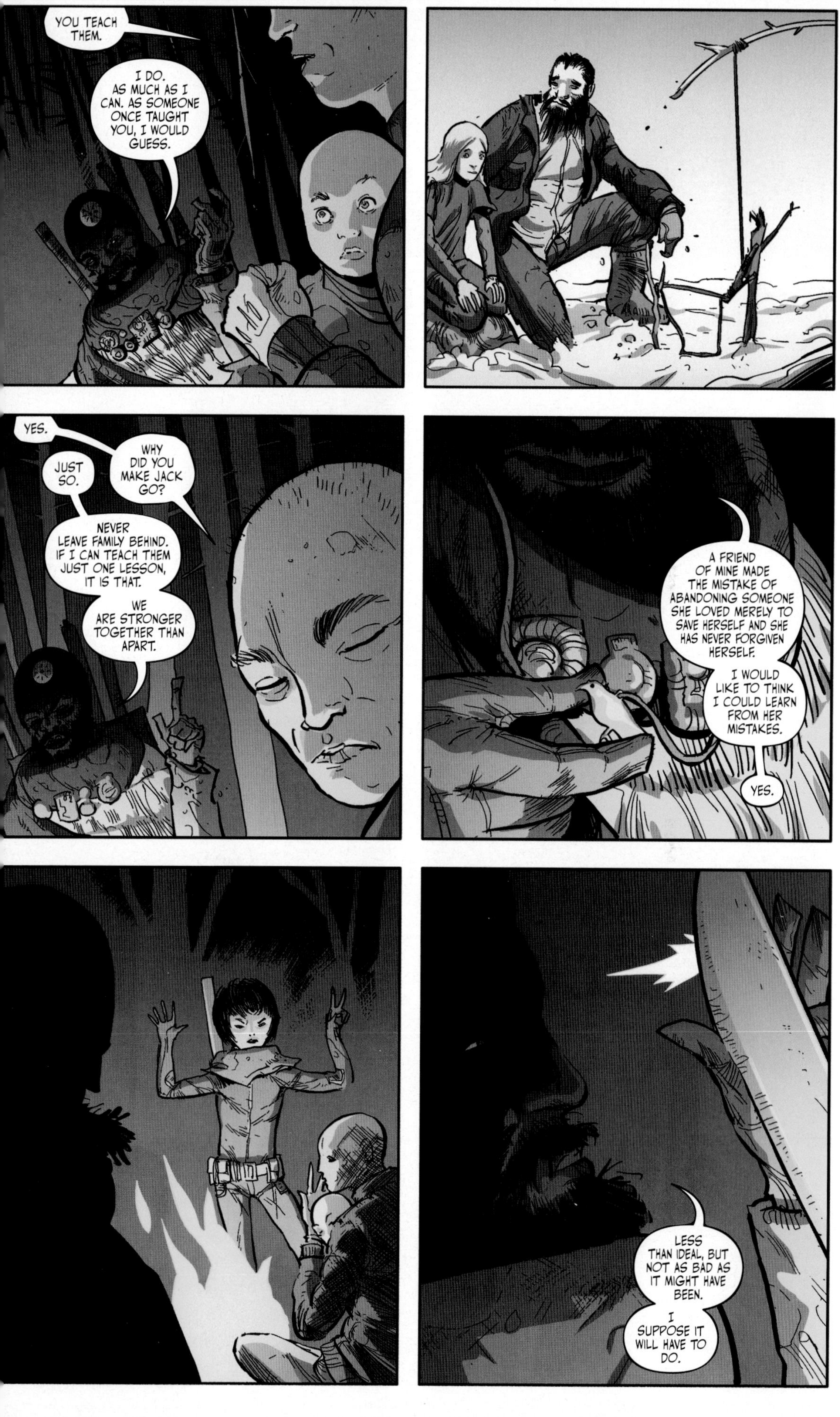
YOU TEACH THEM.
I DO. AS MUCH AS I CAN. AS SOMEONE ONCE TAUGHT YOU, I WOULD GUESS.
YES.
WHY DID YOU MAKE JACK GO?
JUST SO.
NEVER LEAVE FAMILY BEHIND. IF I CAN TEACH THEM JUST ONE LESSON, IT IS THAT.
WE ARE STRONGER TOGETHER THAN APART.
A FRIEND OF MINE MADE THE MISTAKE OF ABANDONING SOMEONE SHE LOVED MERELY TO SAVE HERSELF AND SHE HAS NEVER FORGIVEN HERSELF.
I WOULD LIKE TO THINK I COULD LEARN FROM HER MISTAKES.
YES.
LESS THAN IDEAL, BUT NOT AS BAD AS IT MIGHT HAVE BEEN.
I SUPPOSE IT WILL HAVE TO DO.

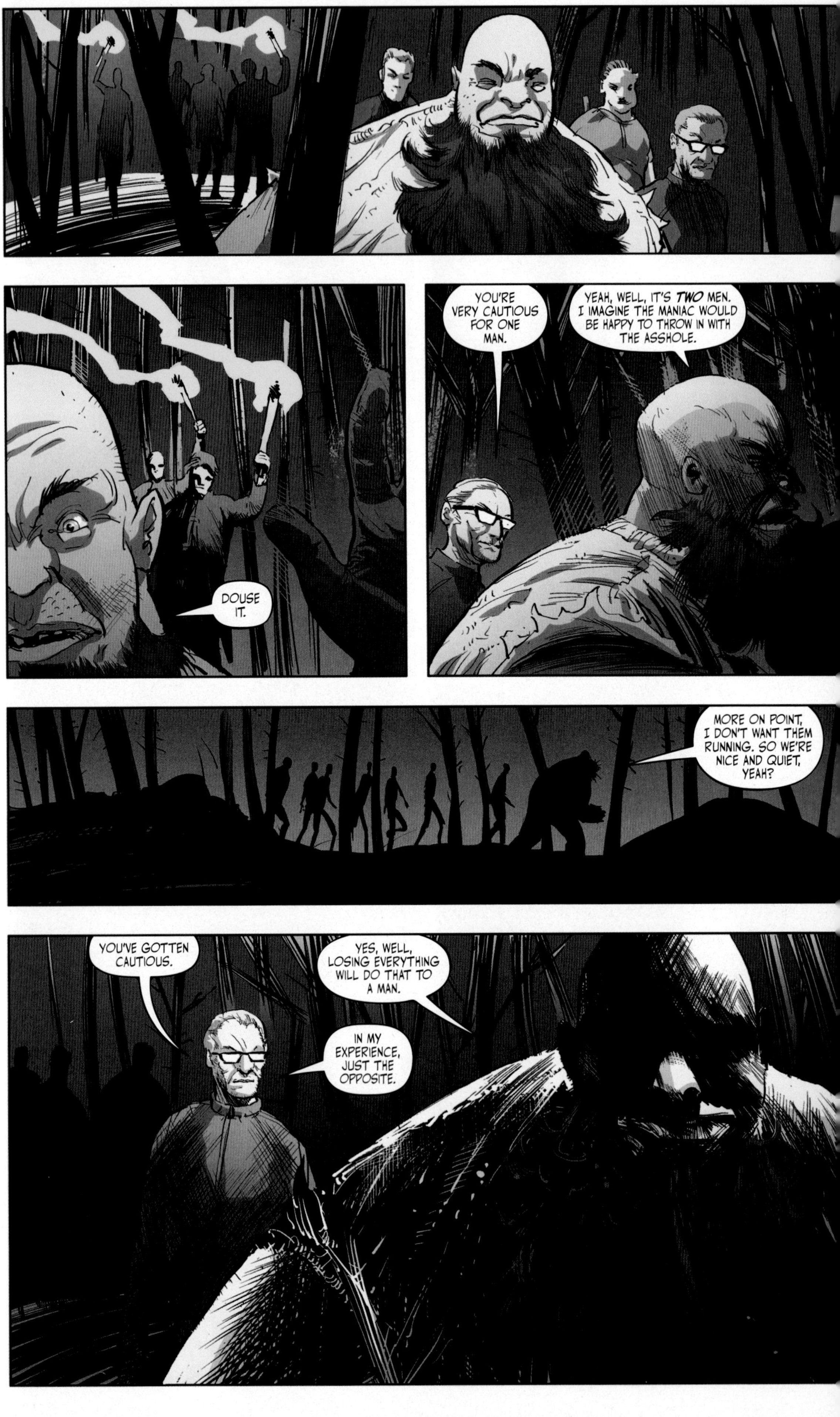
DOUSE IT.
YOU'RE VERY CAUTIOUS FOR ONE MAN.
YEAH, WELL, IT'S TWO MEN. I IMAGINE THE MANIAC WOULD BE HAPPY TO THROW IN WITH THE ASSHOLE.
MORE ON POINT, I DON'T WANT THEM RUNNING. SO WE'RE NICE AND QUIET, YEAH?
YOU'VE GOTTEN CAUTIOUS.
YES, WELL, LOSING EVERYTHING WILL DO THAT TO A MAN.
IN MY EXPERIENCE, JUST THE OPPOSITE.

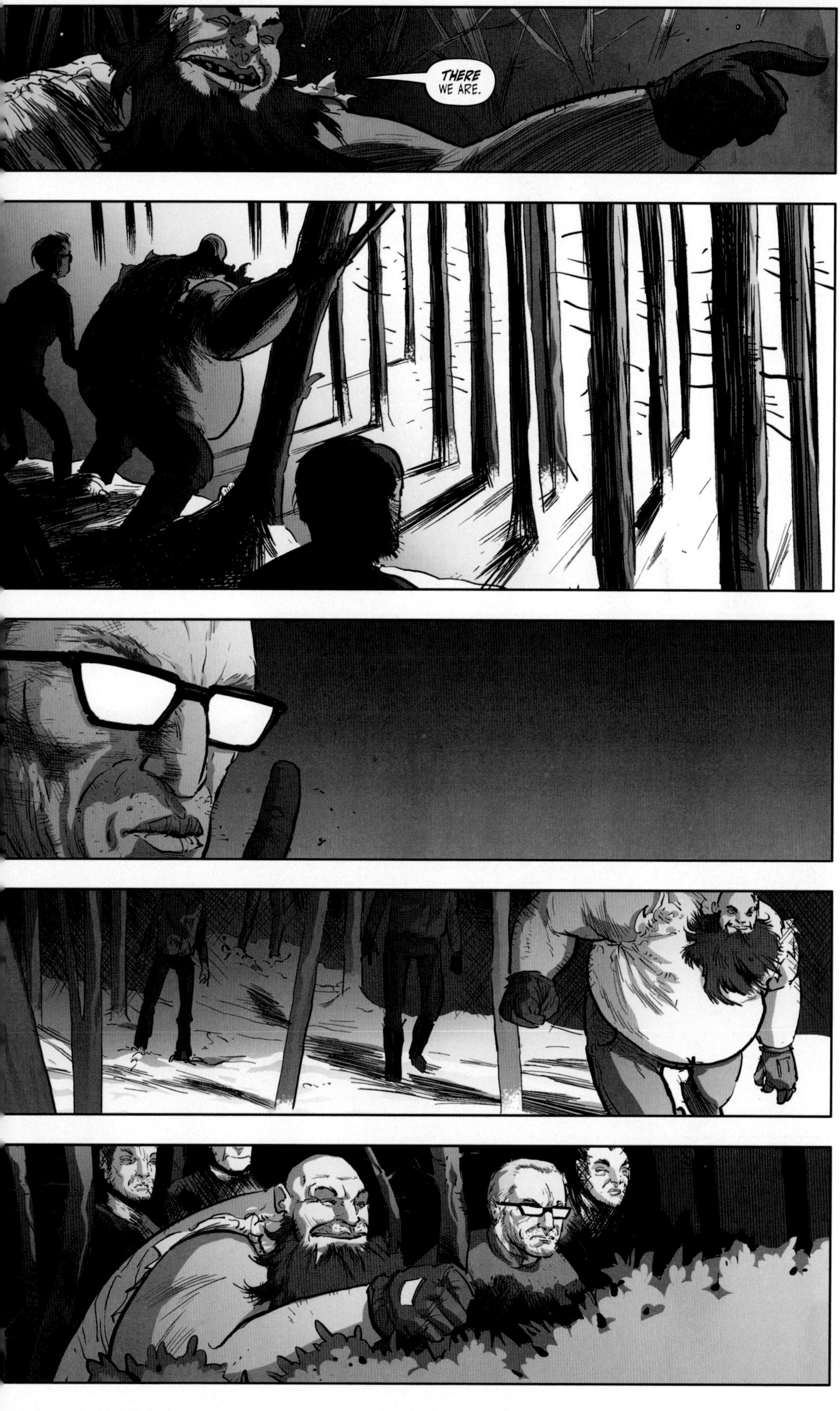
THERE WE ARE.

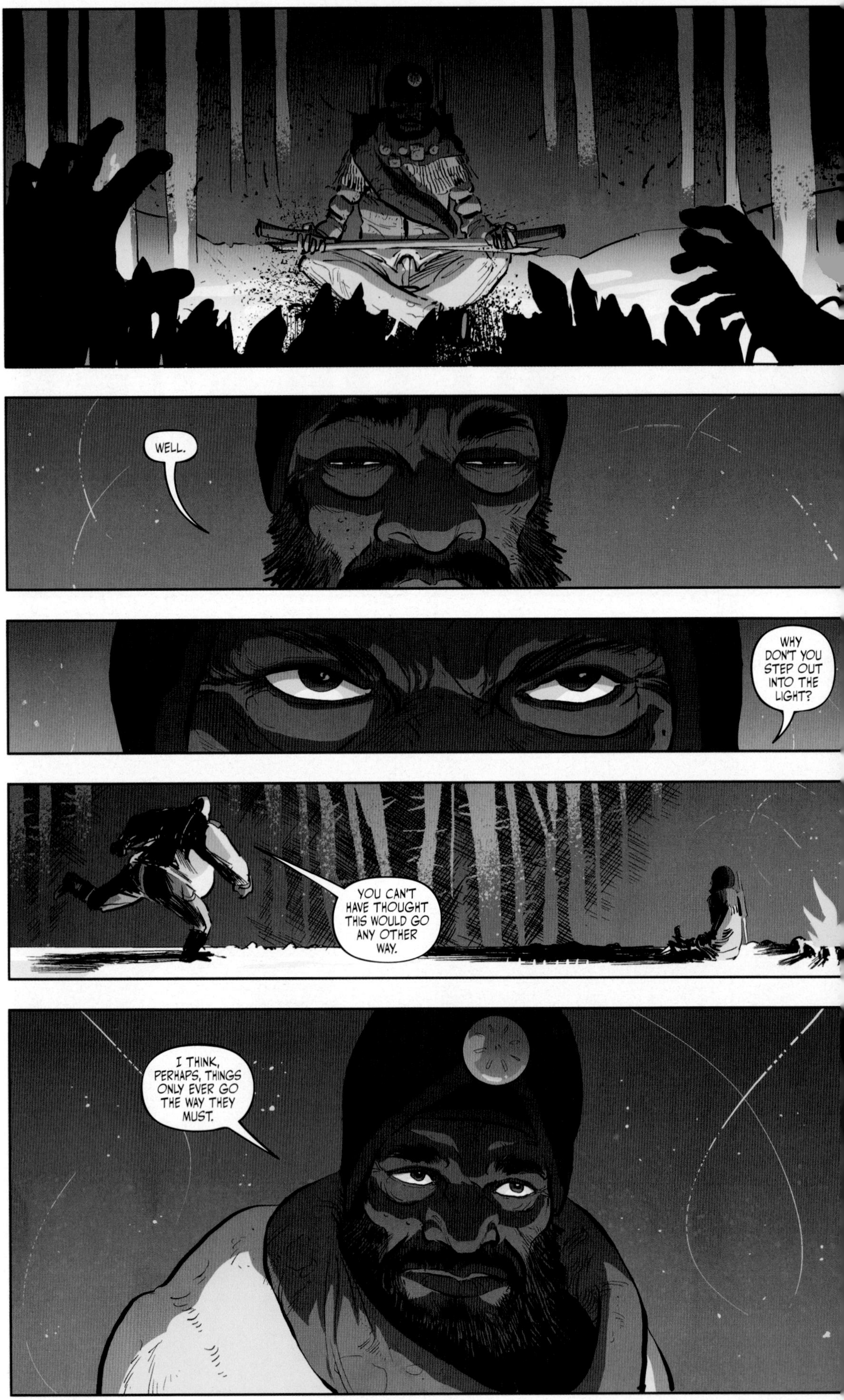
WELL.
WHY DON'T YOU STEP OUT INTO THE LIGHT?
YOU CAN'T HAVE THOUGHT THIS WOULD GO ANY OTHER WAY.
I THINK, PERHAPS, THINGS ONLY EVER GO THE WAY THEY MUST.

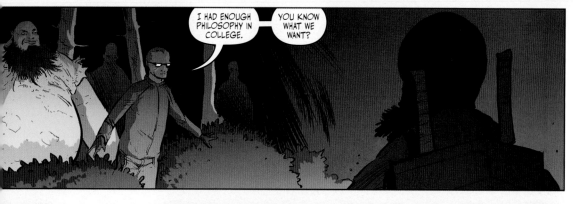

I HAD ENOUGH PHILOSOPHY IN COLLEGE.

YOU KNOW WHAT WE WANT?

I SURELY DO. IF YOU DON'T LIKE PHILOSOPHY, FRIEND, THEN MAY I SUGGEST SOME *ROCK AND ROLL?*

"YOU CAN'T ALWAYS GET WHAT YOU WANT."

JESUS.

I WOULDN'T NORMALLY WASTE THE BULLET, BUT I'M NOT ENTIRELY SURE I CAN STAND TO HEAR *THE STONES* BUTCHERED LIKE THAT.

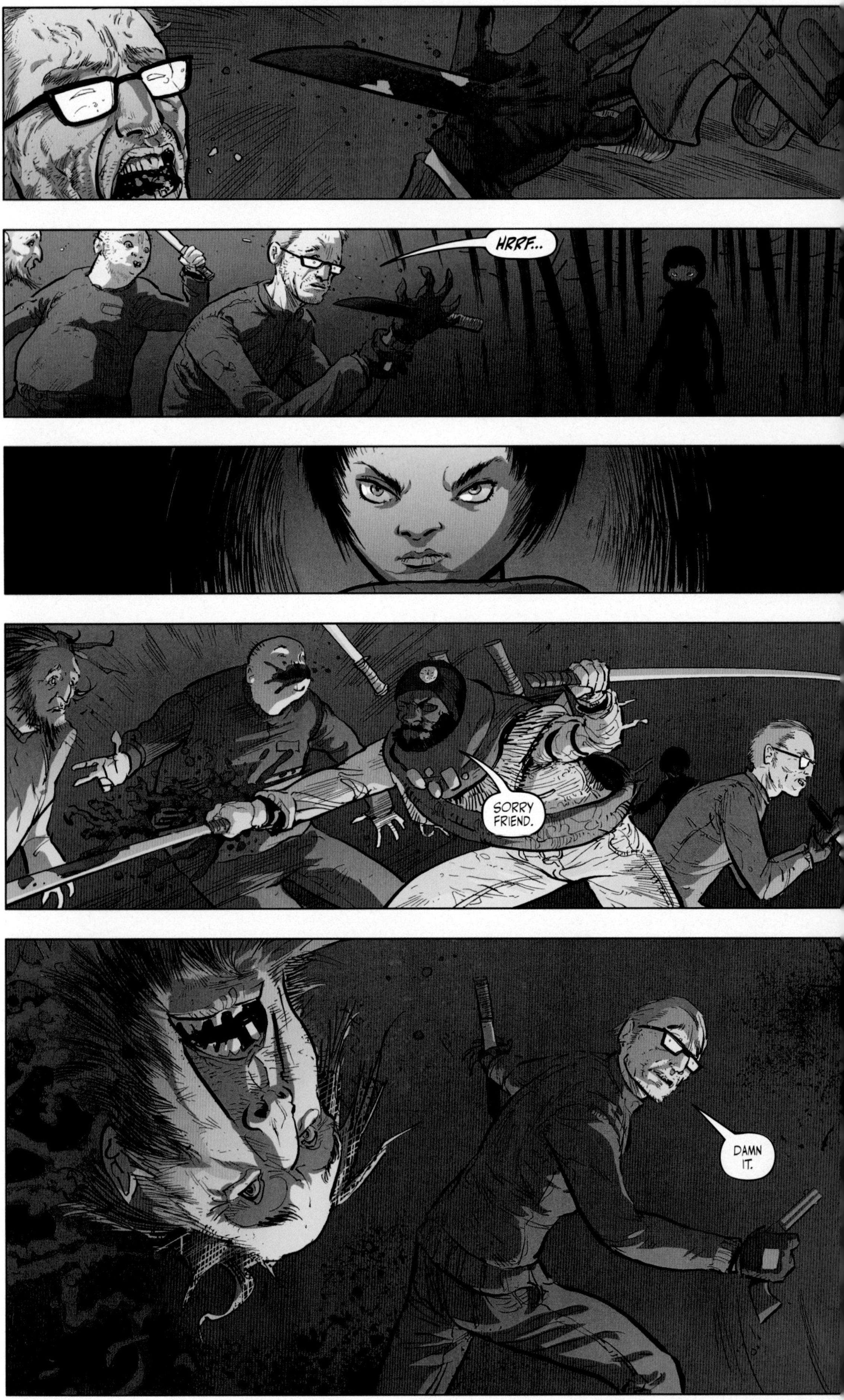
HRRF...
SORRY FRIEND.
DAMN IT.

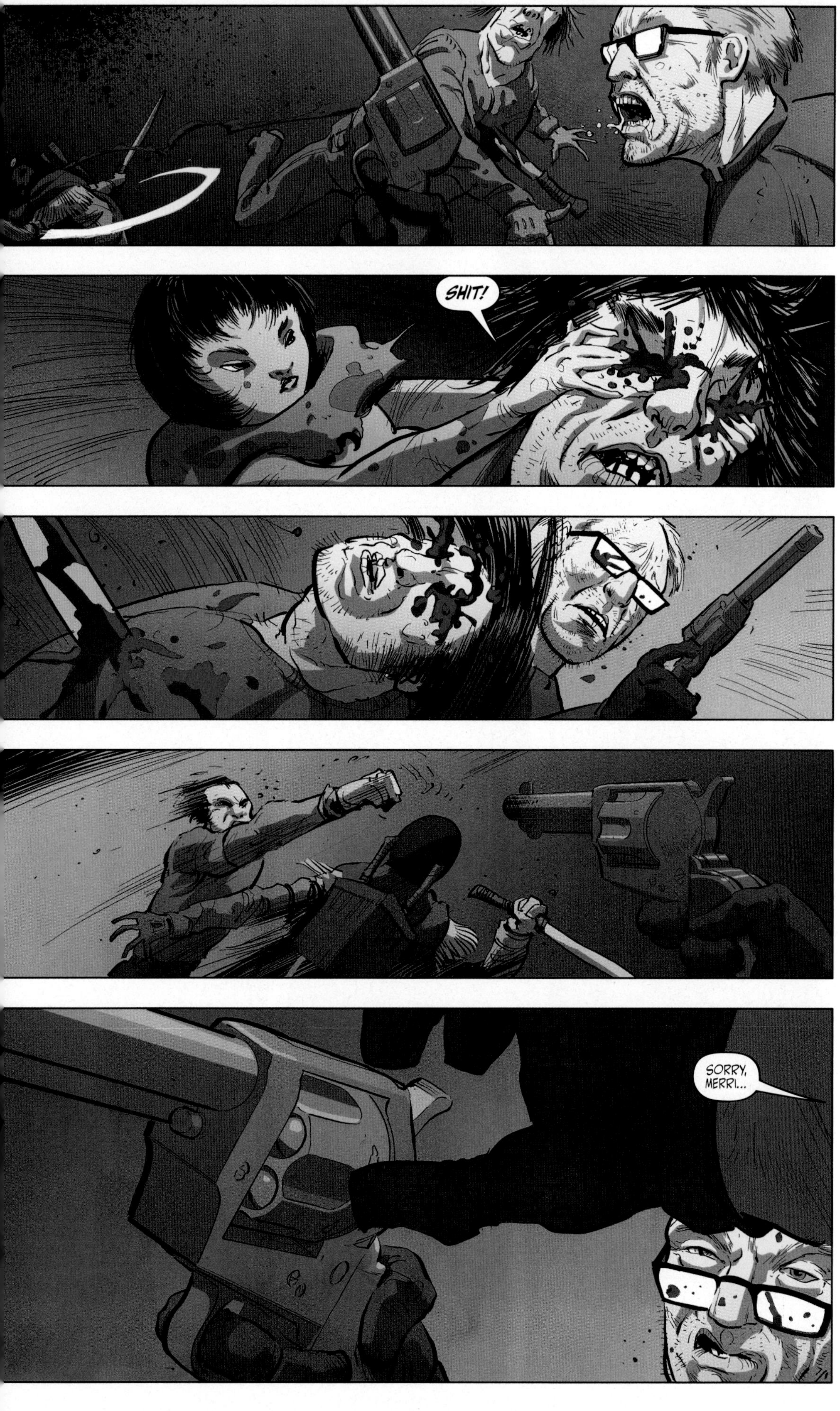
SHIT!
SORRY, MERRI...

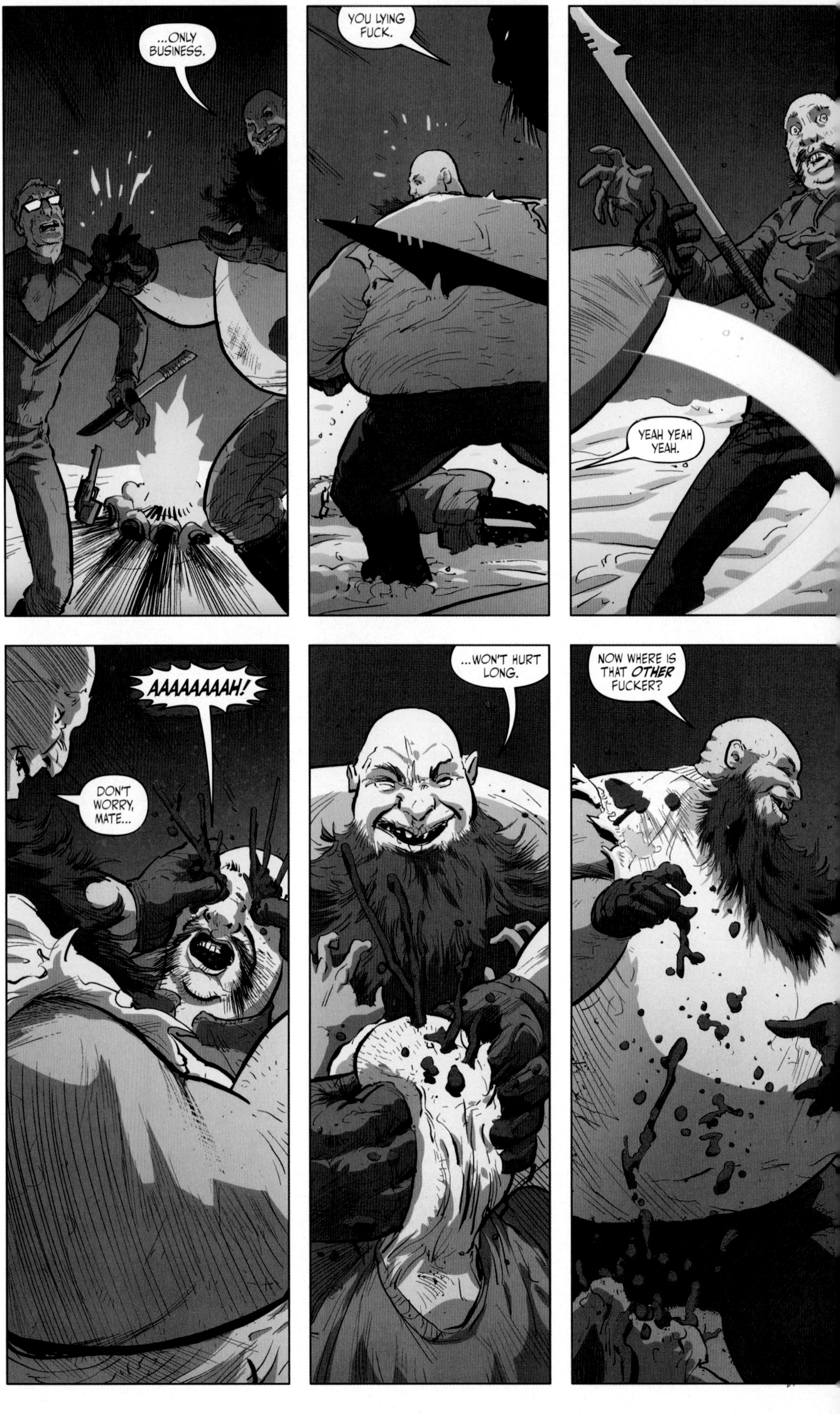

...ONLY BUSINESS.
YOU LYING FUCK.
YEAH YEAH YEAH.
AAAAAAAAH!
DON'T WORRY, MATE...
...WON'T HURT LONG.
NOW WHERE IS THAT *OTHER* FUCKER?

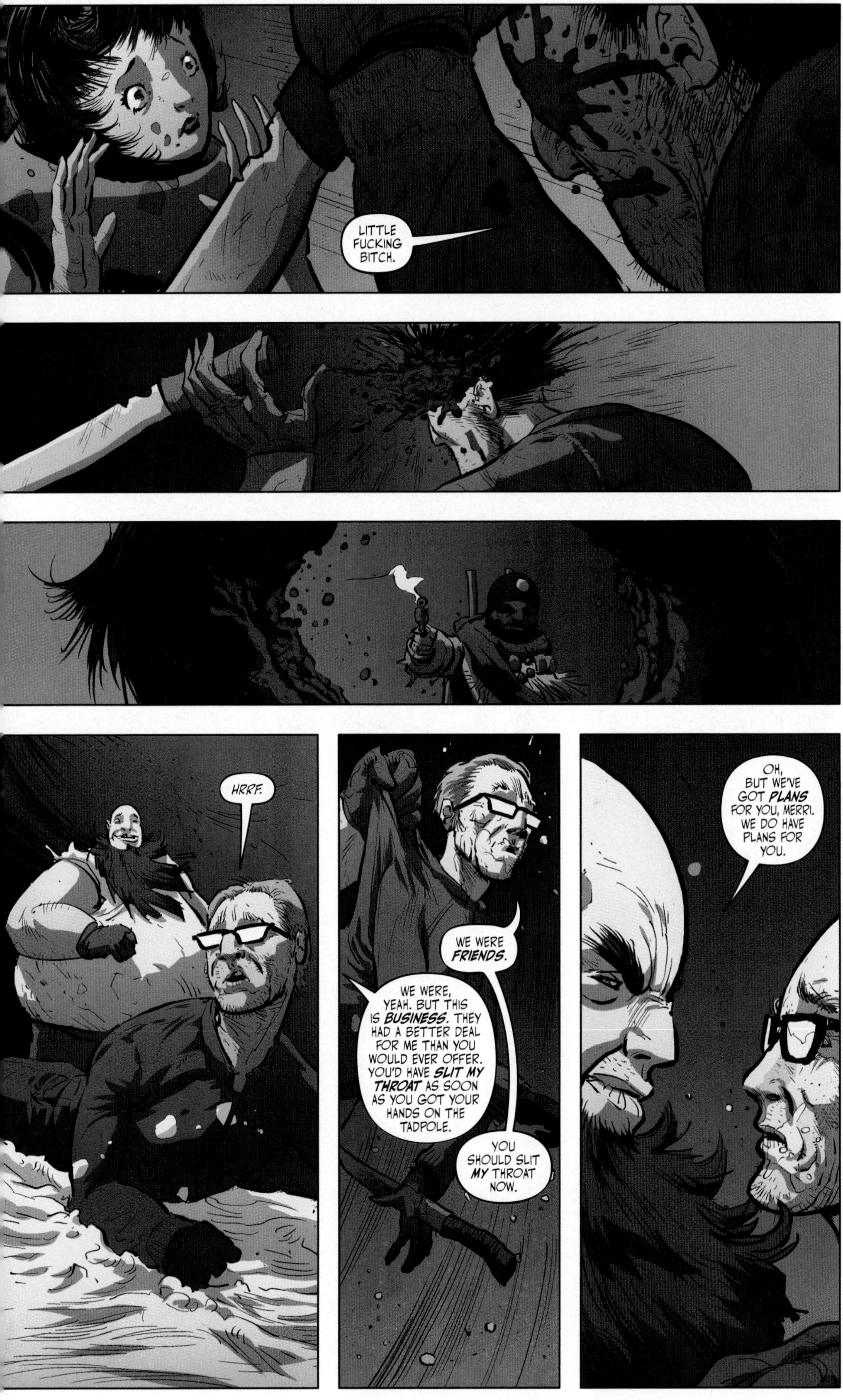
LITTLE FUCKING BITCH.
HRRF.
WE WERE FRIENDS.
WE WERE, YEAH. BUT THIS IS BUSINESS. THEY HAD A BETTER DEAL FOR ME THAN YOU WOULD EVER OFFER. YOU'D HAVE SLIT MY THROAT AS SOON AS YOU GOT YOUR HANDS ON THE TADPOLE.
YOU SHOULD SLIT MY THROAT NOW.
OH, BUT WE'VE GOT PLANS FOR YOU, MERRI. WE DO HAVE PLANS FOR YOU.

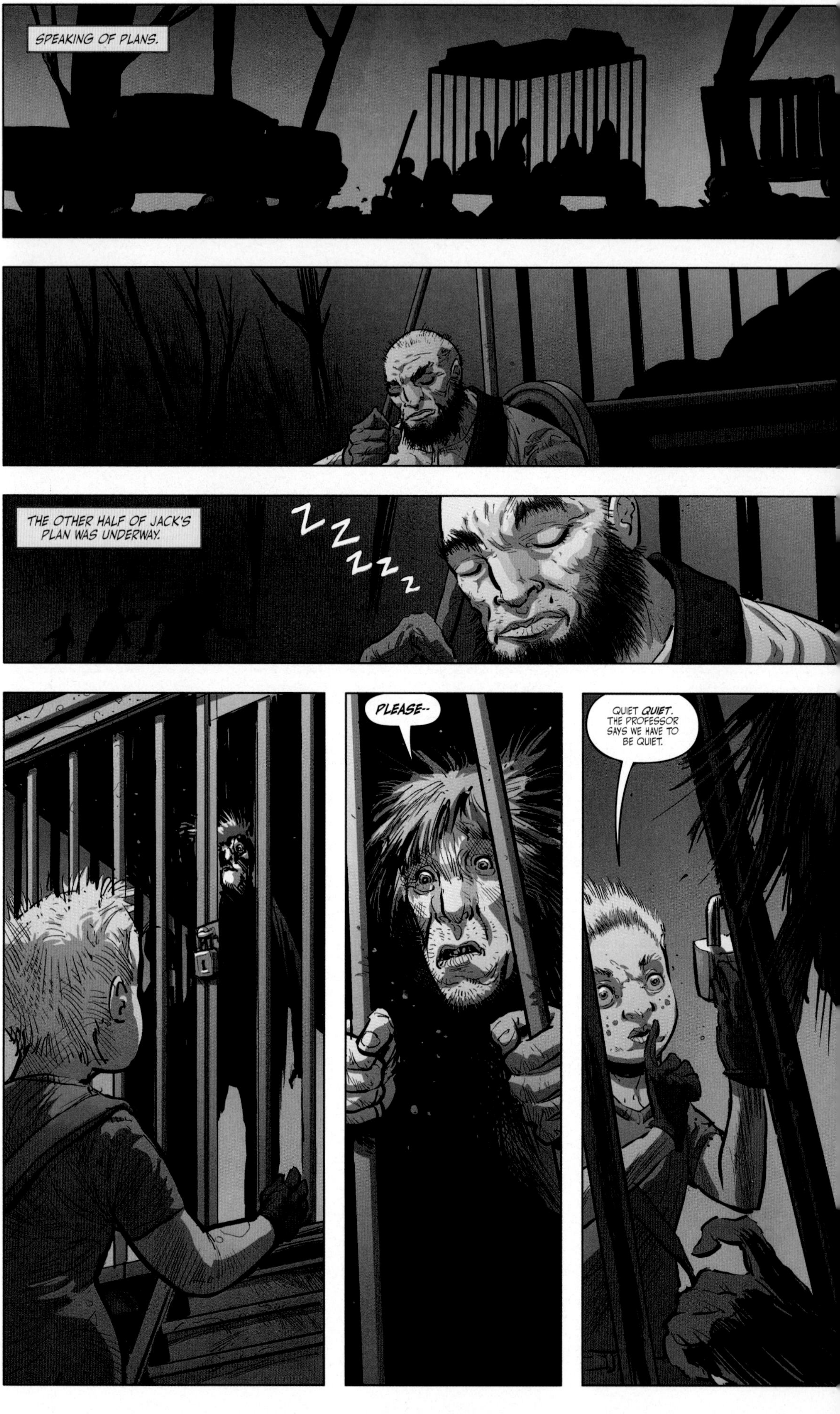
SPEAKING OF PLANS.
THE OTHER HALF OF JACK'S PLAN WAS UNDERWAY.
ZZZZZ
PLEASE--
QUIET QUIET. THE PROFESSOR SAYS WE HAVE TO BE QUIET.

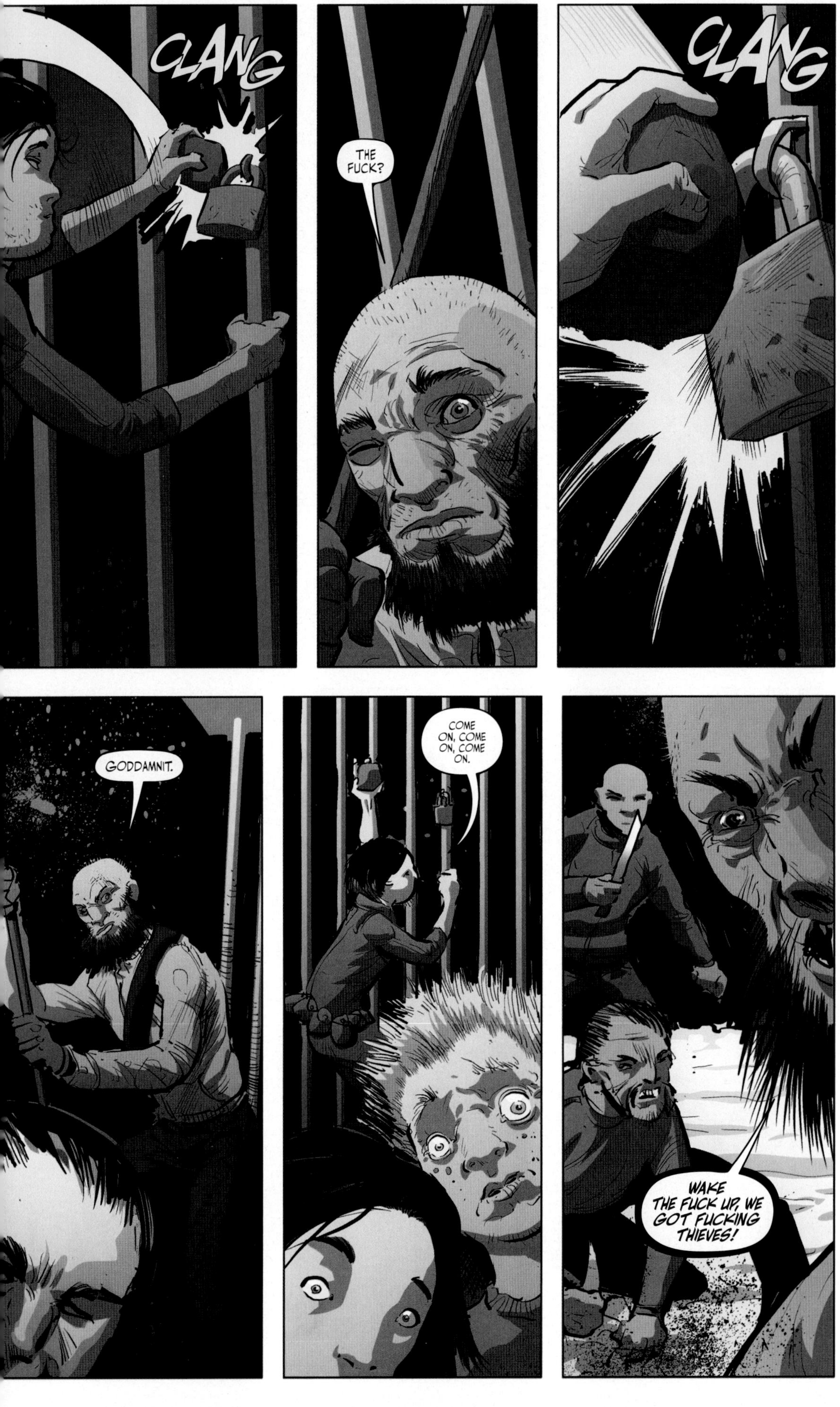
CLANG
THE FUCK?
CLANG
GODDAMNIT.
COME ON, COME ON, COME ON.
WAKE THE FUCK UP, WE GOT FUCKING THIEVES!

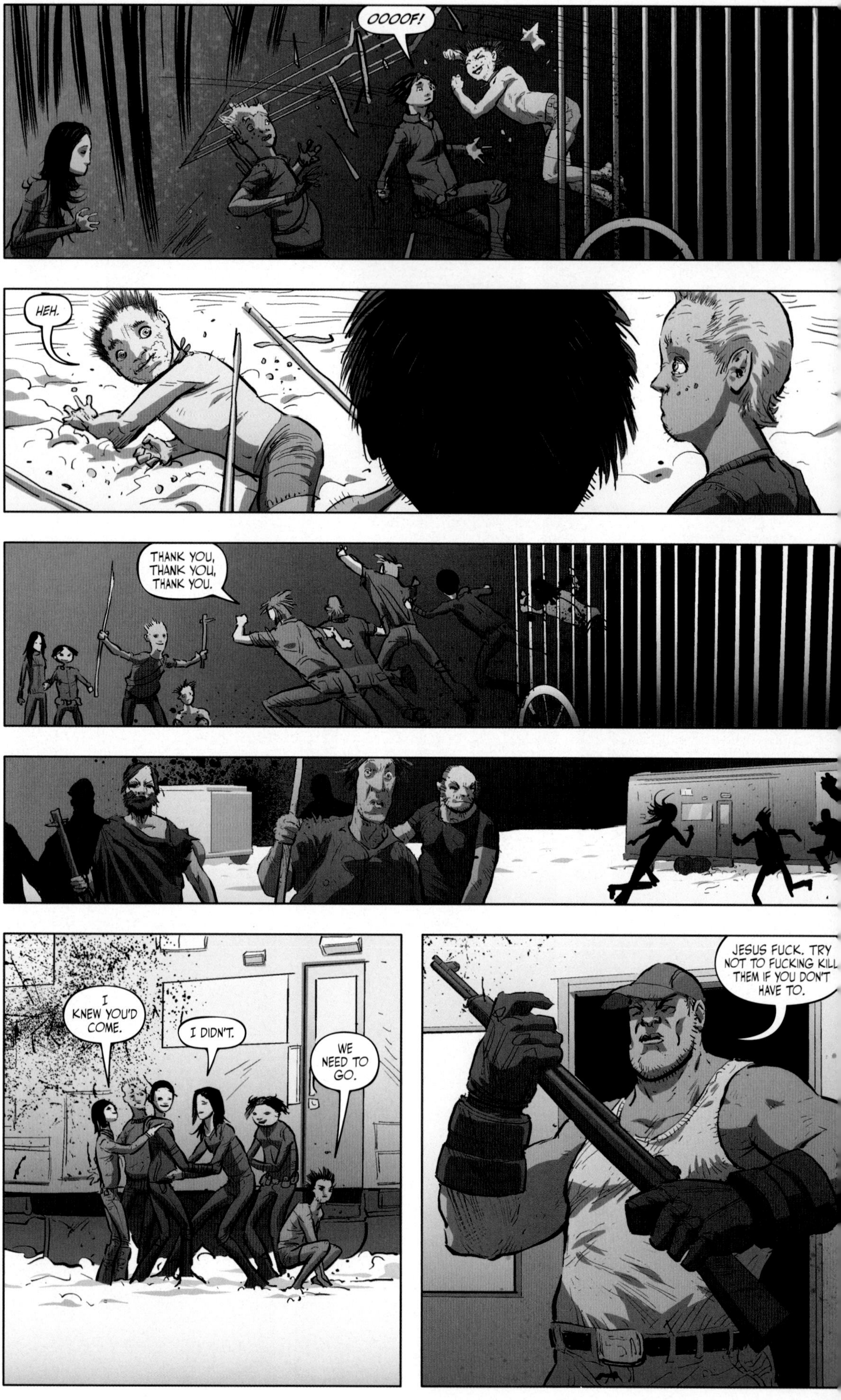

OOOOF!
HEH.
THANK YOU, THANK YOU, THANK YOU.
I KNEW YOU'D COME.
I DIDN'T.
WE NEED TO GO.
JESUS FUCK. TRY NOT TO FUCKING KILL THEM IF YOU DON'T HAVE TO.

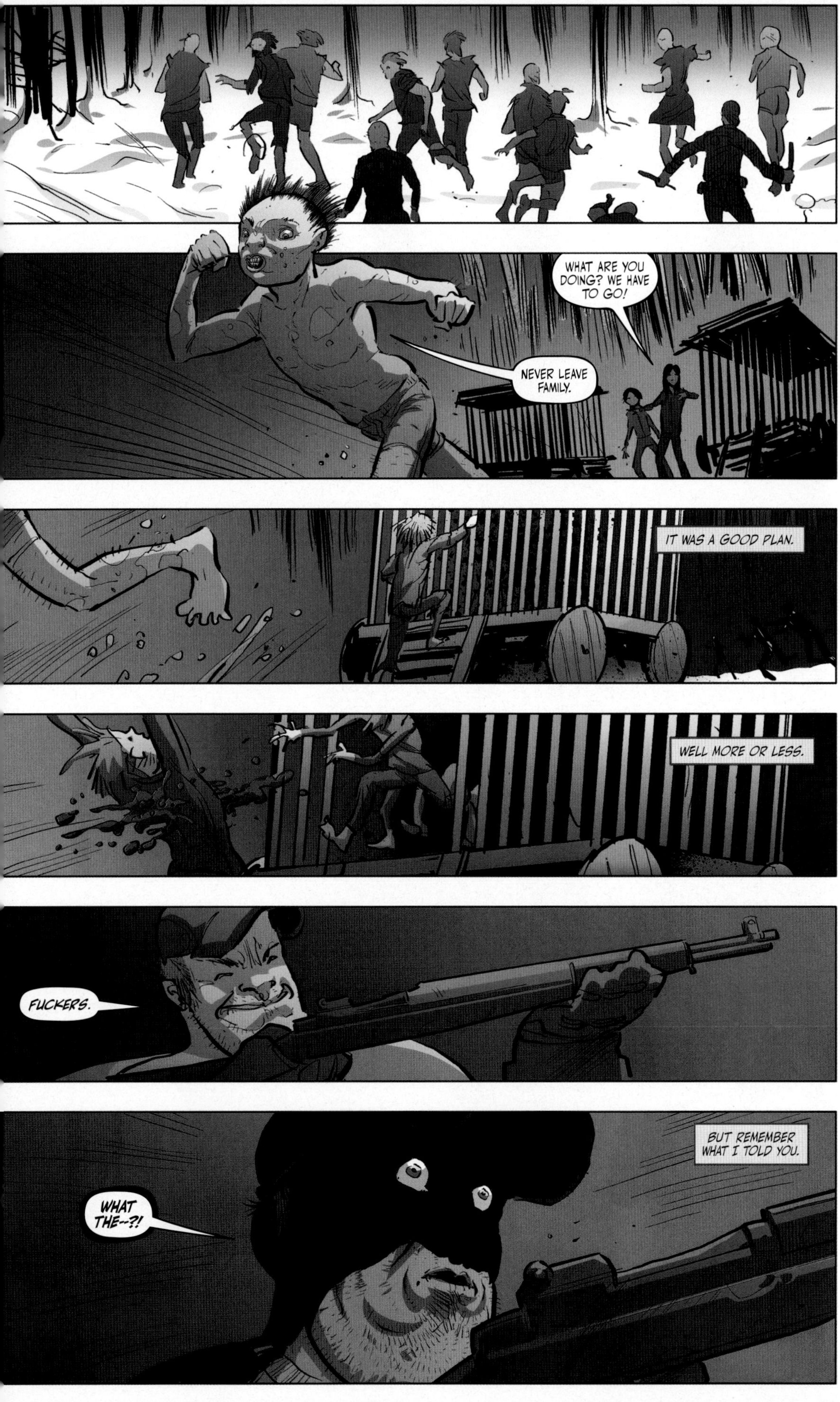
WHAT ARE YOU DOING? WE HAVE TO GO!
NEVER LEAVE FAMILY.
IT WAS A GOOD PLAN.
WELL MORE OR LESS.
FUCKERS.
BUT REMEMBER WHAT I TOLD YOU.
WHAT THE--?!

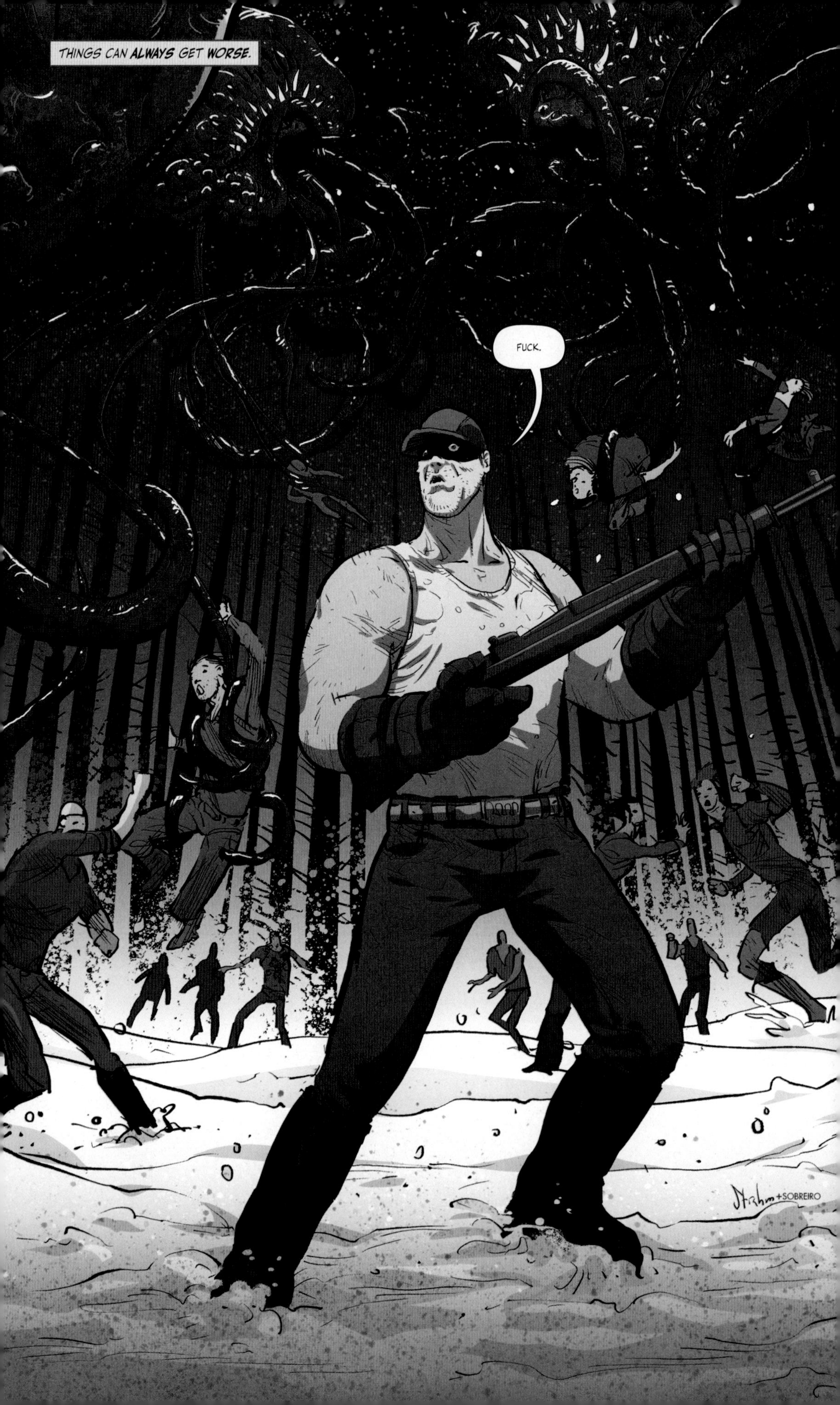
THINGS CAN ALWAYS GET WORSE.
FUCK.
SOBREIRO

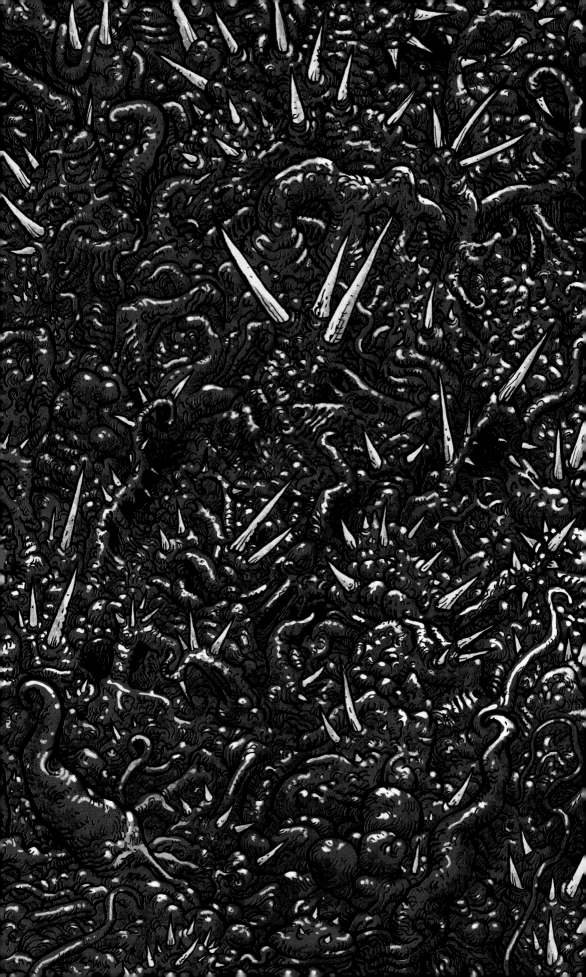

CHAPTER FIVE

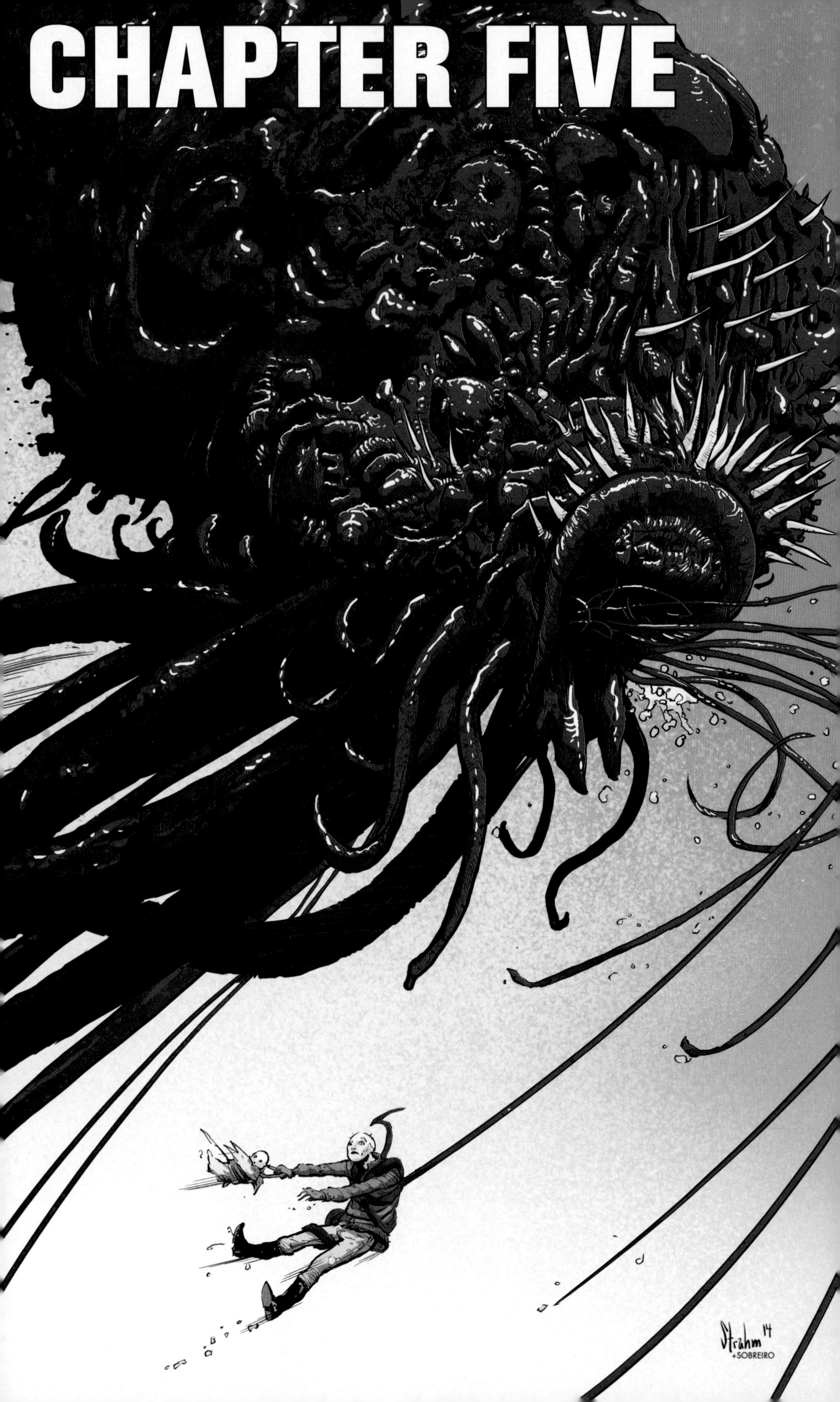
Strahm '14
+SOBREIRO

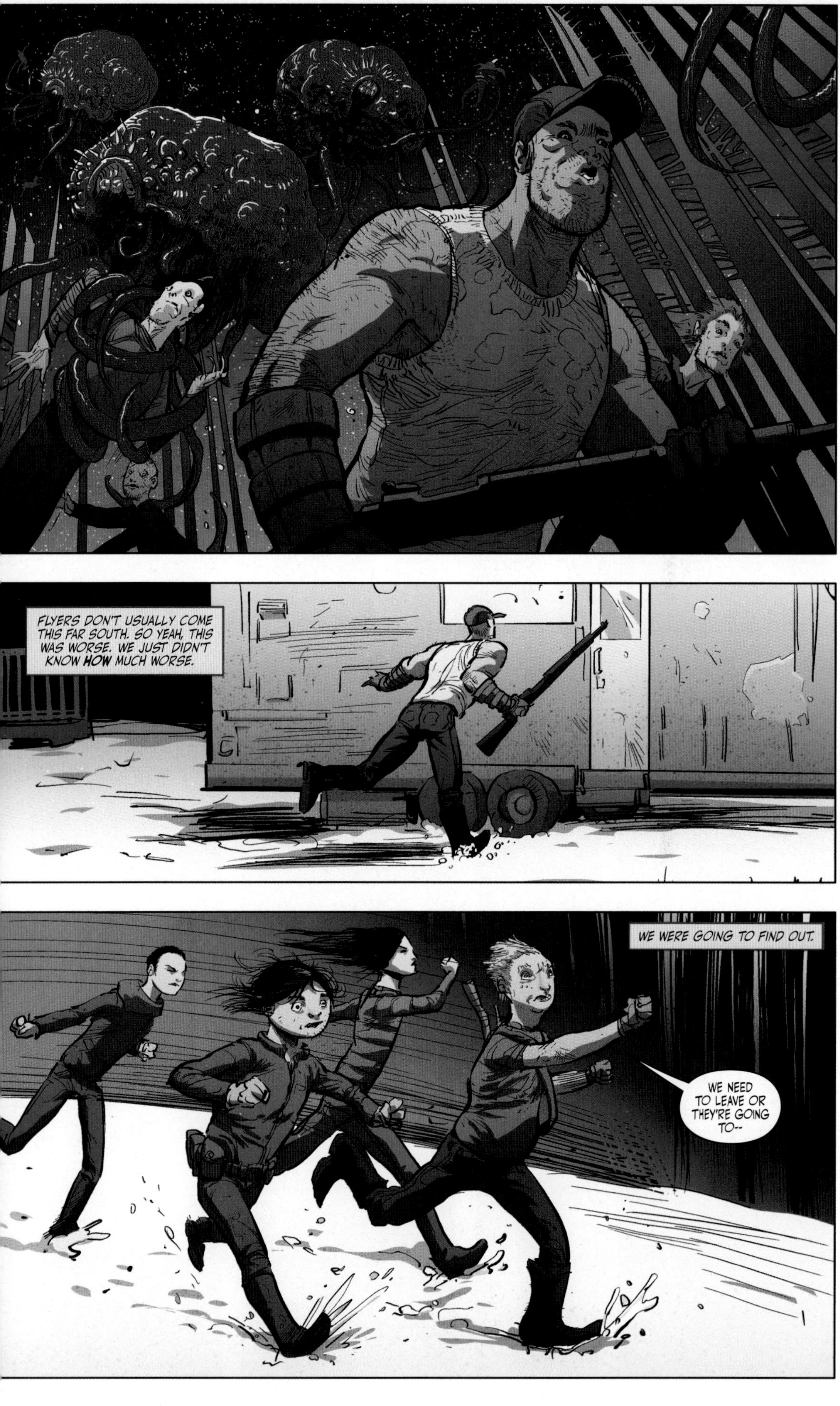
FLYERS DON'T USUALLY COME THIS FAR SOUTH. SO YEAH, THIS WAS WORSE. WE JUST DIDN'T KNOW **HOW** MUCH WORSE.
WE WERE GOING TO FIND OUT.
WE NEED TO LEAVE OR THEY'RE GOING TO--

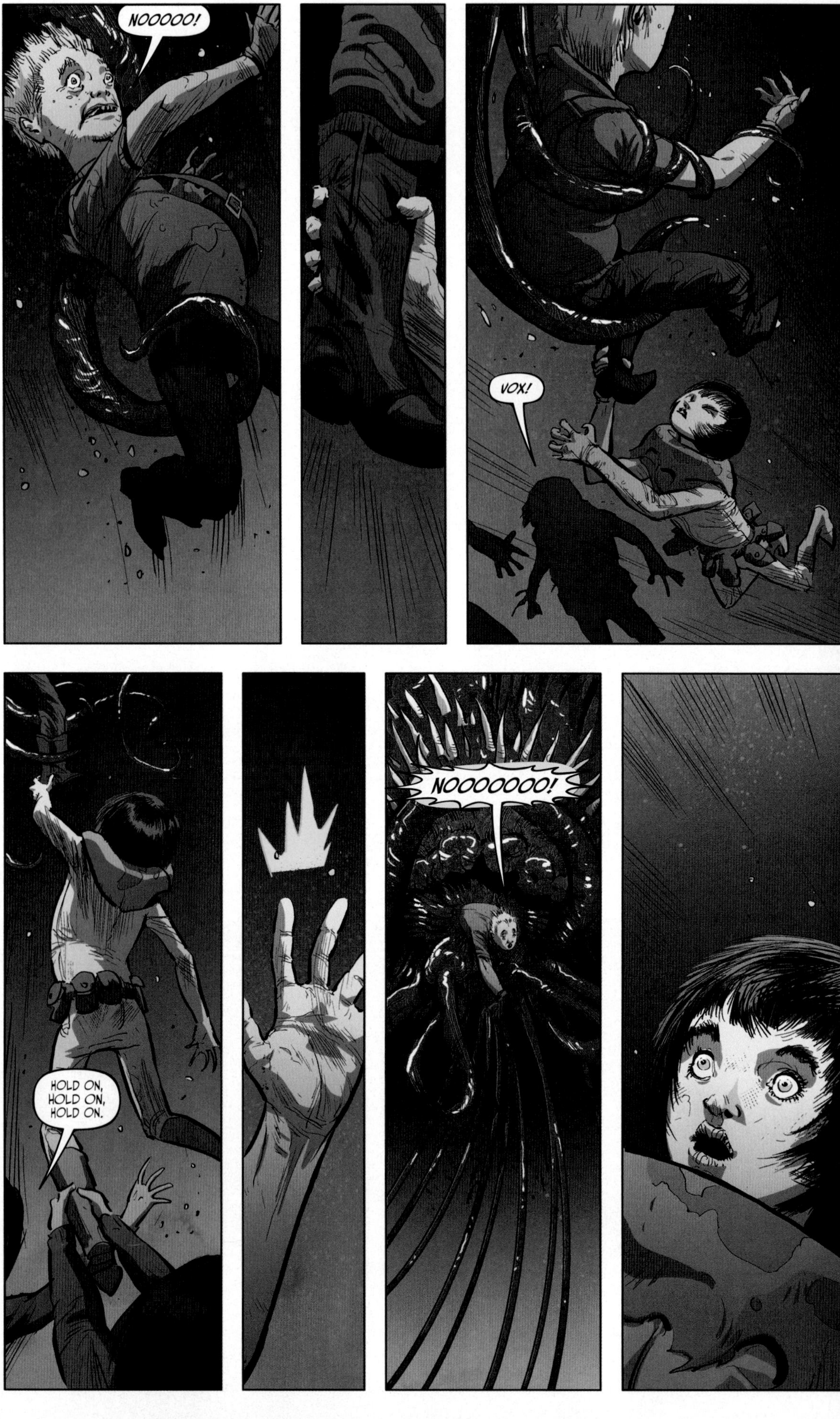
NOOOOO!
VOX!
HOLD ON, HOLD ON, HOLD ON.
NOOOOOOO!

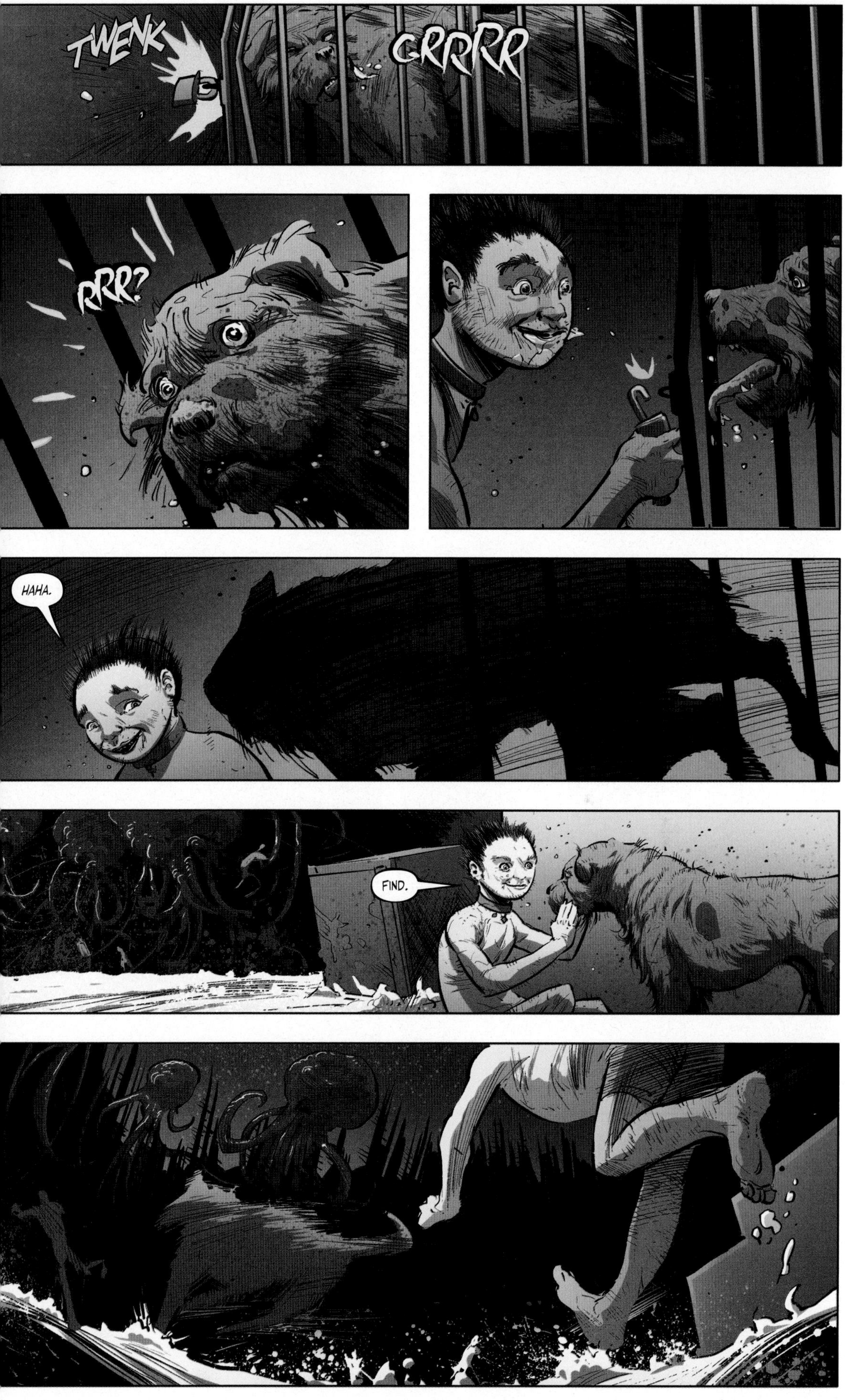
TWENK
GRRRR
RRR?
HAHA.
FIND.

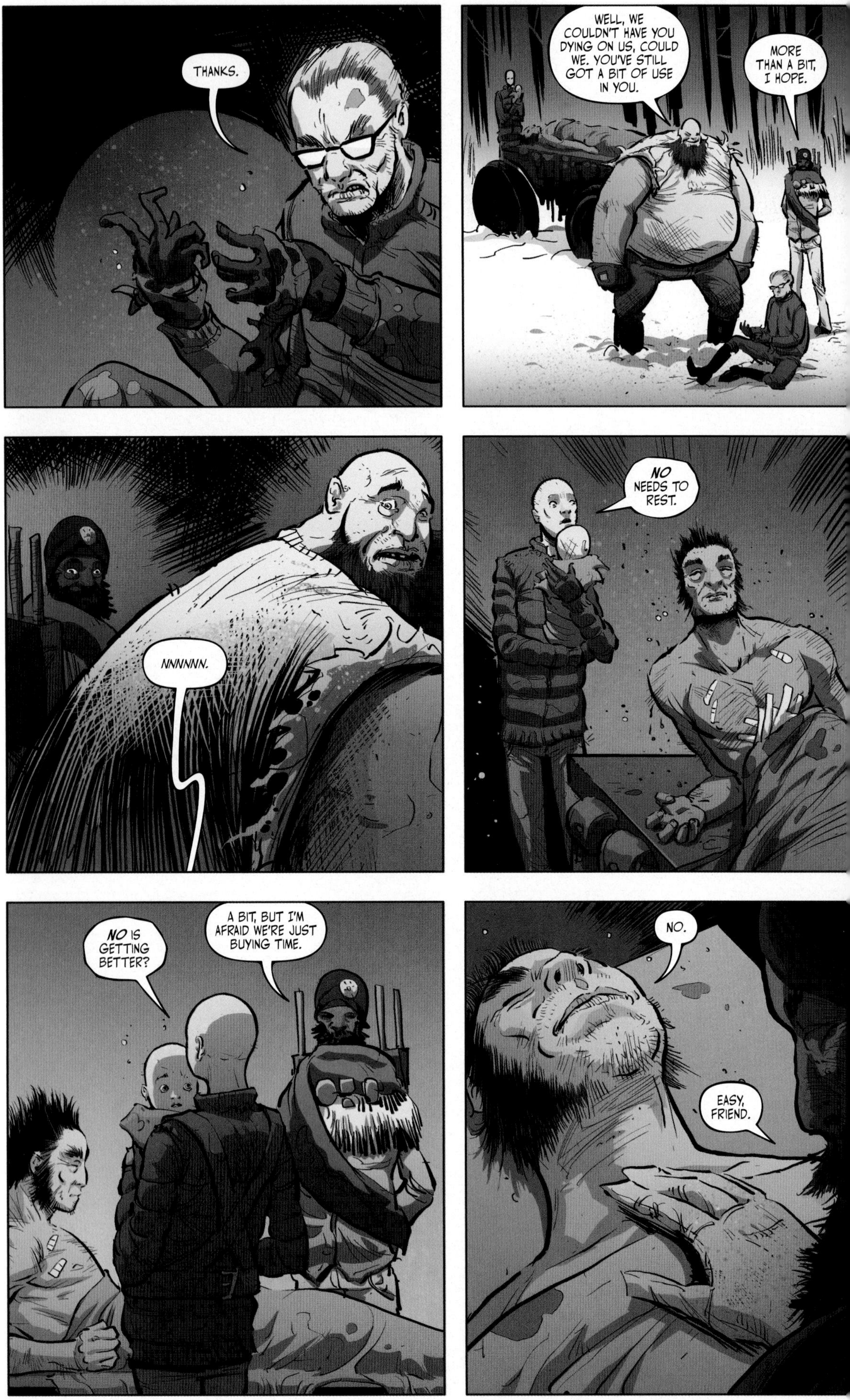
THANKS.
WELL, WE COULDN'T HAVE YOU DYING ON US, COULD WE. YOU'VE STILL GOT A BIT OF USE IN YOU.
MORE THAN A BIT, I HOPE.
NNNNNN.
NO NEEDS TO REST.
NO IS GETTING BETTER?
A BIT, BUT I'M AFRAID WE'RE JUST BUYING TIME.
NO.
EASY, FRIEND.

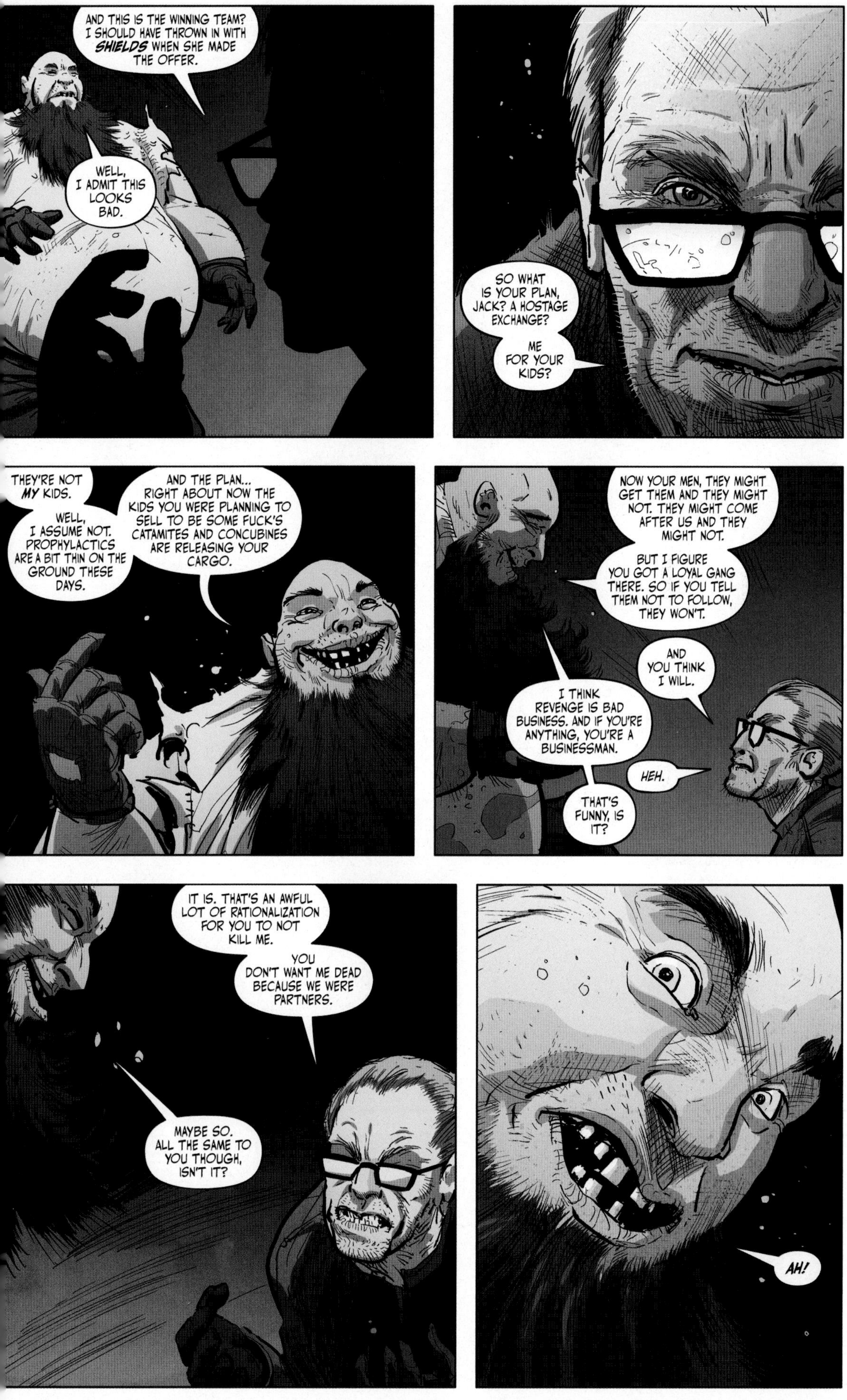
AND THIS IS THE WINNING TEAM? I SHOULD HAVE THROWN IN WITH SHIELDS WHEN SHE MADE THE OFFER.
WELL, I ADMIT THIS LOOKS BAD.
SO WHAT IS YOUR PLAN, JACK? A HOSTAGE EXCHANGE?
ME FOR YOUR KIDS?
THEY'RE NOT MY KIDS.
WELL, I ASSUME NOT. PROPHYLACTICS ARE A BIT THIN ON THE GROUND THESE DAYS.
AND THE PLAN... RIGHT ABOUT NOW THE KIDS YOU WERE PLANNING TO SELL TO BE SOME FUCK'S CATAMITES AND CONCUBINES ARE RELEASING YOUR CARGO.
NOW YOUR MEN, THEY MIGHT GET THEM AND THEY MIGHT NOT. THEY MIGHT COME AFTER US AND THEY MIGHT NOT.
BUT I FIGURE YOU GOT A LOYAL GANG THERE. SO IF YOU TELL THEM NOT TO FOLLOW, THEY WON'T.
AND YOU THINK I WILL.
I THINK REVENGE IS BAD BUSINESS. AND IF YOU'RE ANYTHING, YOU'RE A BUSINESSMAN.
HEH.
THAT'S FUNNY, IS IT?
IT IS. THAT'S AN AWFUL LOT OF RATIONALIZATION FOR YOU TO NOT KILL ME.
YOU DON'T WANT ME DEAD BECAUSE WE WERE PARTNERS.
MAYBE SO. ALL THE SAME TO YOU THOUGH, ISN'T IT?
AH!

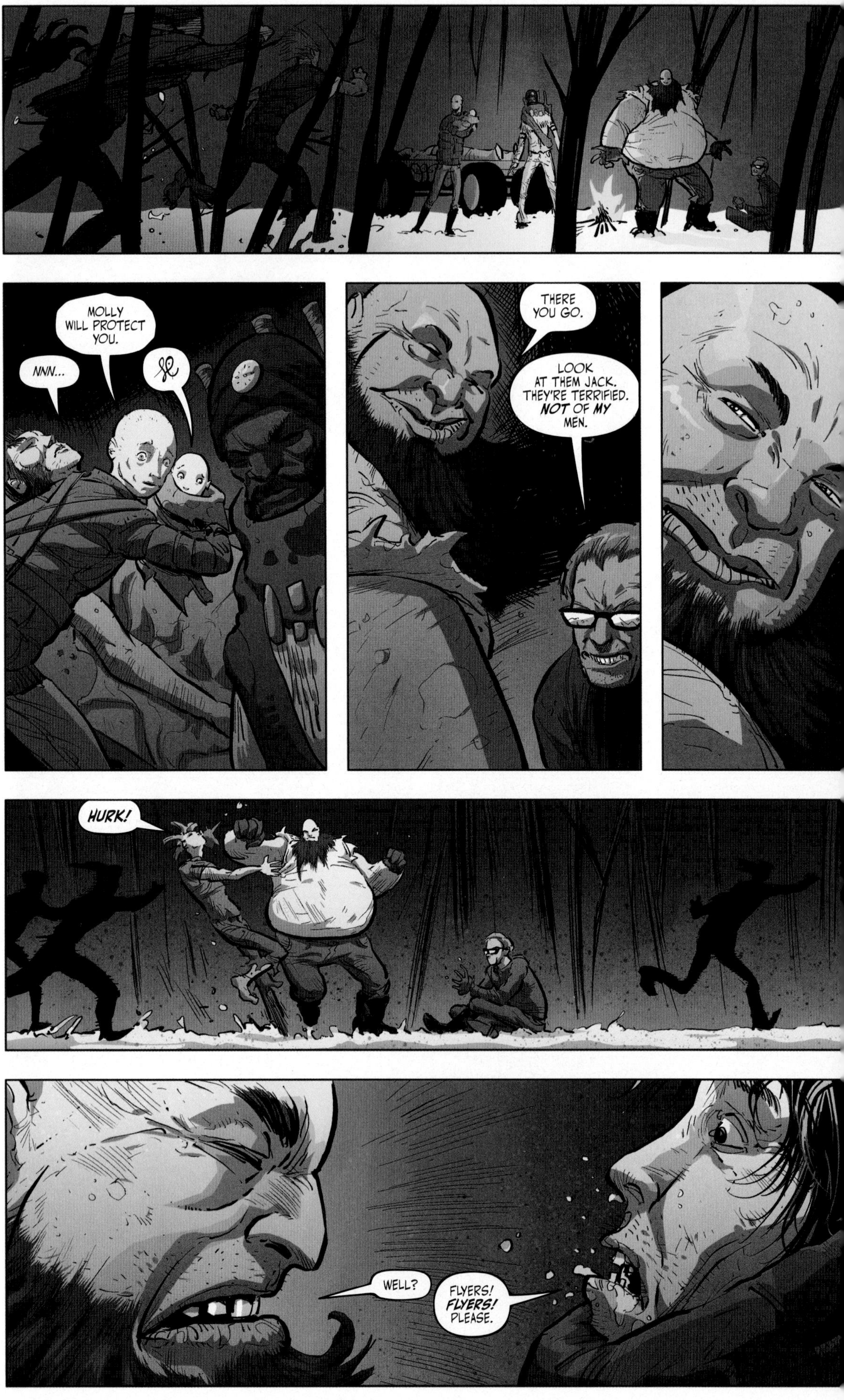
MOLLY WILL PROTECT YOU.
NNN...
THERE YOU GO.
LOOK AT THEM JACK. THEY'RE TERRIFIED. NOT OF MY MEN.
HURK!
WELL?
FLYERS! FLYERS! PLEASE.

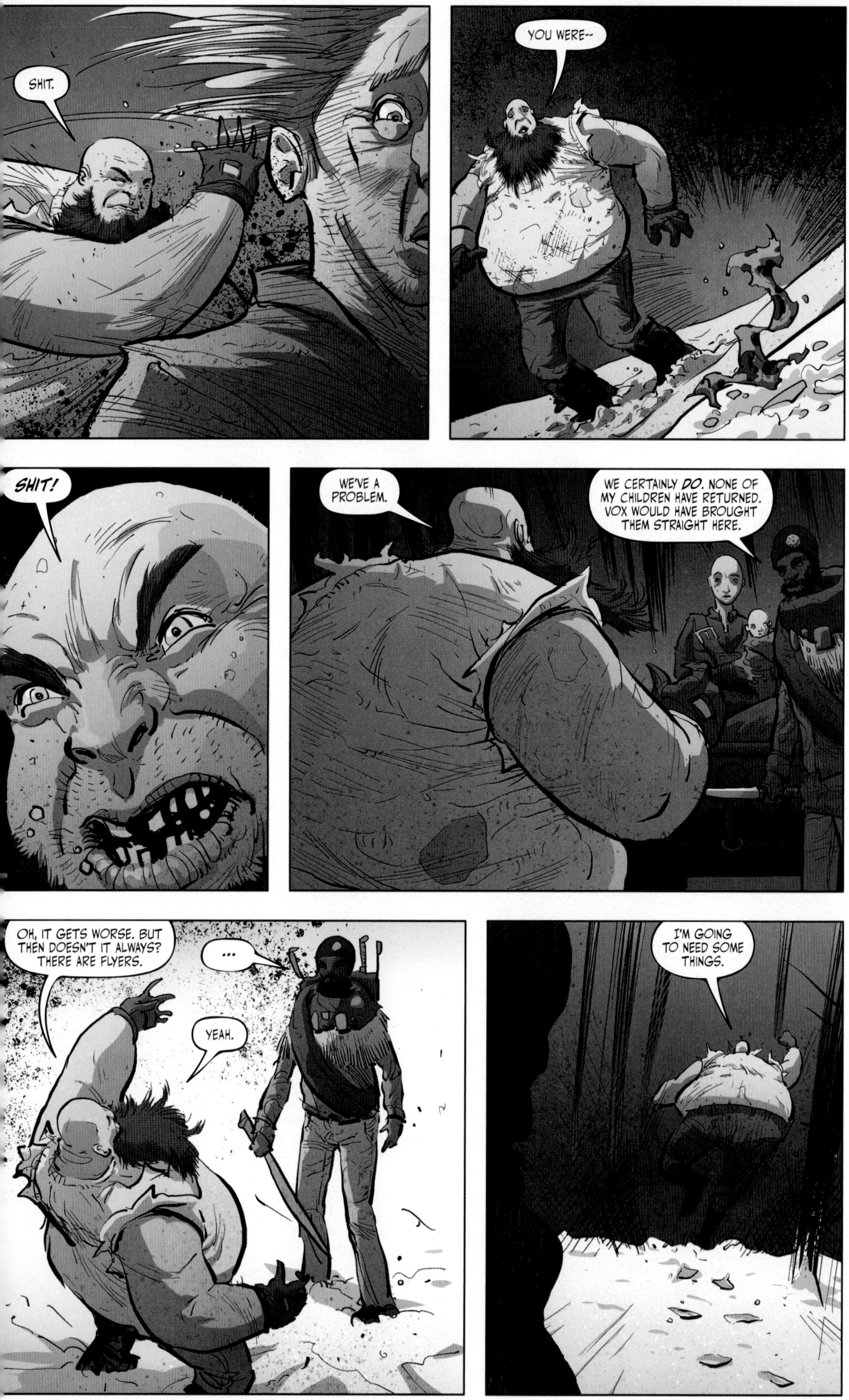
SHIT.
YOU WERE--
SHIT!
WE'VE A PROBLEM.
WE CERTAINLY DO. NONE OF MY CHILDREN HAVE RETURNED. VOX WOULD HAVE BROUGHT THEM STRAIGHT HERE.
OH, IT GETS WORSE. BUT THEN DOESN'T IT ALWAYS? THERE ARE FLYERS.
...
YEAH.
I'M GOING TO NEED SOME THINGS.

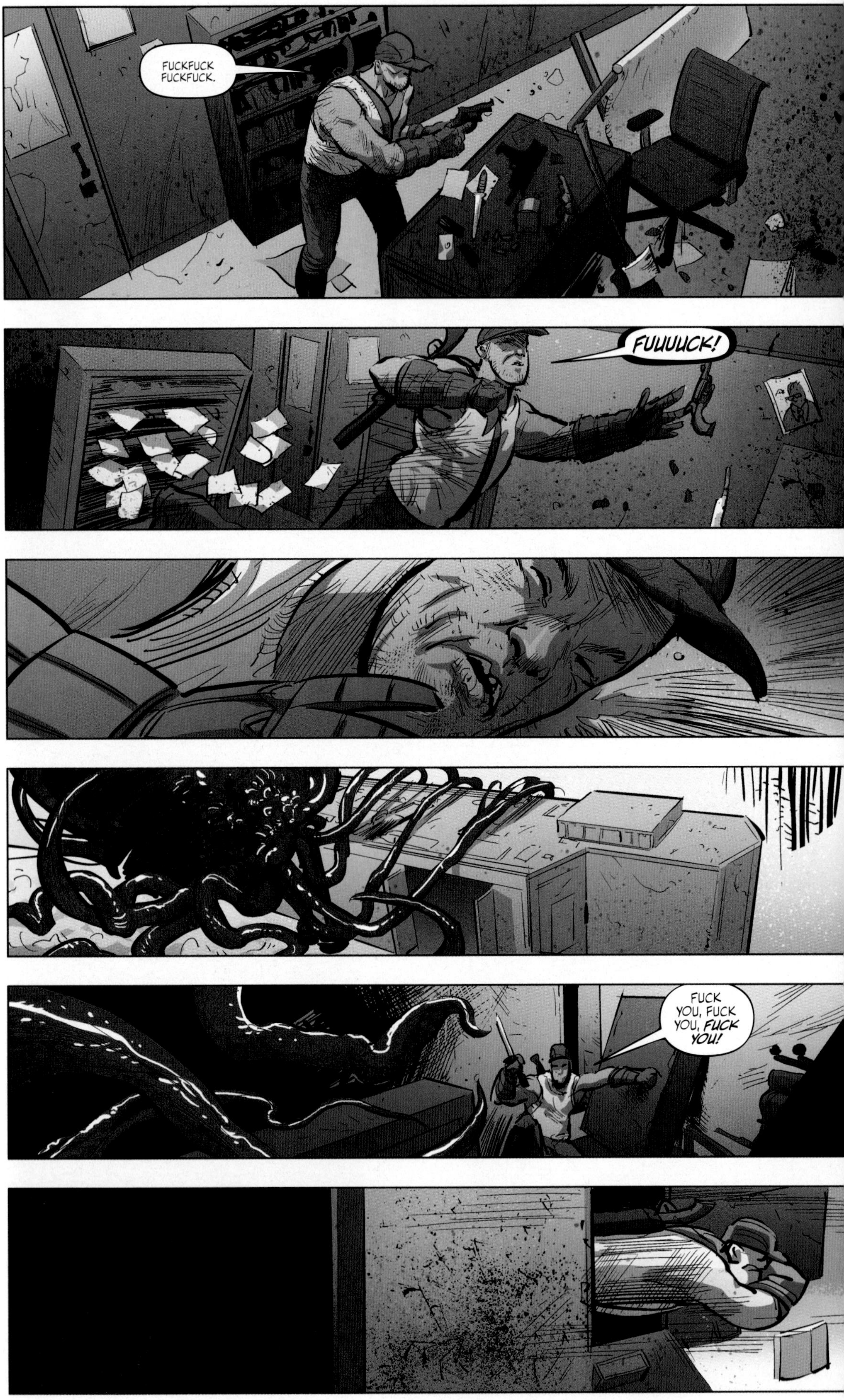
FUCKFUCK FUCKFUCK.
FUUUUCK!
FUCK YOU, FUCK YOU, FUCK YOU!

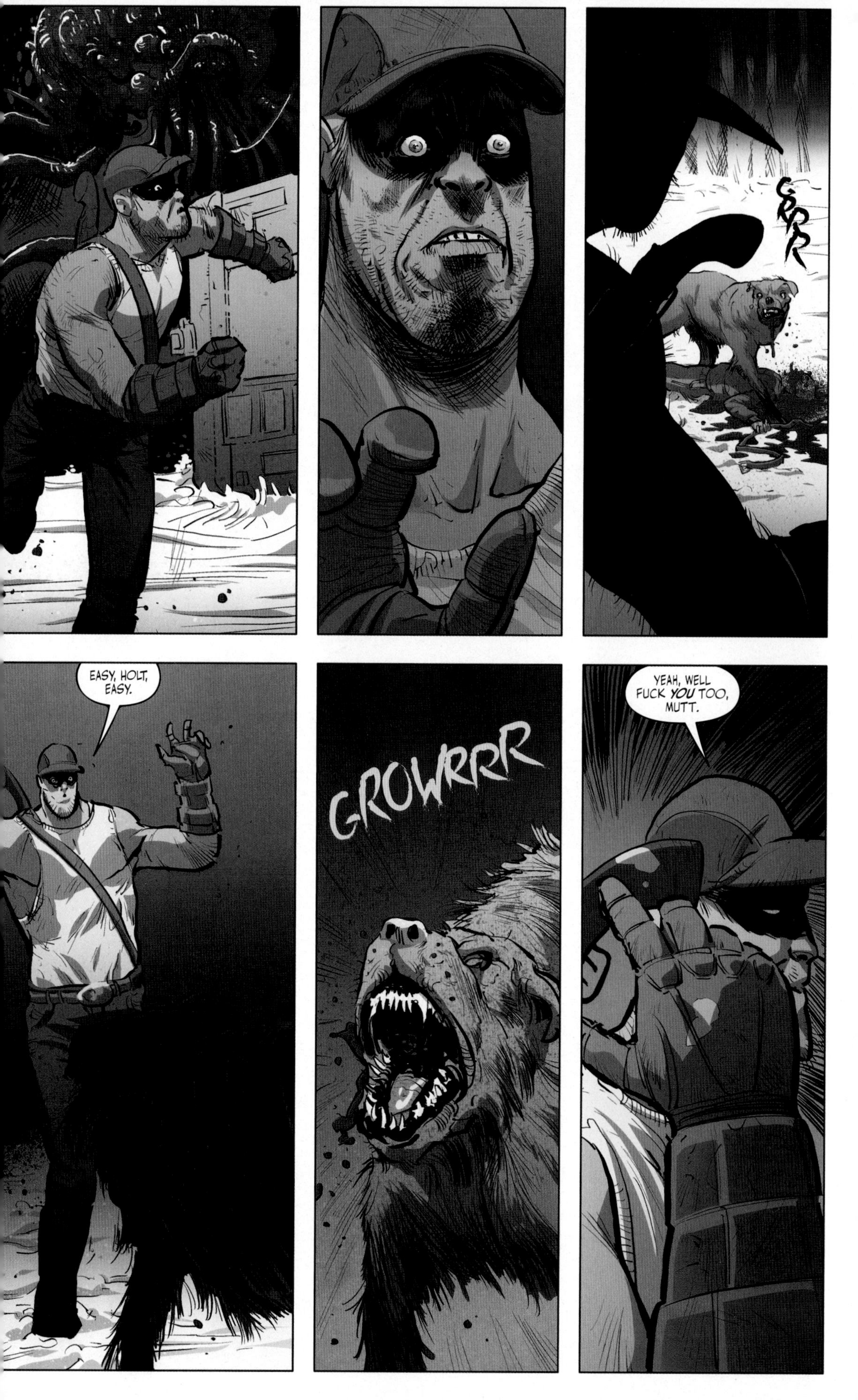
GRRR
EASY, HOLT, EASY.
GROWRRR
YEAH, WELL FUCK *YOU* TOO, MUTT.

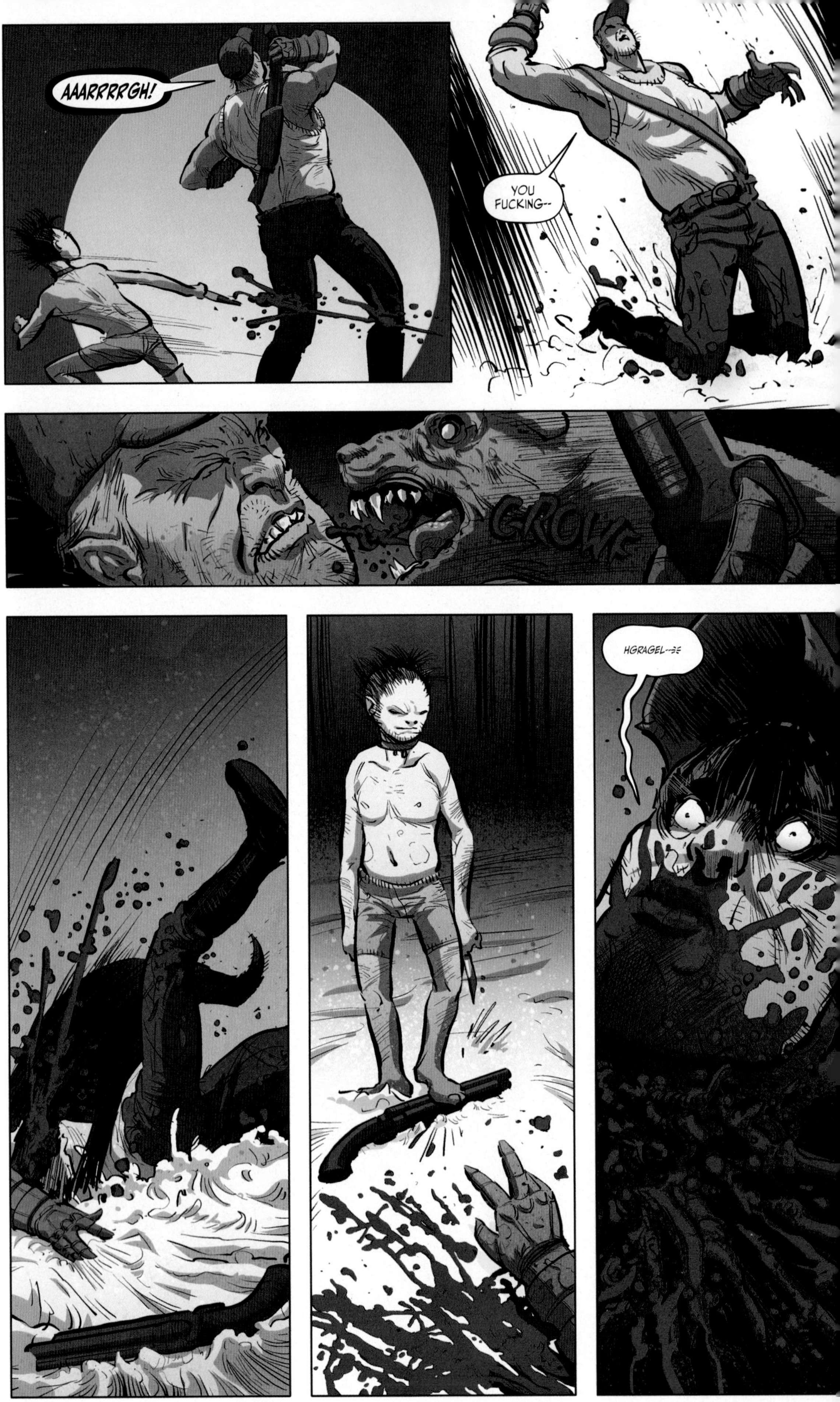
AAARRRRGH!
YOU FUCKING--
GROWF
HGRAGEL--

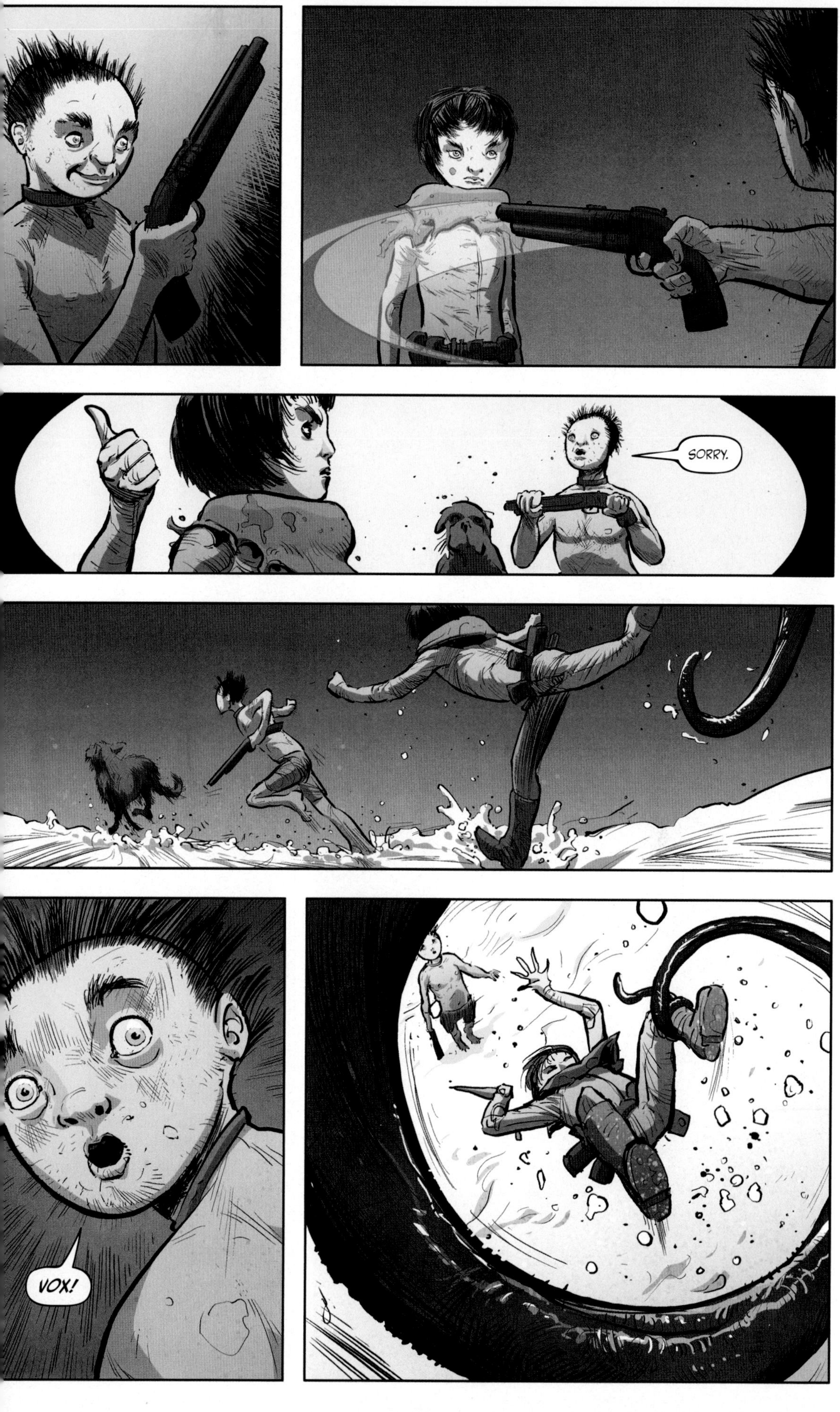
SORRY.
VOX!

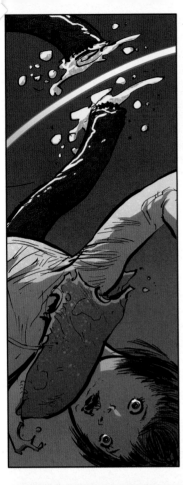

NOT TODAY.
NOT EVER.

PROFESSOR!

DON'T
YOU WORRY,
CHILD.

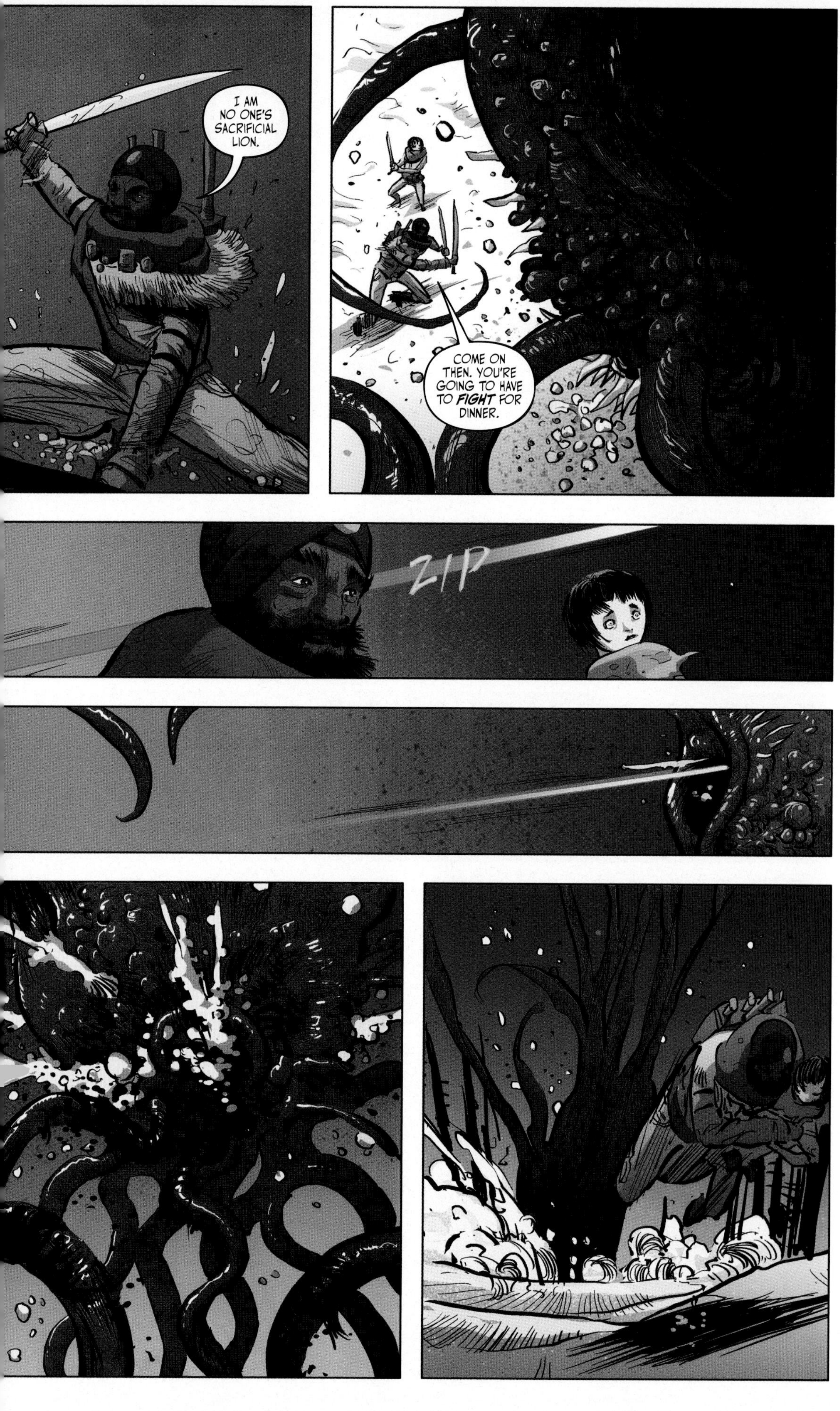
I AM NO ONE'S SACRIFICIAL LION.
COME ON THEN. YOU'RE GOING TO HAVE TO FIGHT FOR DINNER.
ZIP

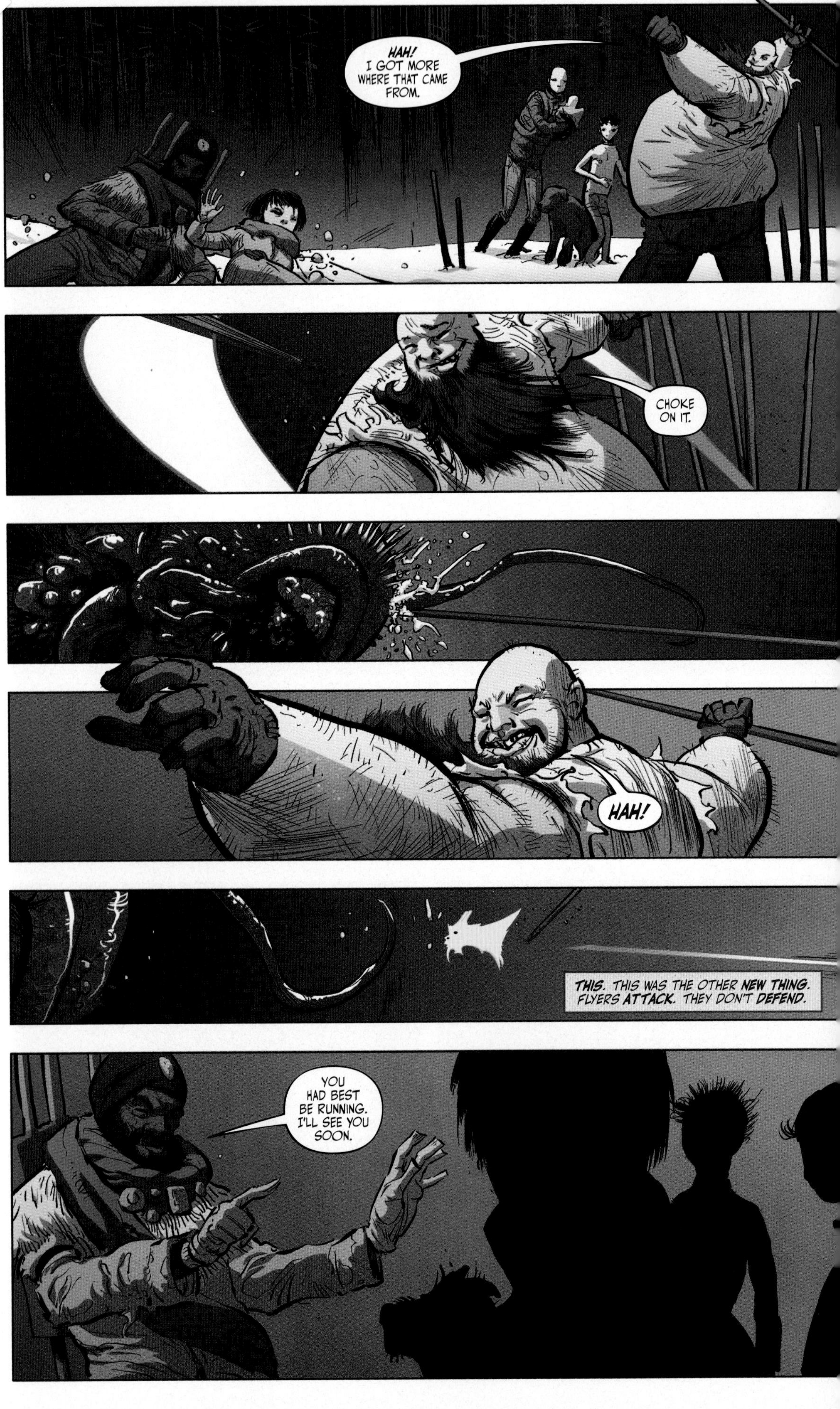
HAH! I GOT MORE WHERE THAT CAME FROM.
CHOKE ON IT.
HAH!
THIS. THIS WAS THE OTHER NEW THING. FLYERS ATTACK. THEY DON'T DEFEND.
YOU HAD BEST BE RUNNING. I'LL SEE YOU SOON.

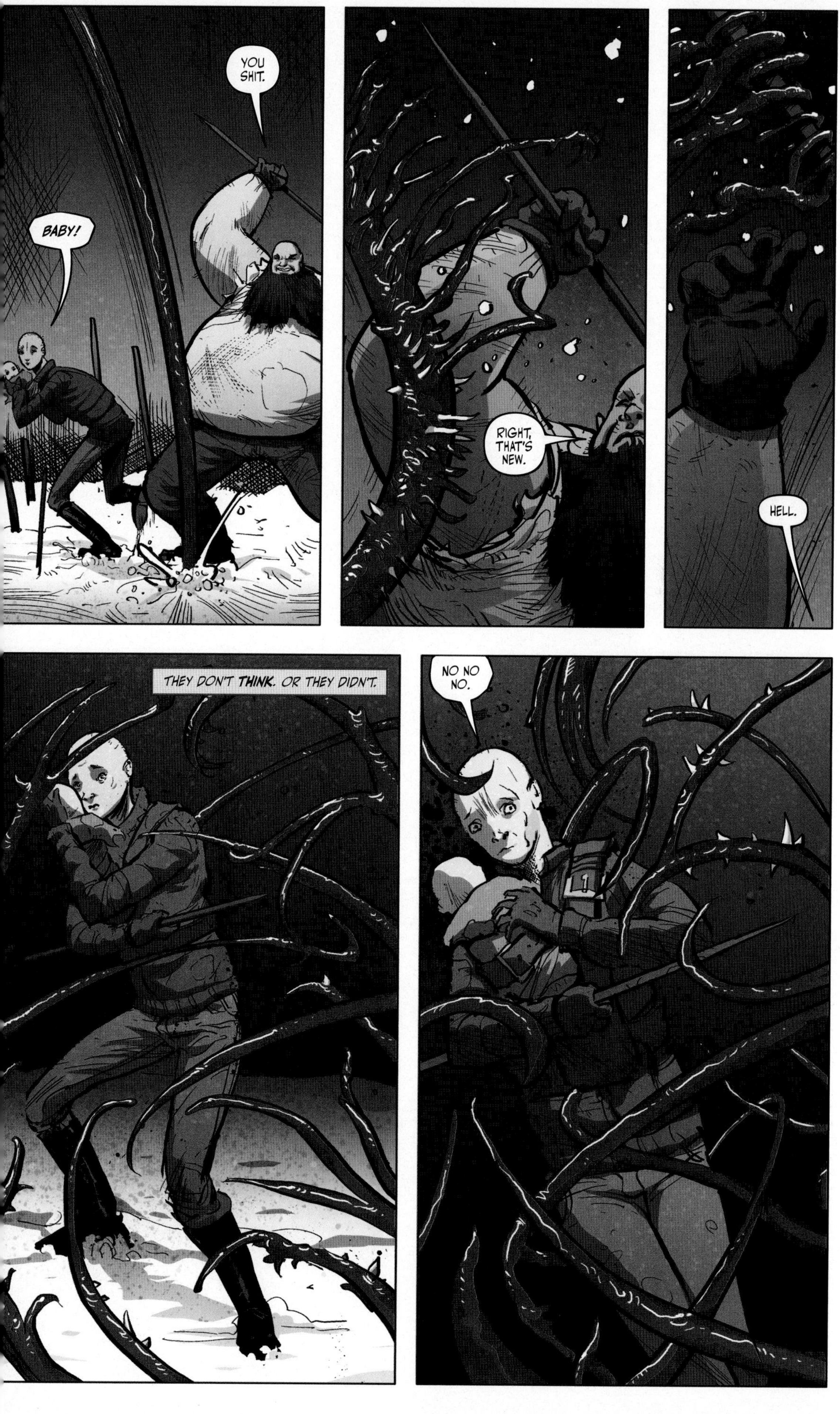
YOU SHIT.
BABY!
RIGHT, THAT'S NEW.
HELL.
THEY DON'T **THINK**. OR THEY DIDN'T.
NO NO NO.

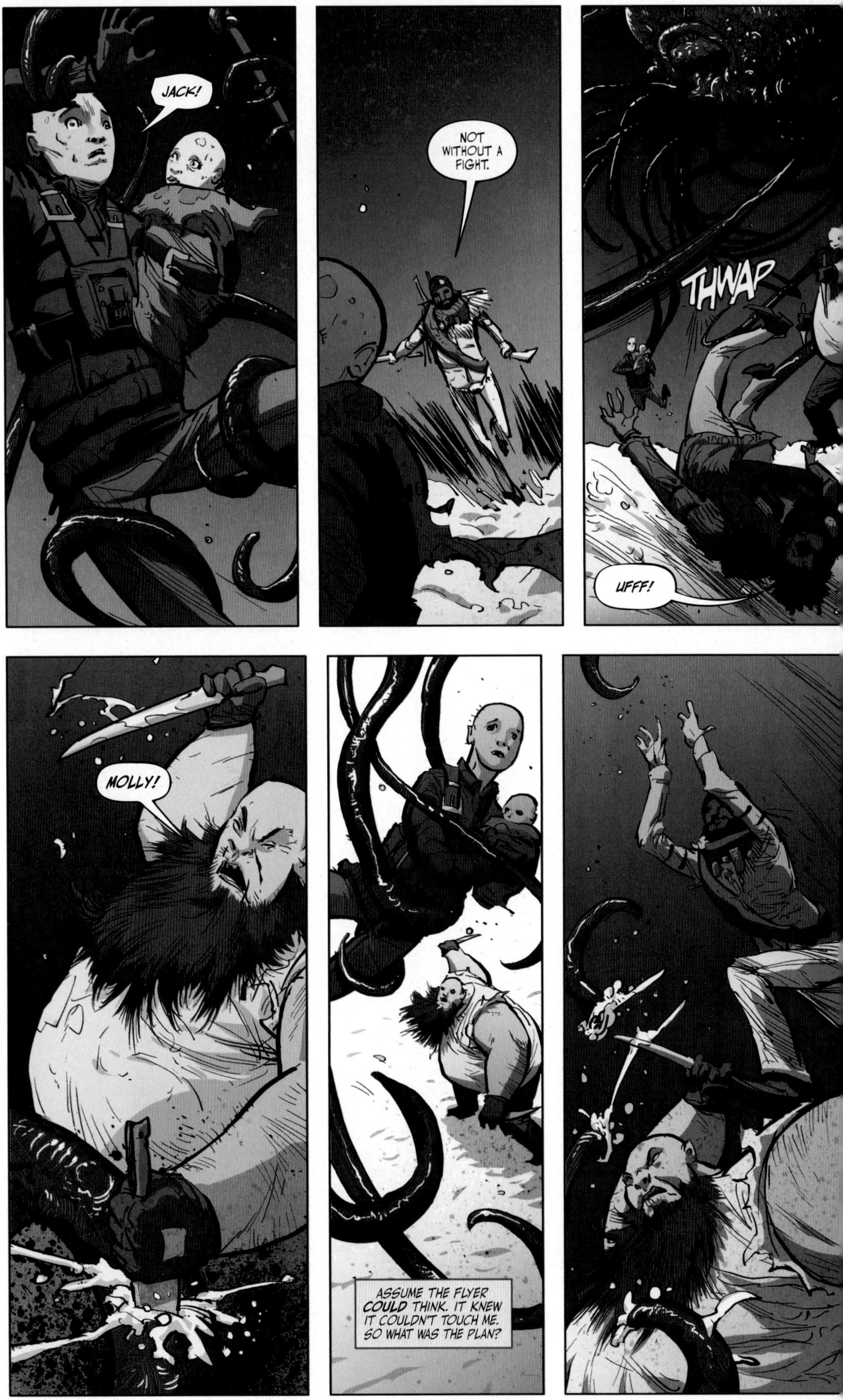
JACK!
NOT WITHOUT A FIGHT.
THWAP
UFFF!
MOLLY!
ASSUME THE FLYER COULD THINK. IT KNEW IT COULDN'T TOUCH ME. SO WHAT WAS THE PLAN?

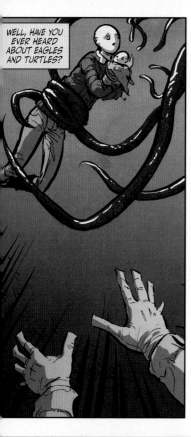

WELL, HAVE YOU EVER HEARD ABOUT EAGLES AND TURTLES?

THE SPREAD COULDN'T KILL ME DIRECTLY.

JACK.

BUT **GRAVITY** IS A DIFFERENT STORY.

FUCKING HELL.

JACK'S GOT YOU. THANK FUCK, JACK'S GOT YOU.

GOODBYE, BABY.

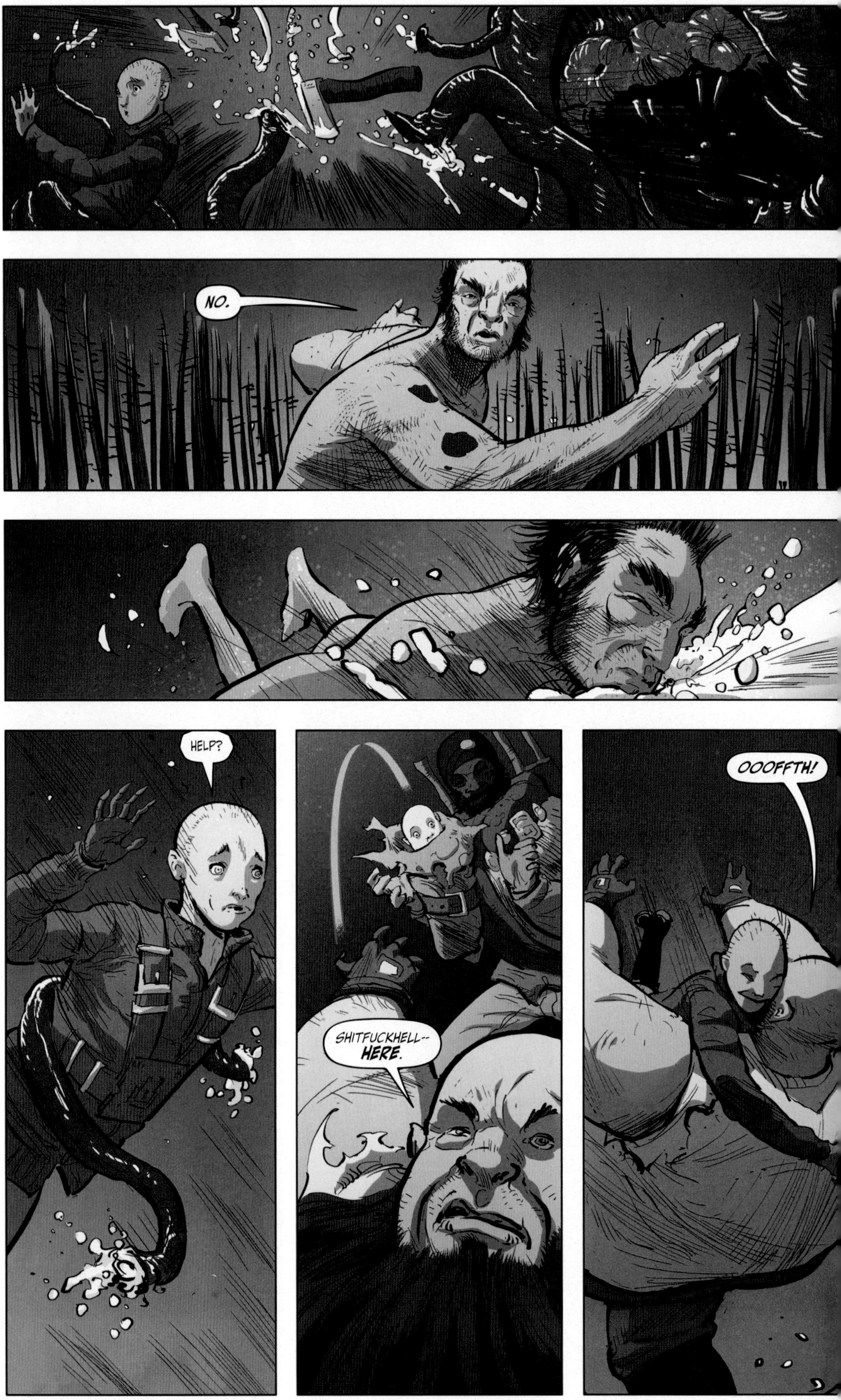
NO.
HELP?
SHITFUCKHELL--
HERE.
OOOFFTH!

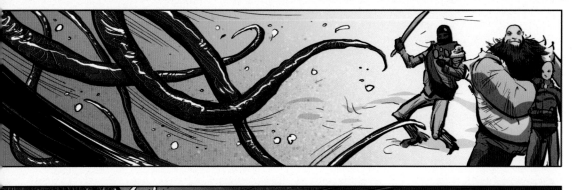

DON'T LEAVE FAMILY BEHIND.

I GUESS I TAUGHT YOU TOO WELL.

NO!

I'M FINE, THANKS.

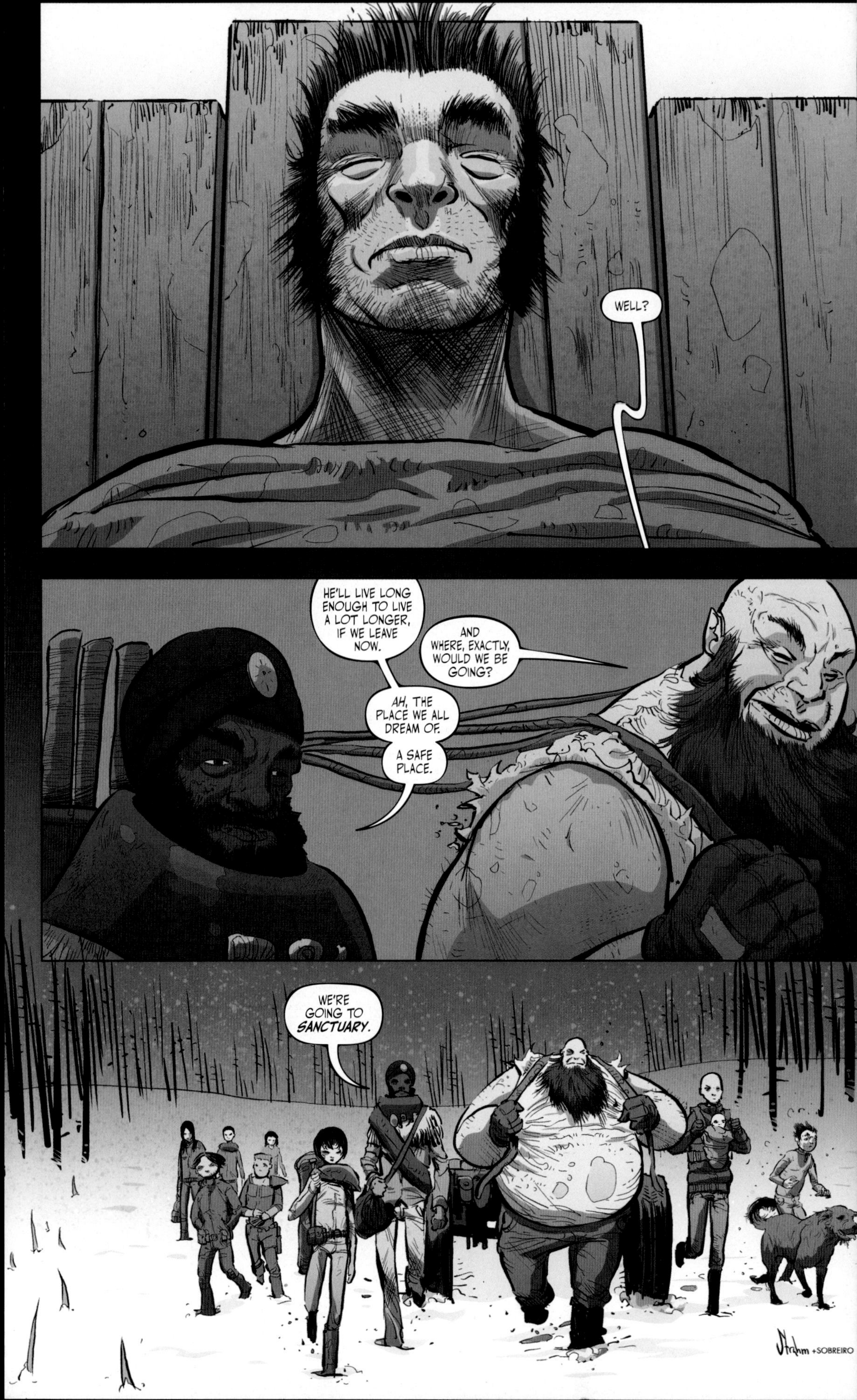
WELL?
HE'LL LIVE LONG ENOUGH TO LIVE A LOT LONGER, IF WE LEAVE NOW.
AND WHERE, EXACTLY, WOULD WE BE GOING?
AH, THE PLACE WE ALL DREAM OF.
A SAFE PLACE.
WE'RE GOING TO SANCTUARY.
+SOBREIRO

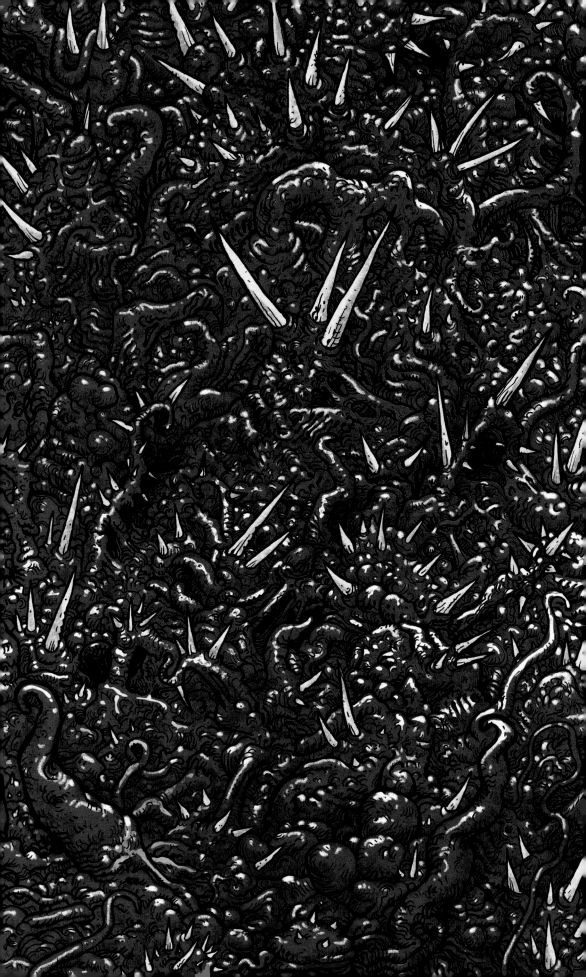

GALLERY

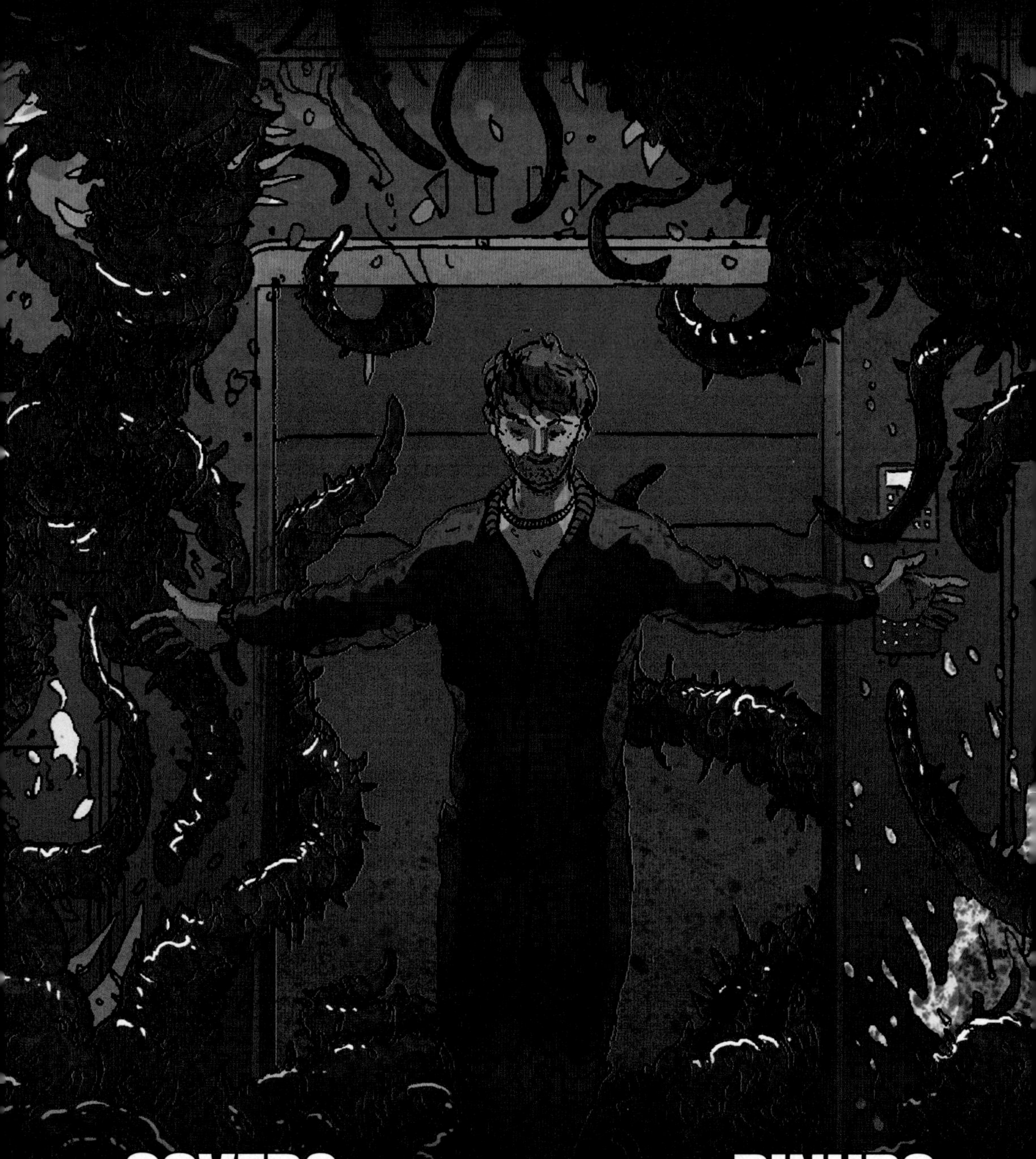

COVERS

SPREAD #7A: Kyle Strahm & Felipe Sobreiro
SPREAD #7B: Liam Cobb & Felipe Sobreiro
SPREAD #7 FLEA MARKET VARIANT: Kyle Strahm & Michael Adams
SPREAD #7 BACK COVER: Felipe Sobreiro
SPREAD #8: Kyle Strahm & Felipe Sobreiro
SPREAD #9: Kyle Strahm & Felipe Sobreiro
SPREAD NYCC EXCLUSIVE: Ben Templesmith
SPREAD #10: Kyle Strahm & Felipe Sobreiro
SPREAD #11: Kyle Strahm & Felipe Sobreiro
SPREAD C2E2 EXCLUSIVE: Buster Moody

PINUPS

Juan Gedeon
Buster Moody
Carlos Cabrera
Bruno Stahl
Chris Bolton
Zakuro Aoyama
John Bivens
Michael Adams

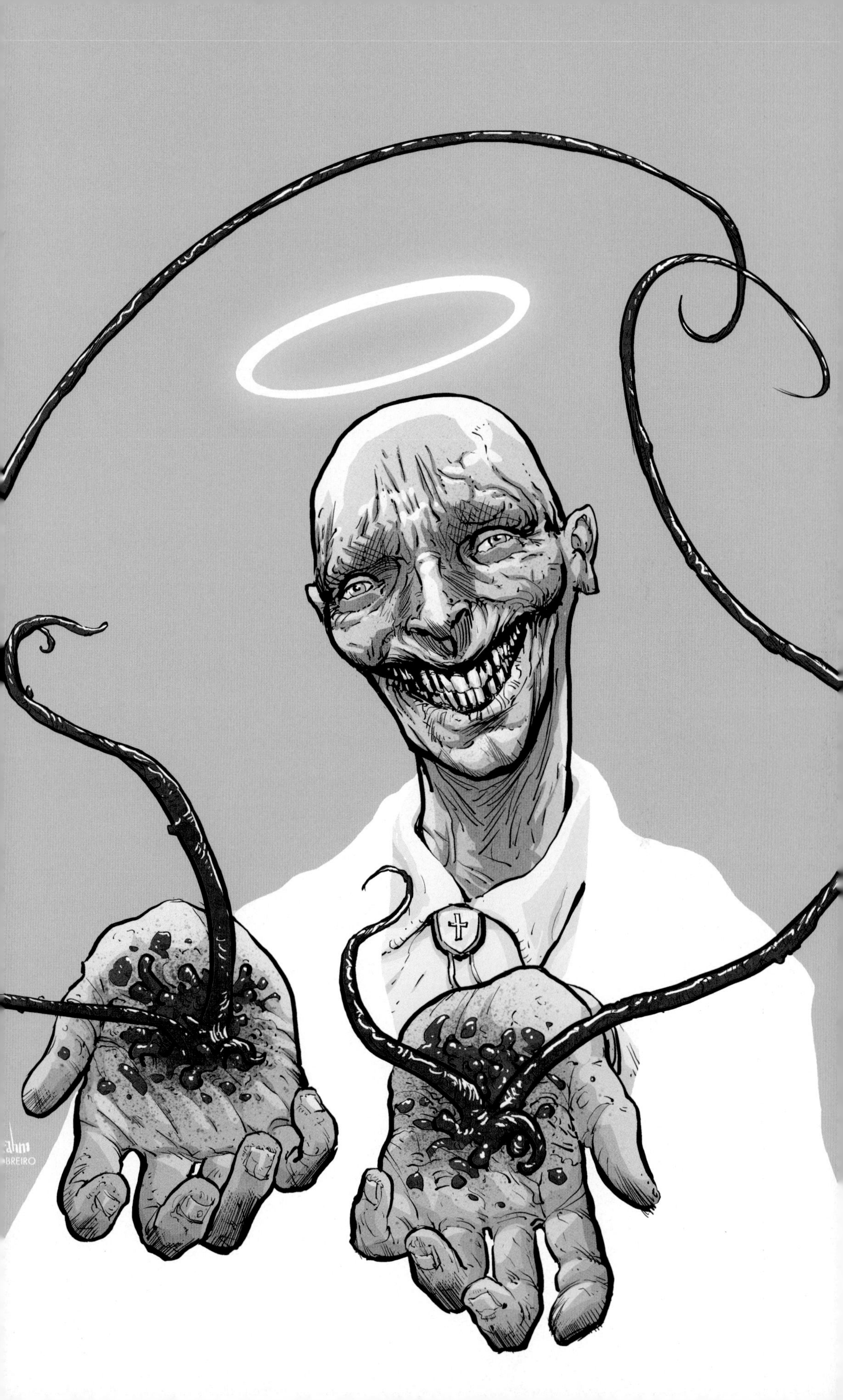

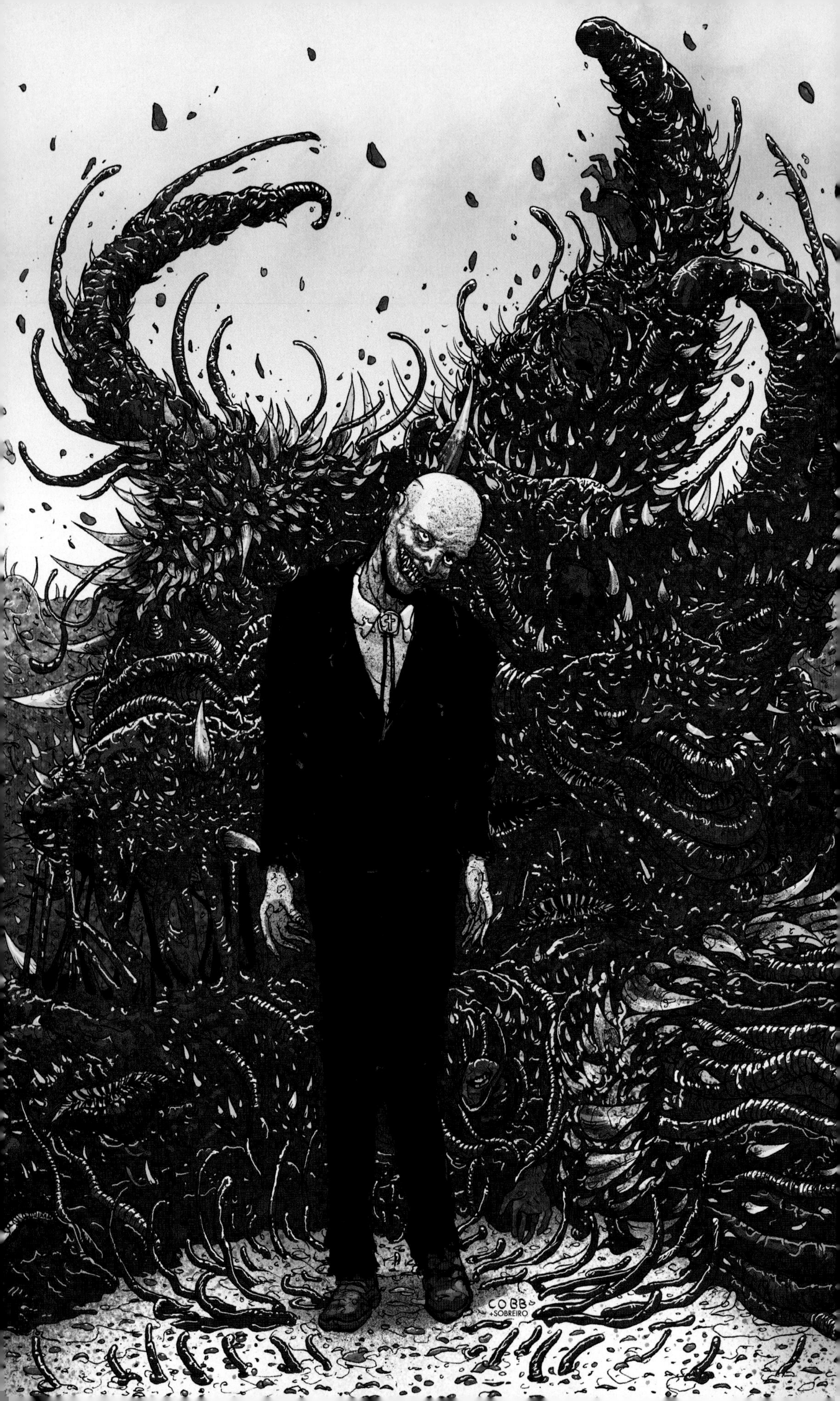
COBB
+SOBREIRO

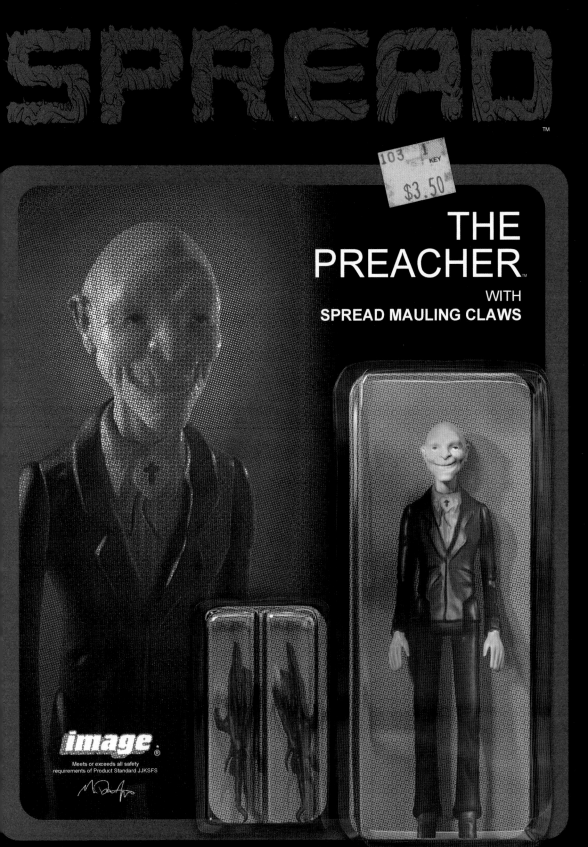

No. 00007

Ages 18 and up

SPREAD ™

103 1 KEY
$3.50

THE
PREACHER ™
WITH
SPREAD MAULING CLAWS

image ®

Meets or exceeds all safety
requirements of Product Standard JJKSFS

Jordan - Cobb - Sobreiro
Cover by Michael Adams and Kyle Strahm

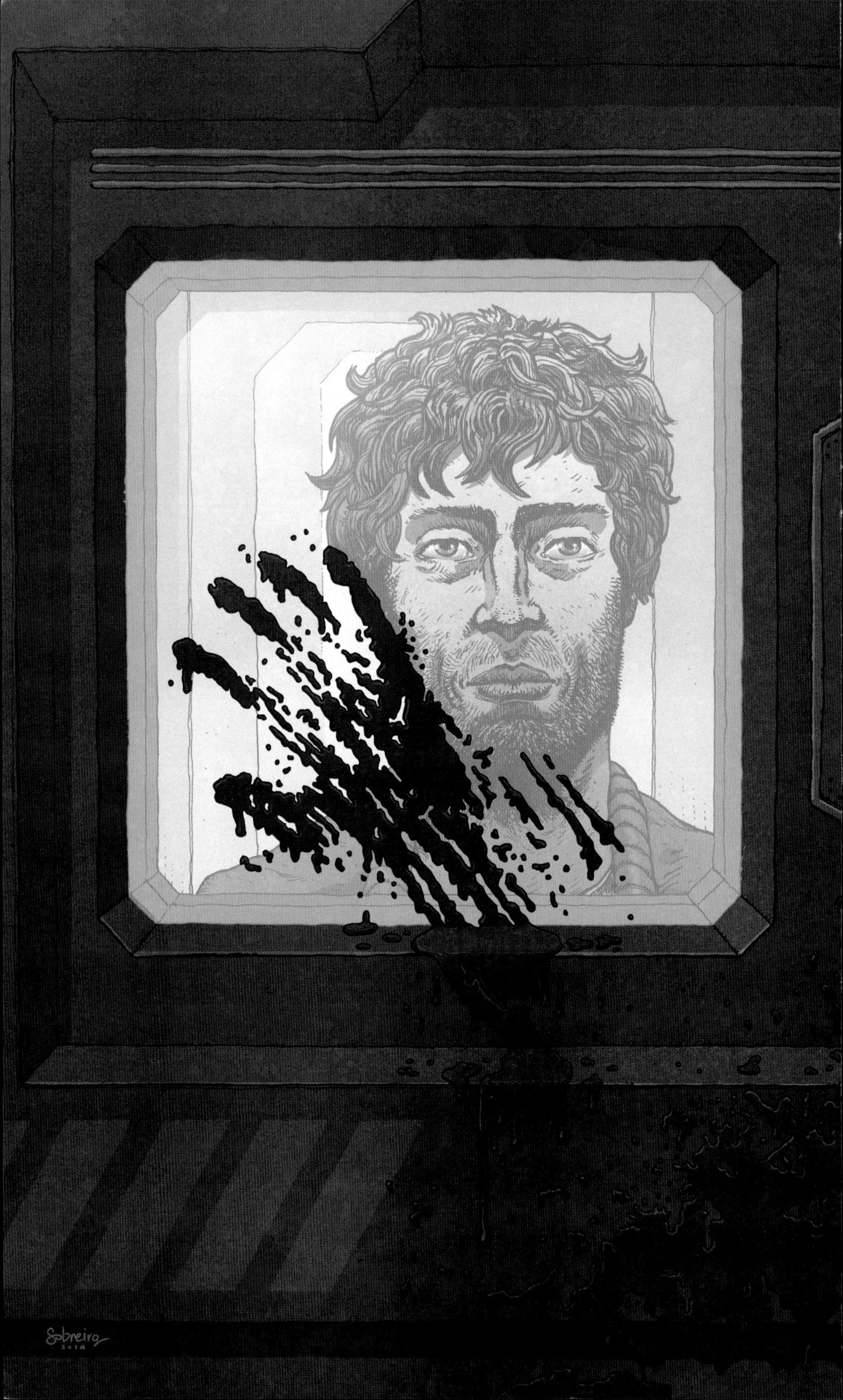
Sobreiro
2014

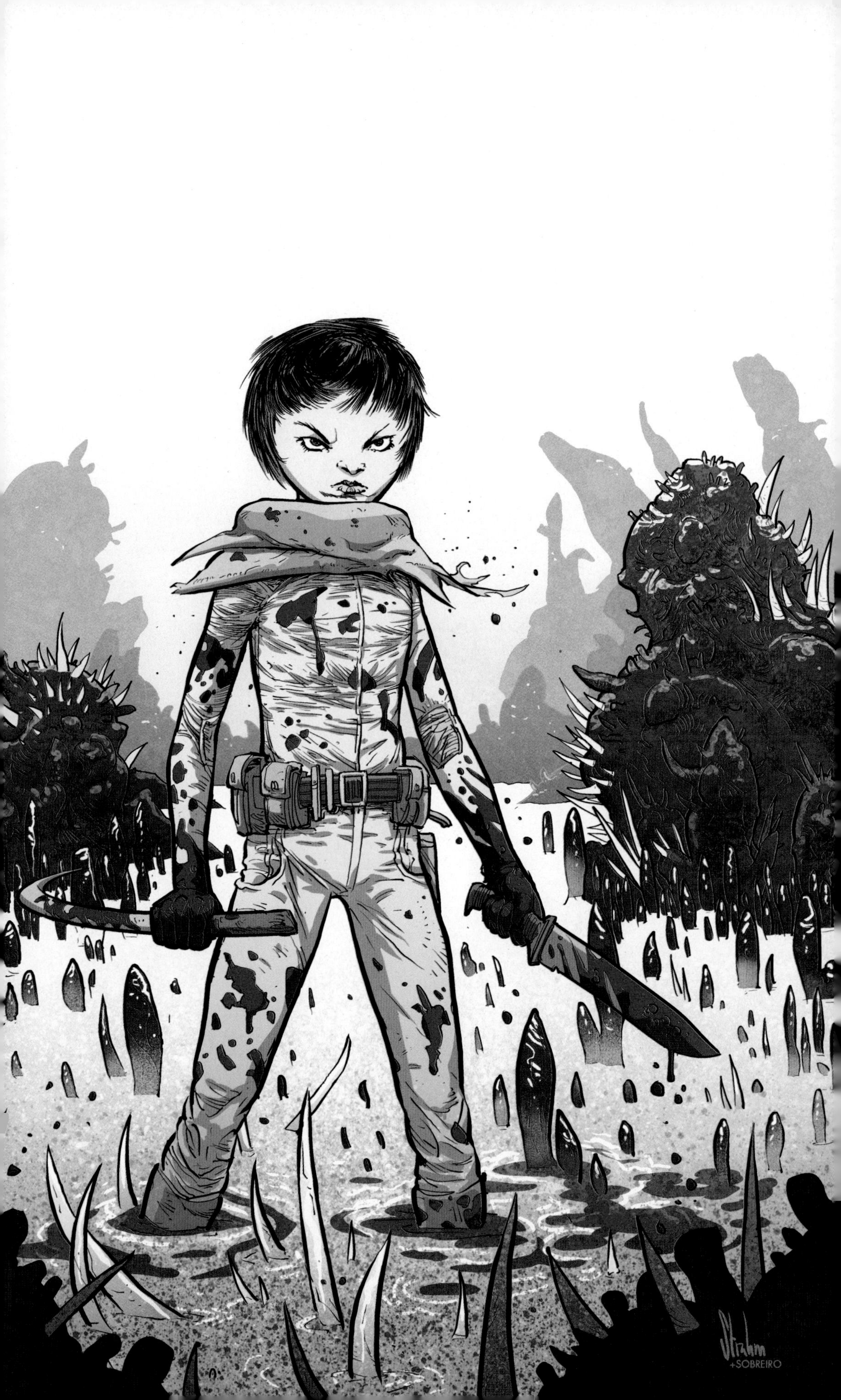
+SOBREIRO

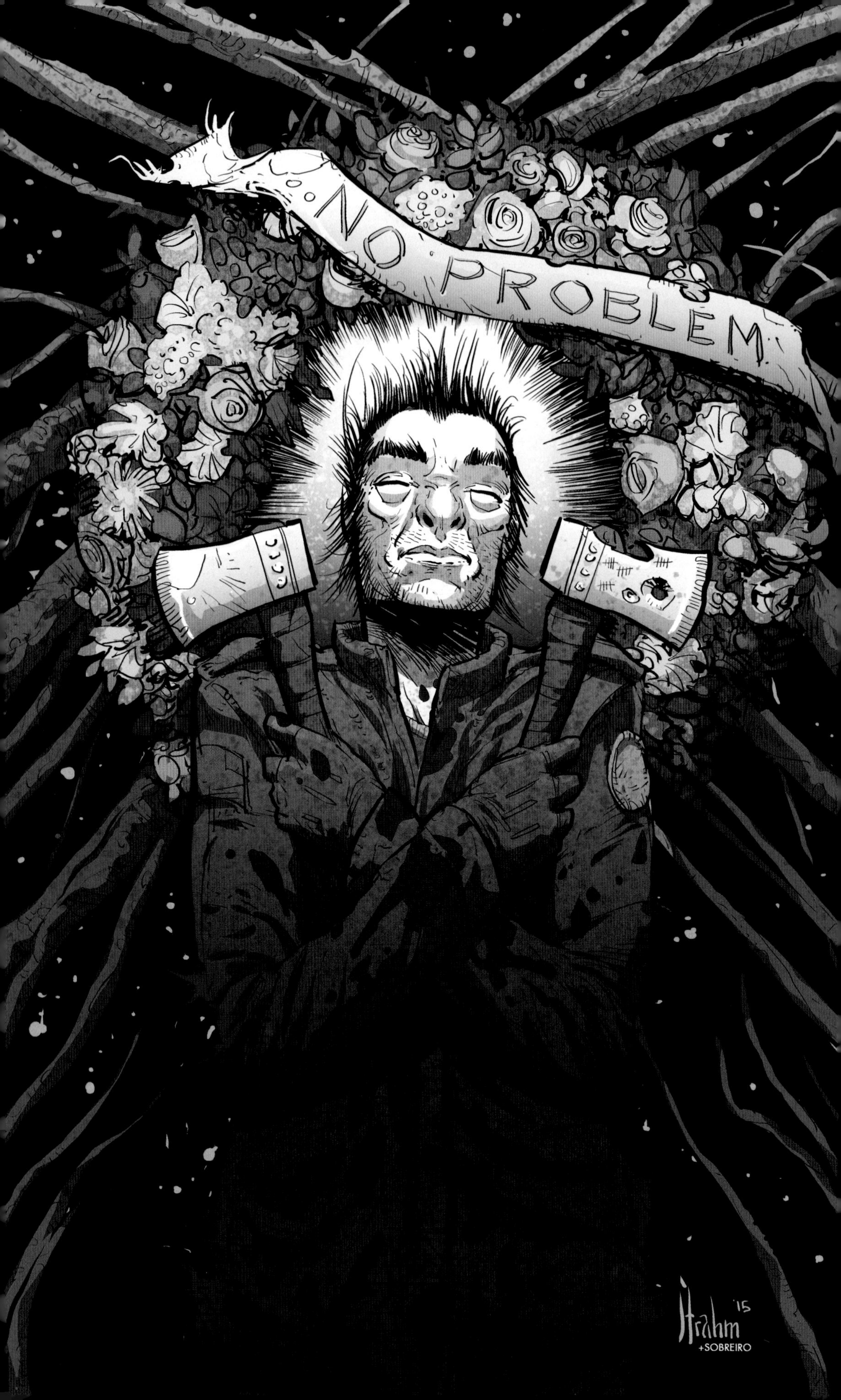
NO PROBLEM
Strahm '15
+SOBREIRO

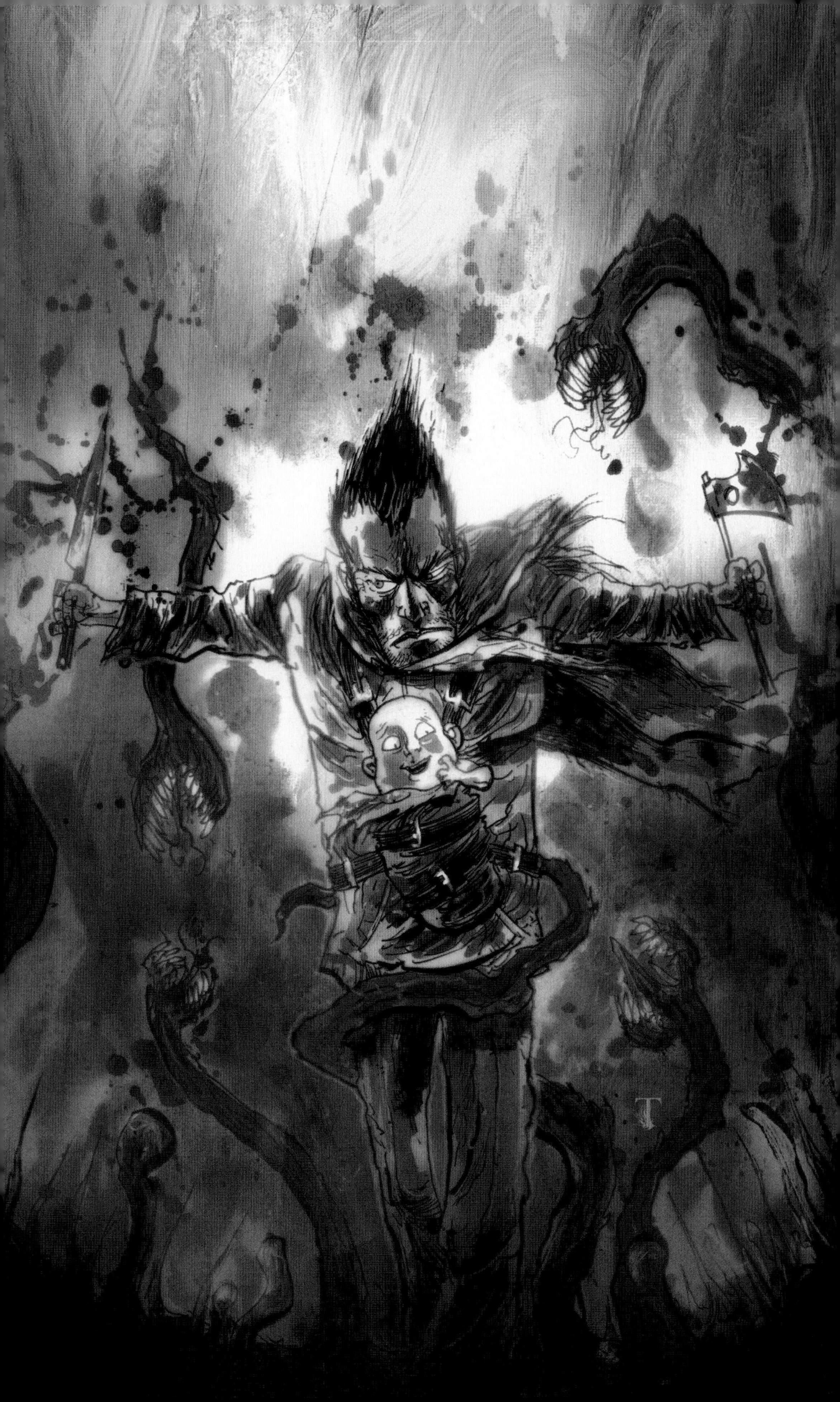

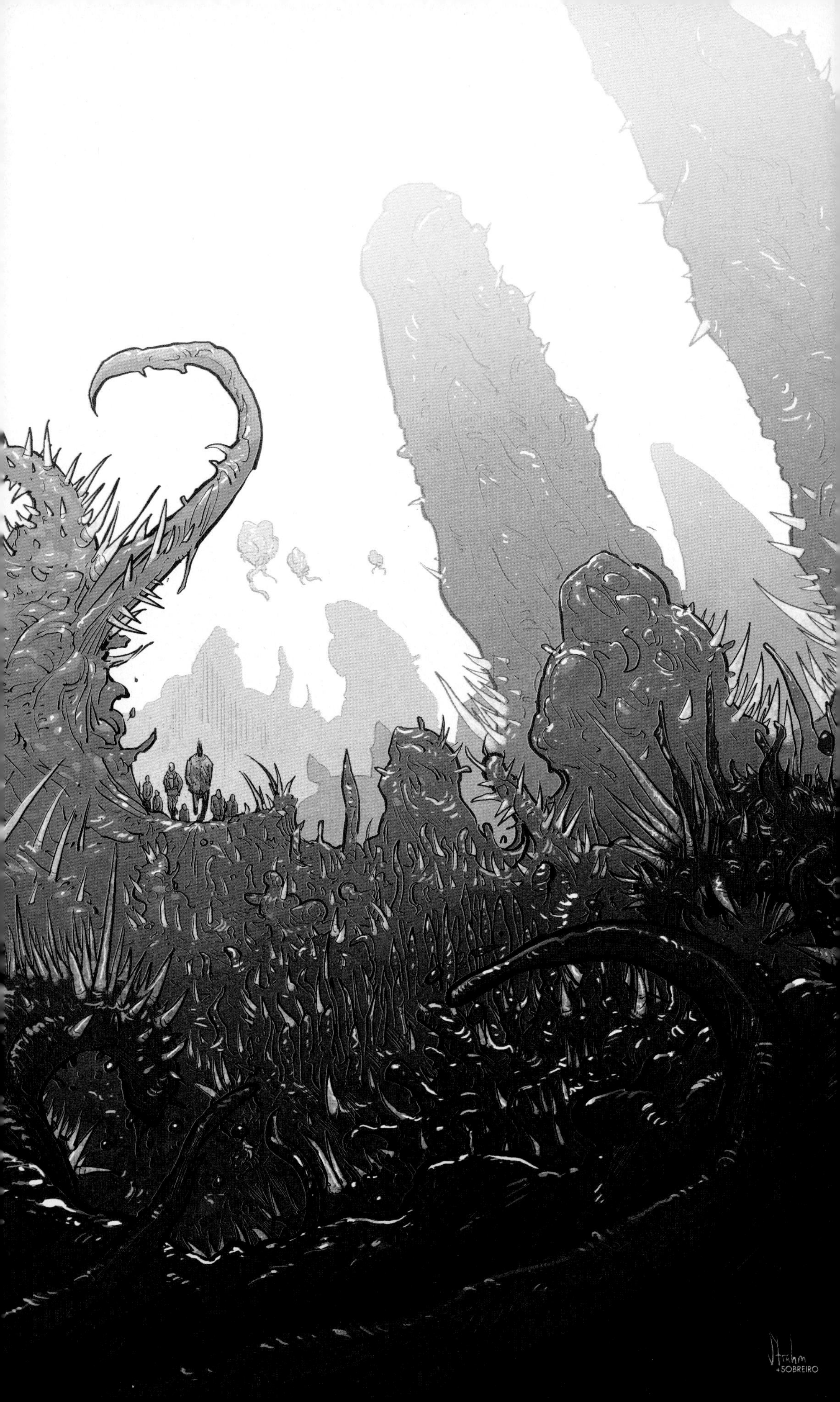
Strahm
+SOBREIRO

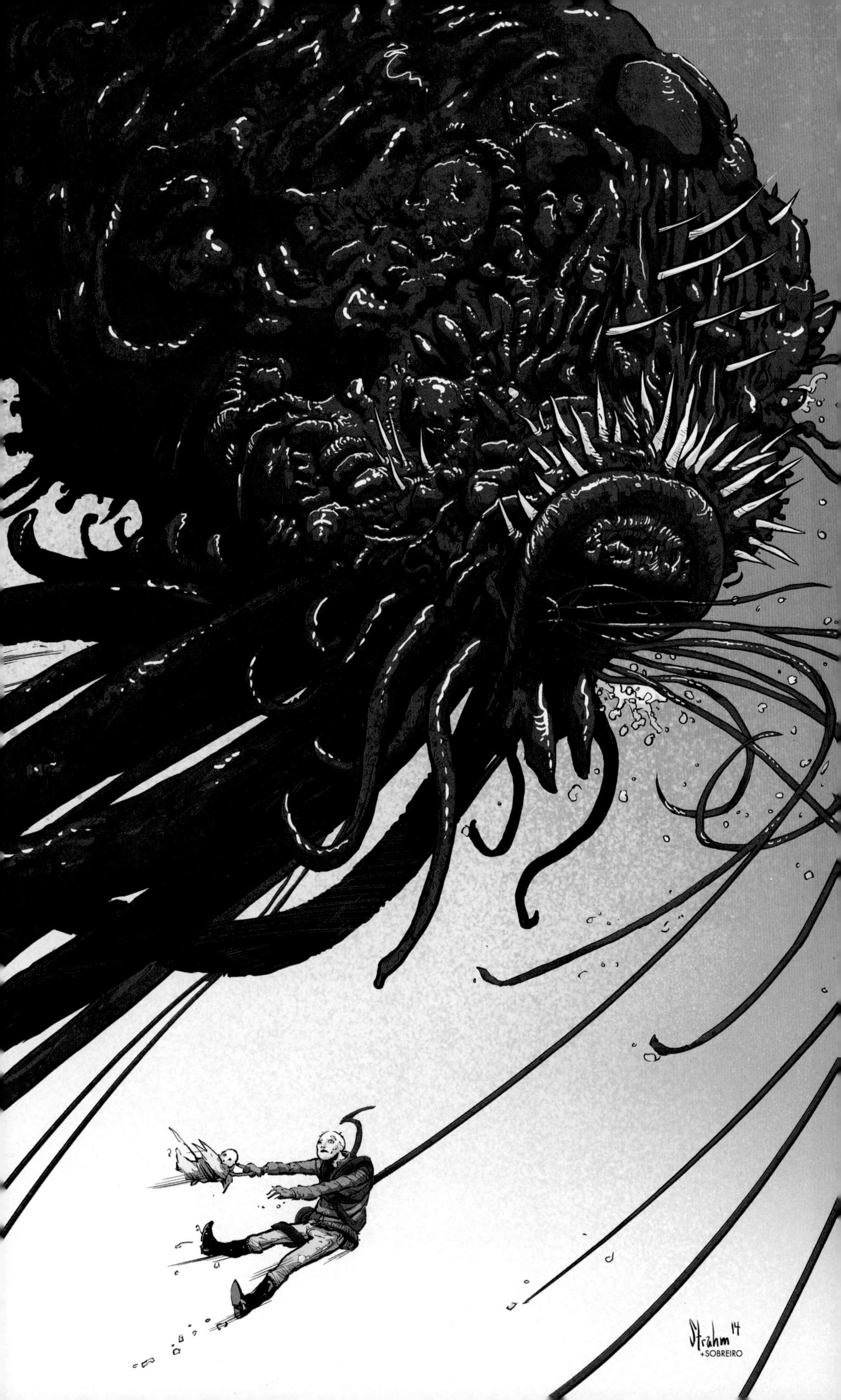
Strahm 14
+SOBREIRO

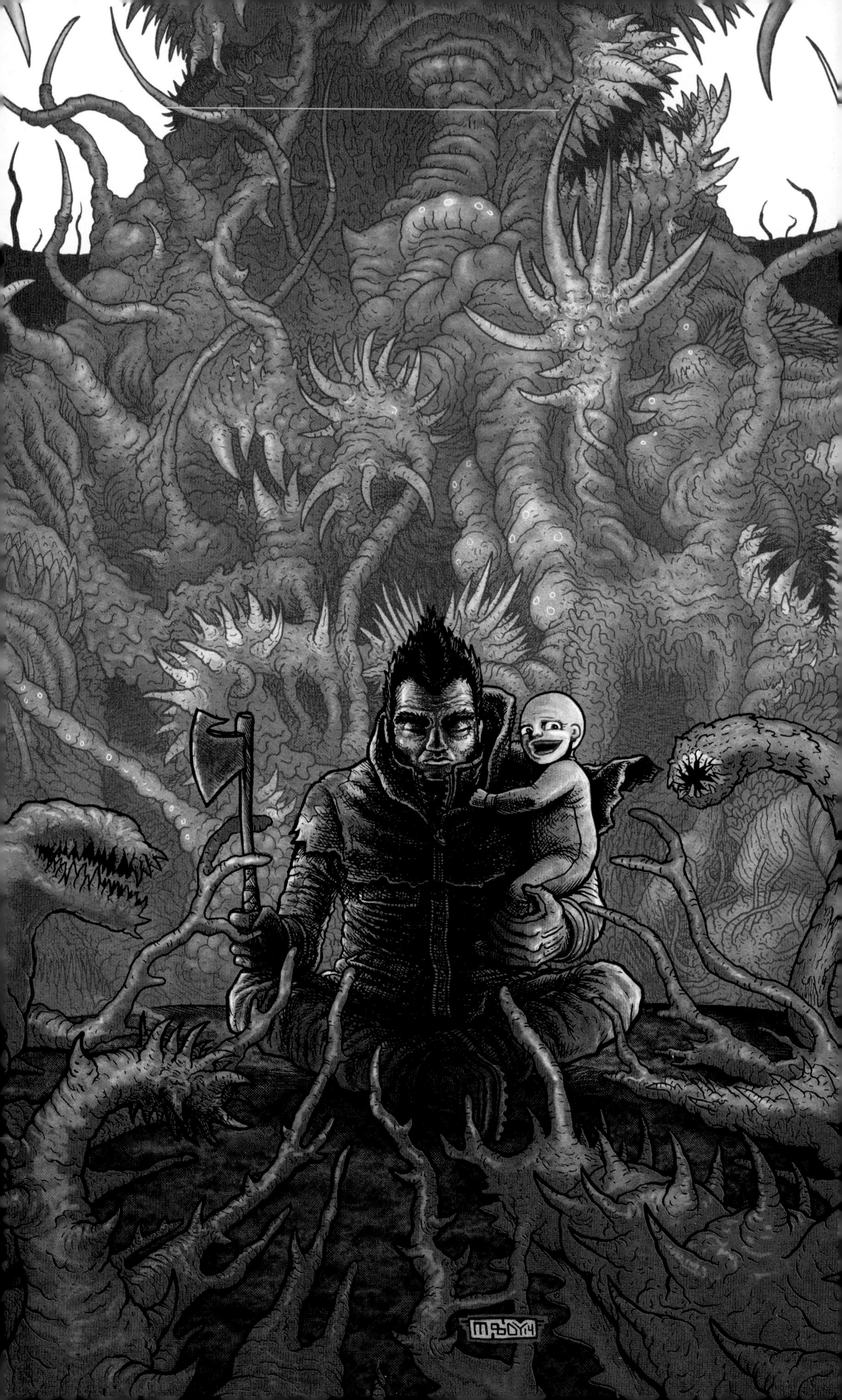

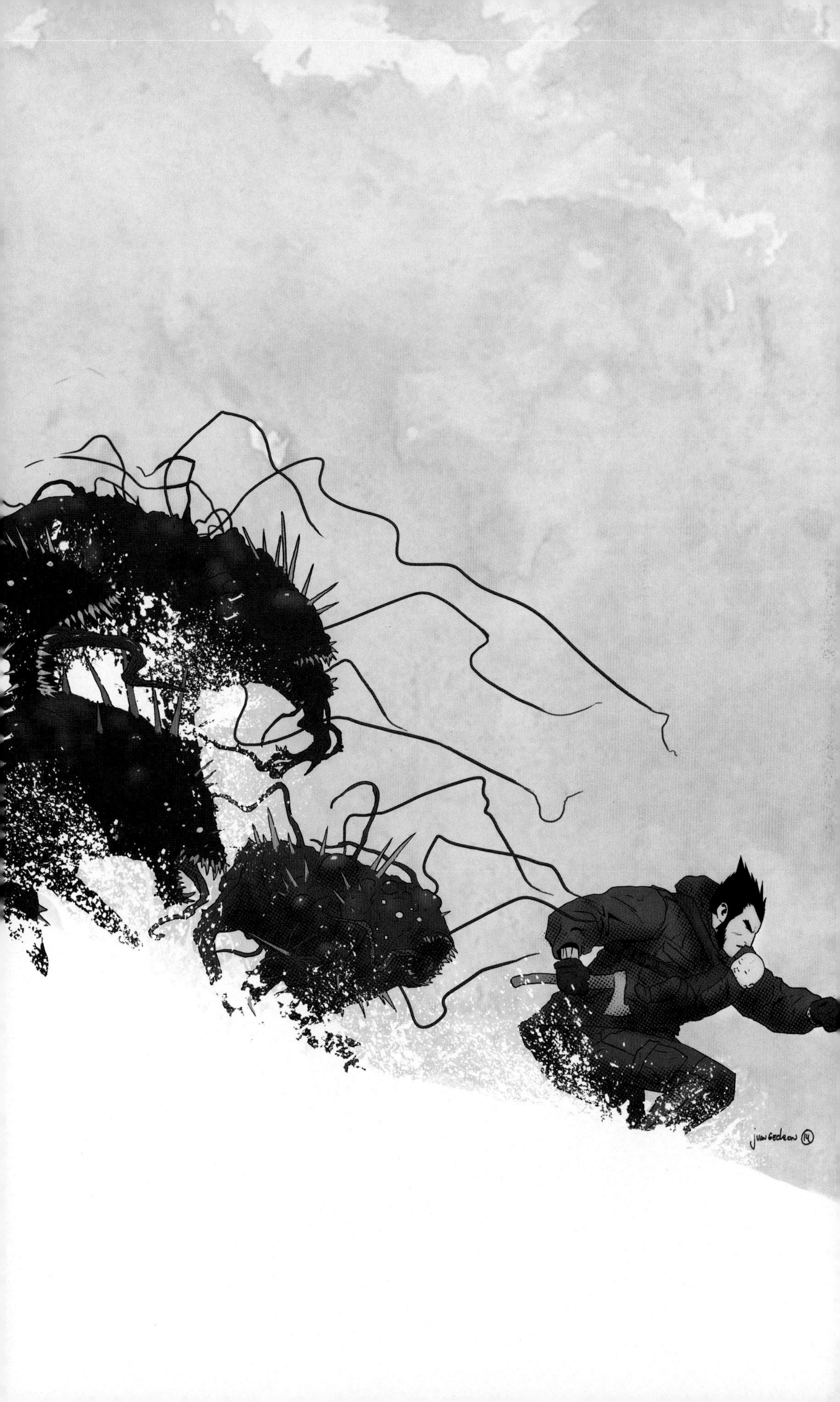

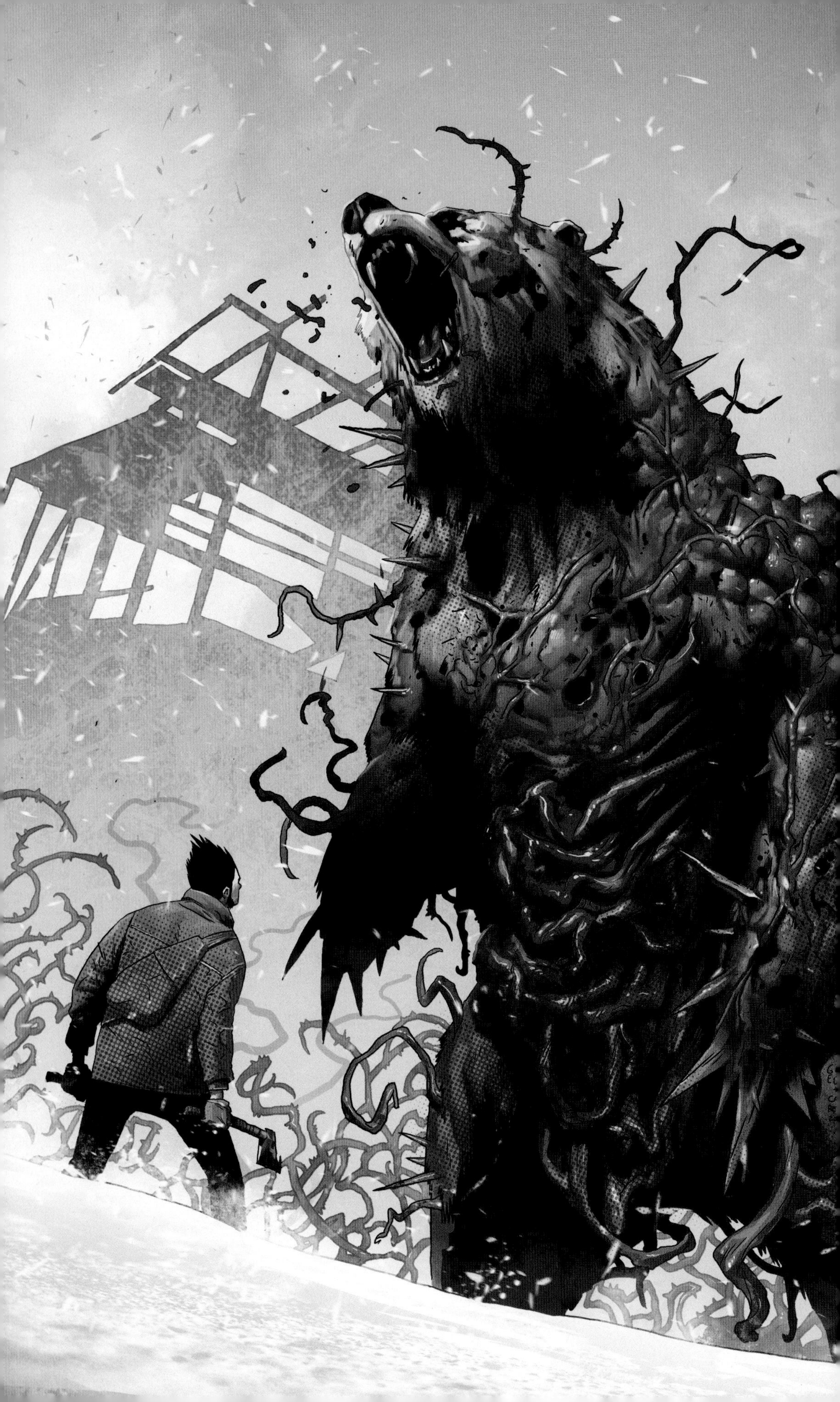

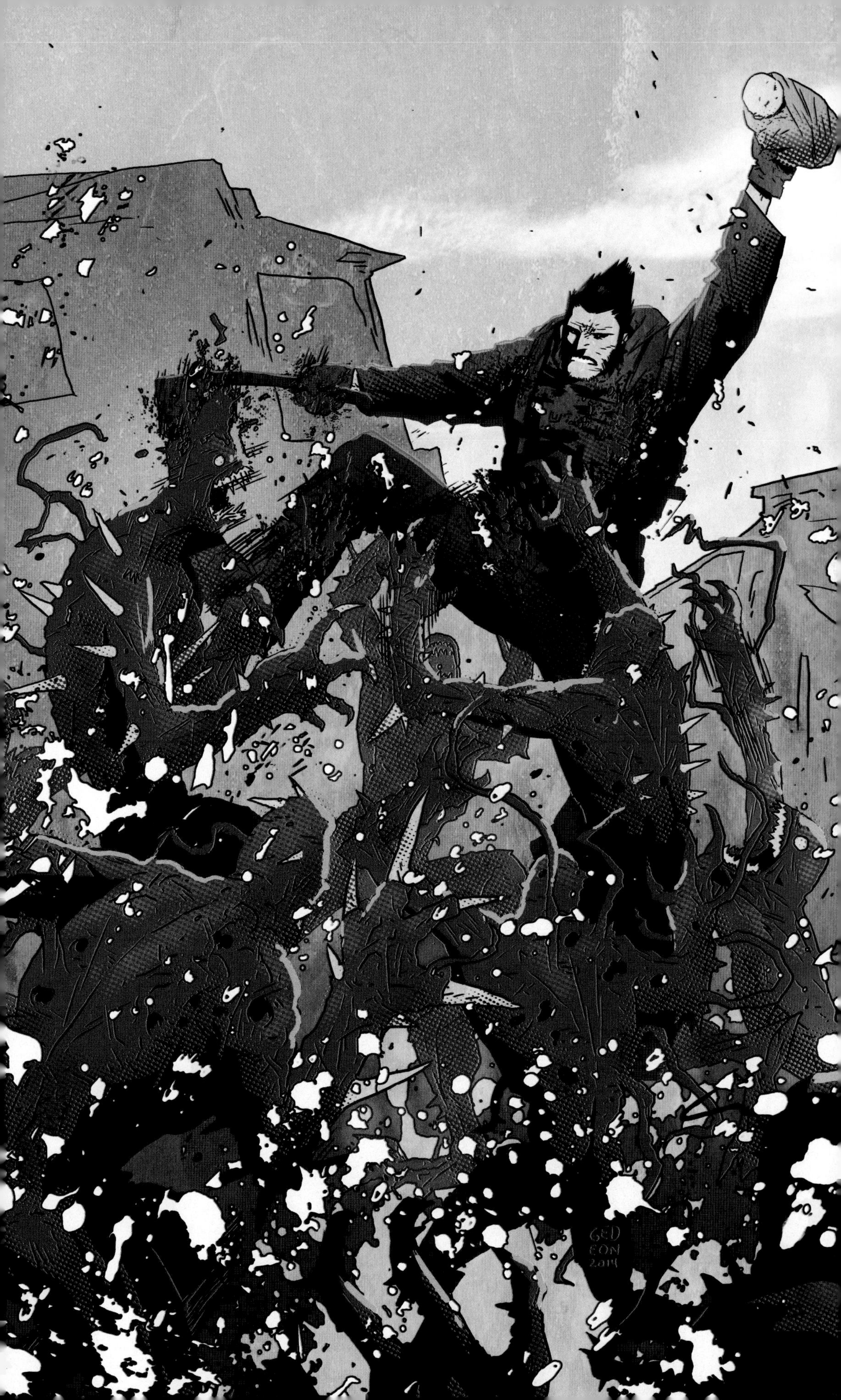

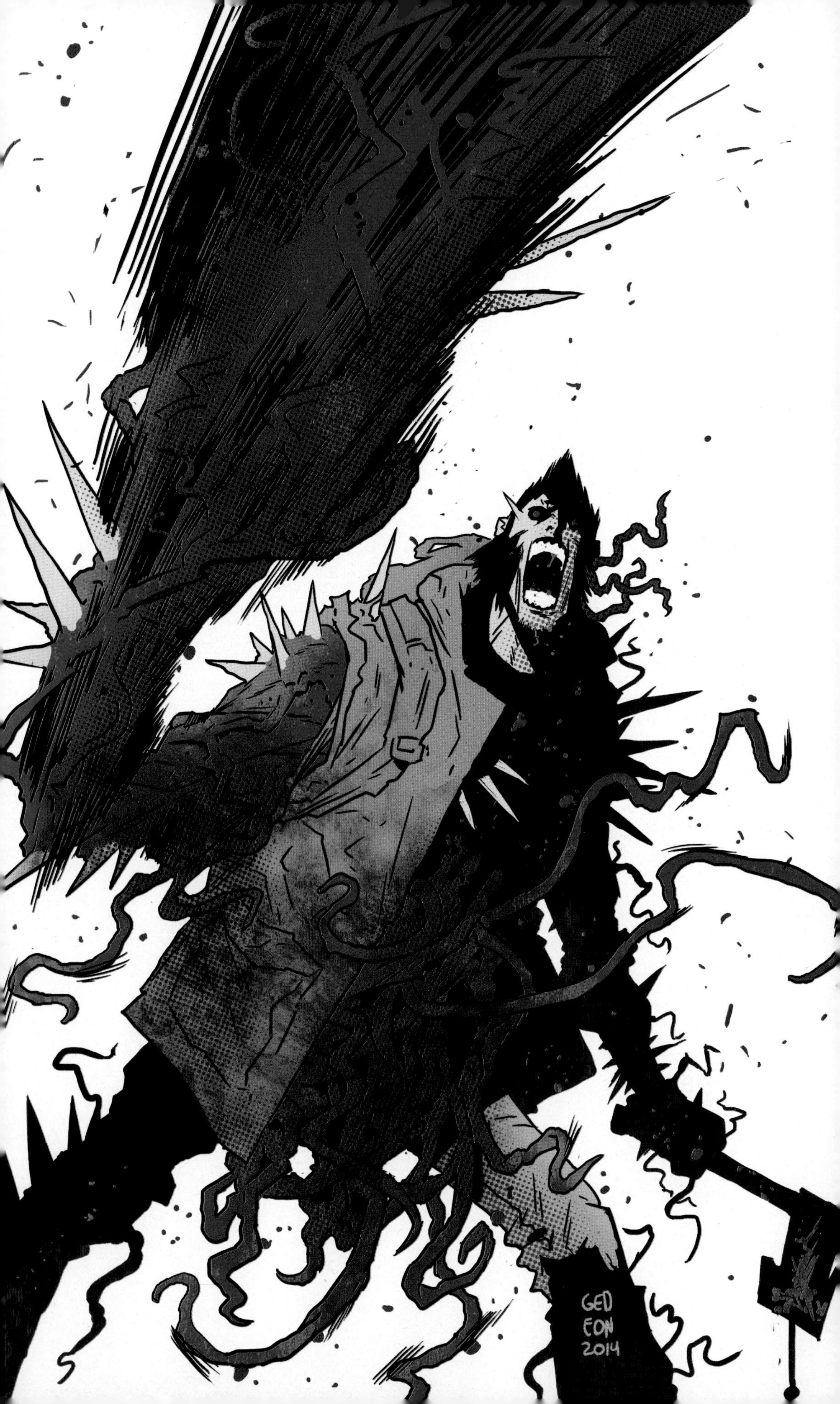
GED
EON
2014

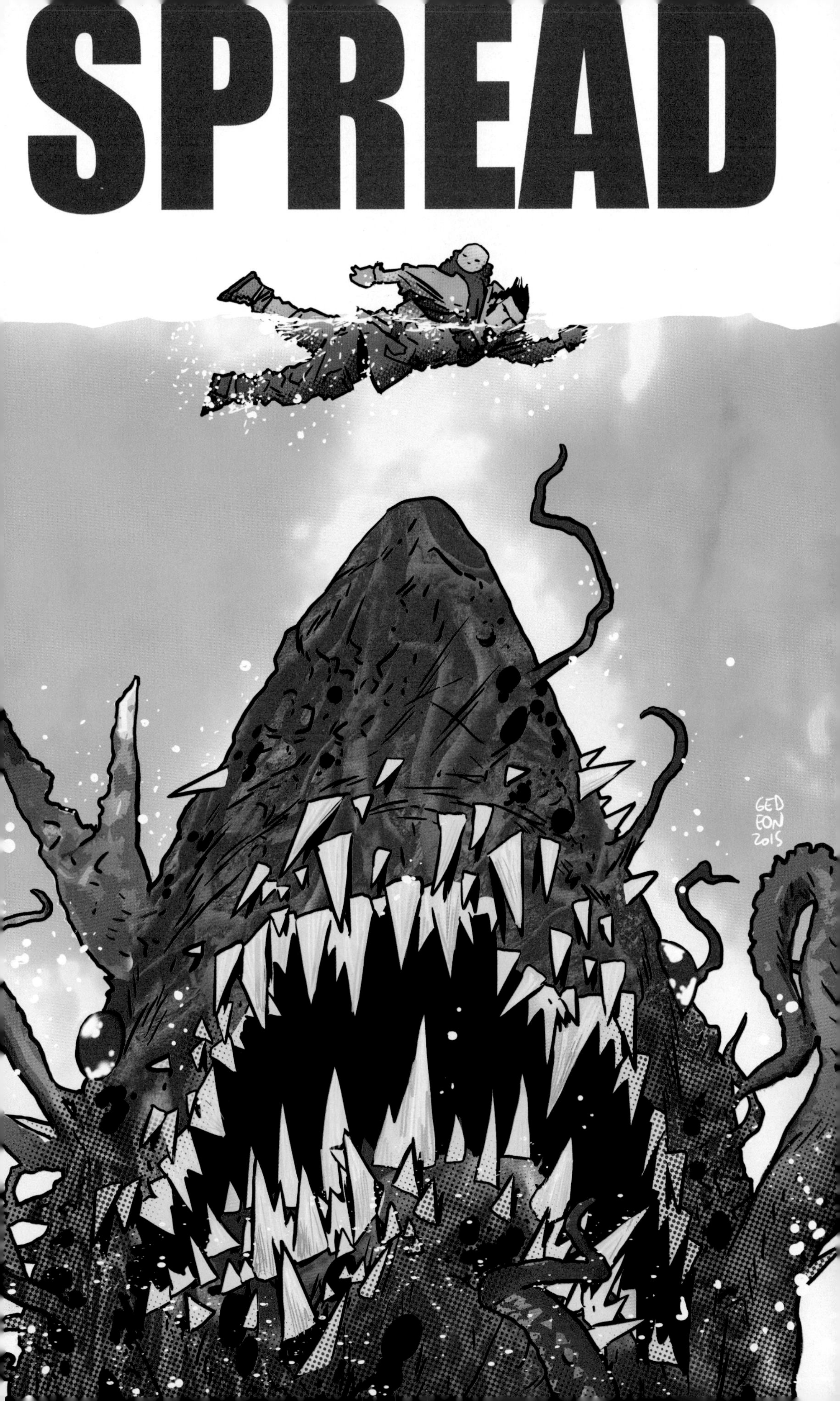
SPREAD
GED
EON
2015

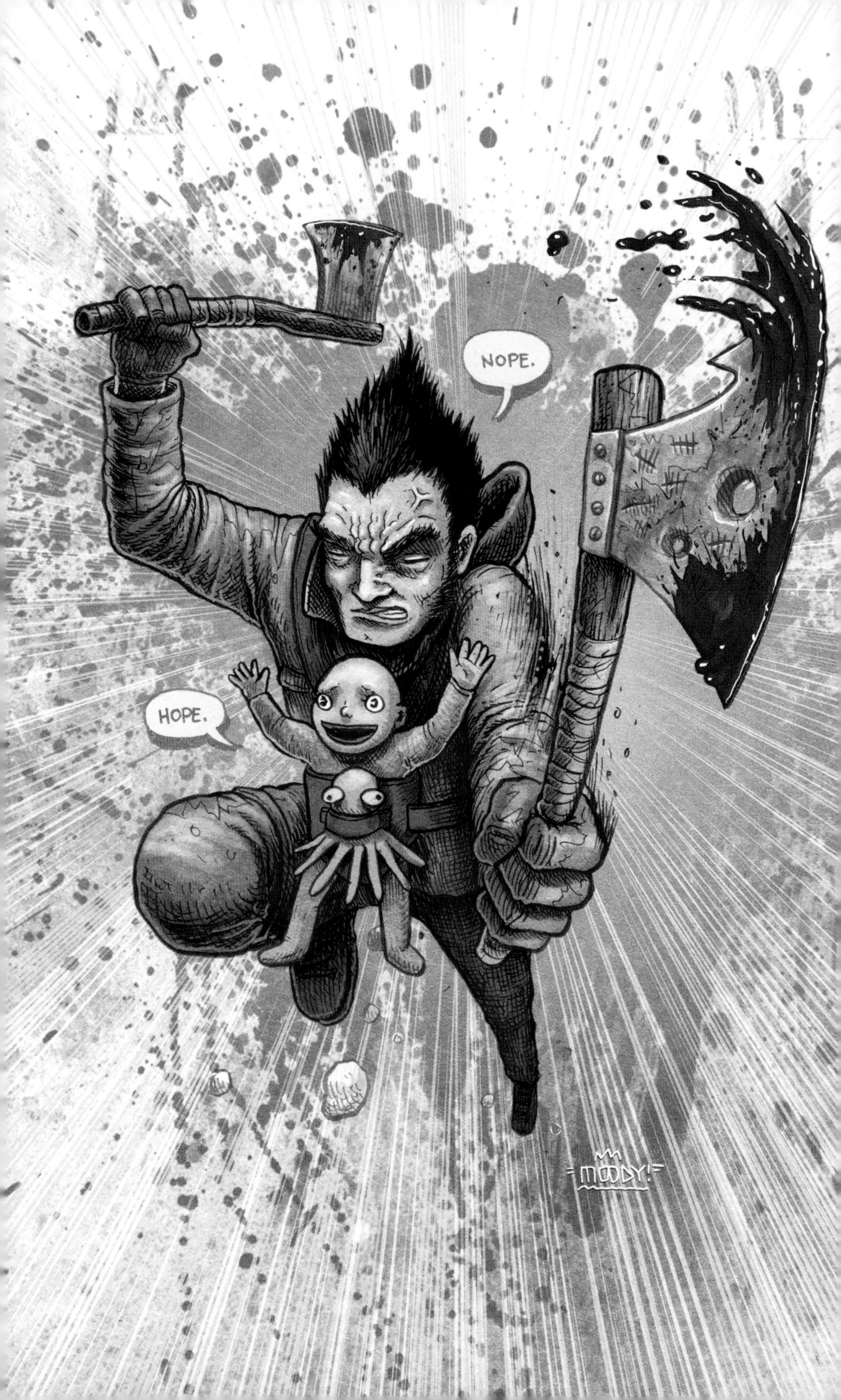
NOPE.
HOPE.
MOODY!

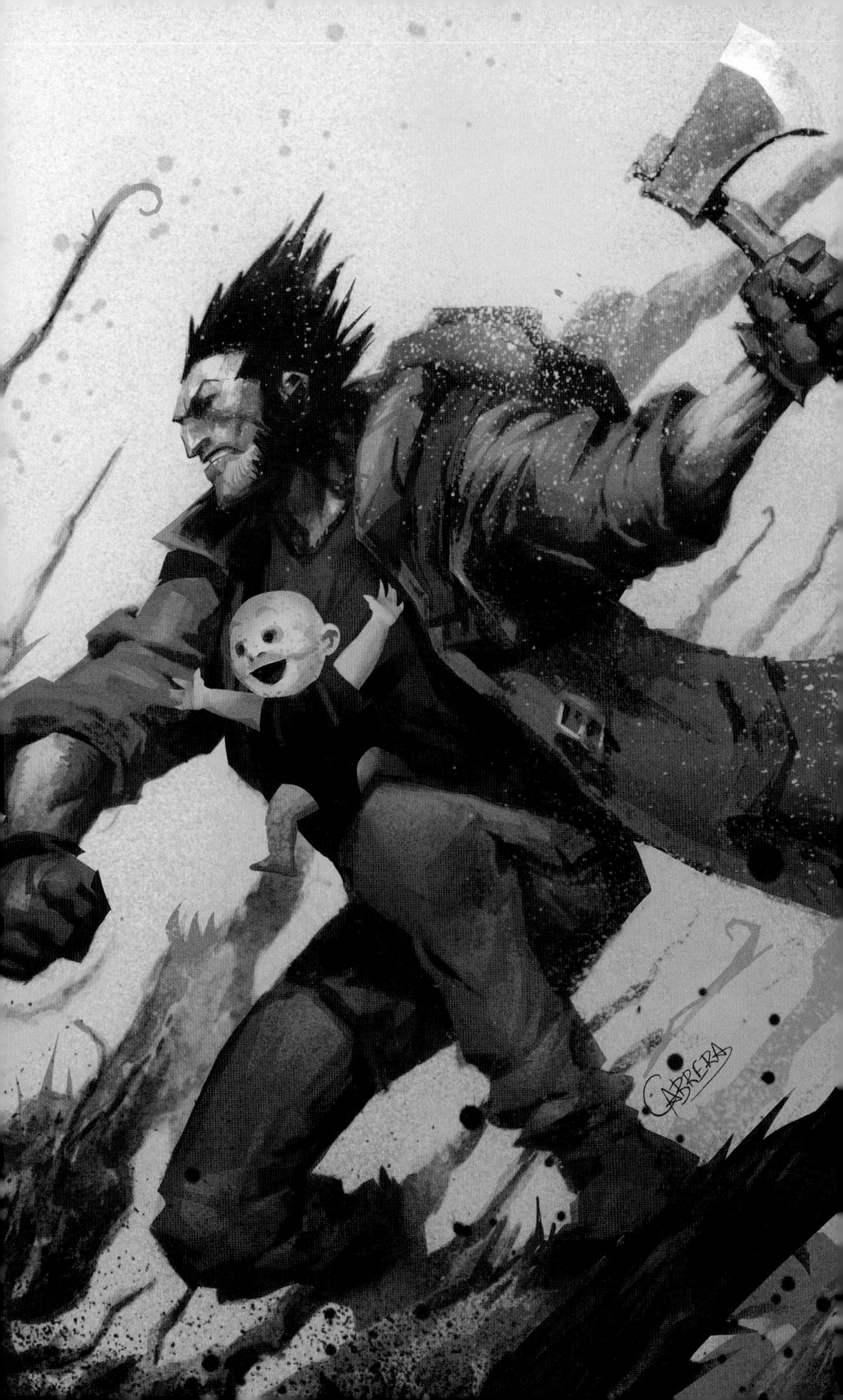
CABRERA

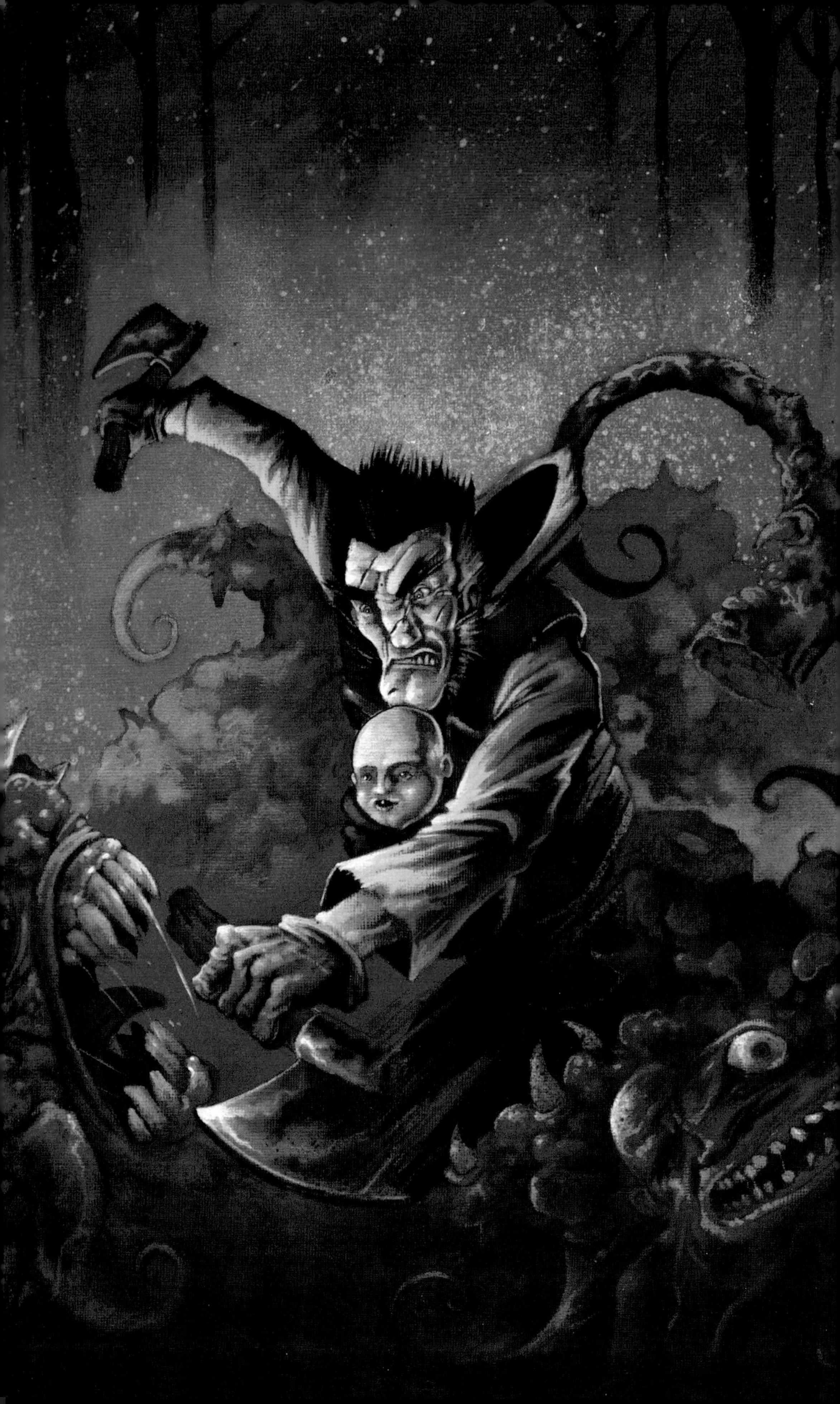

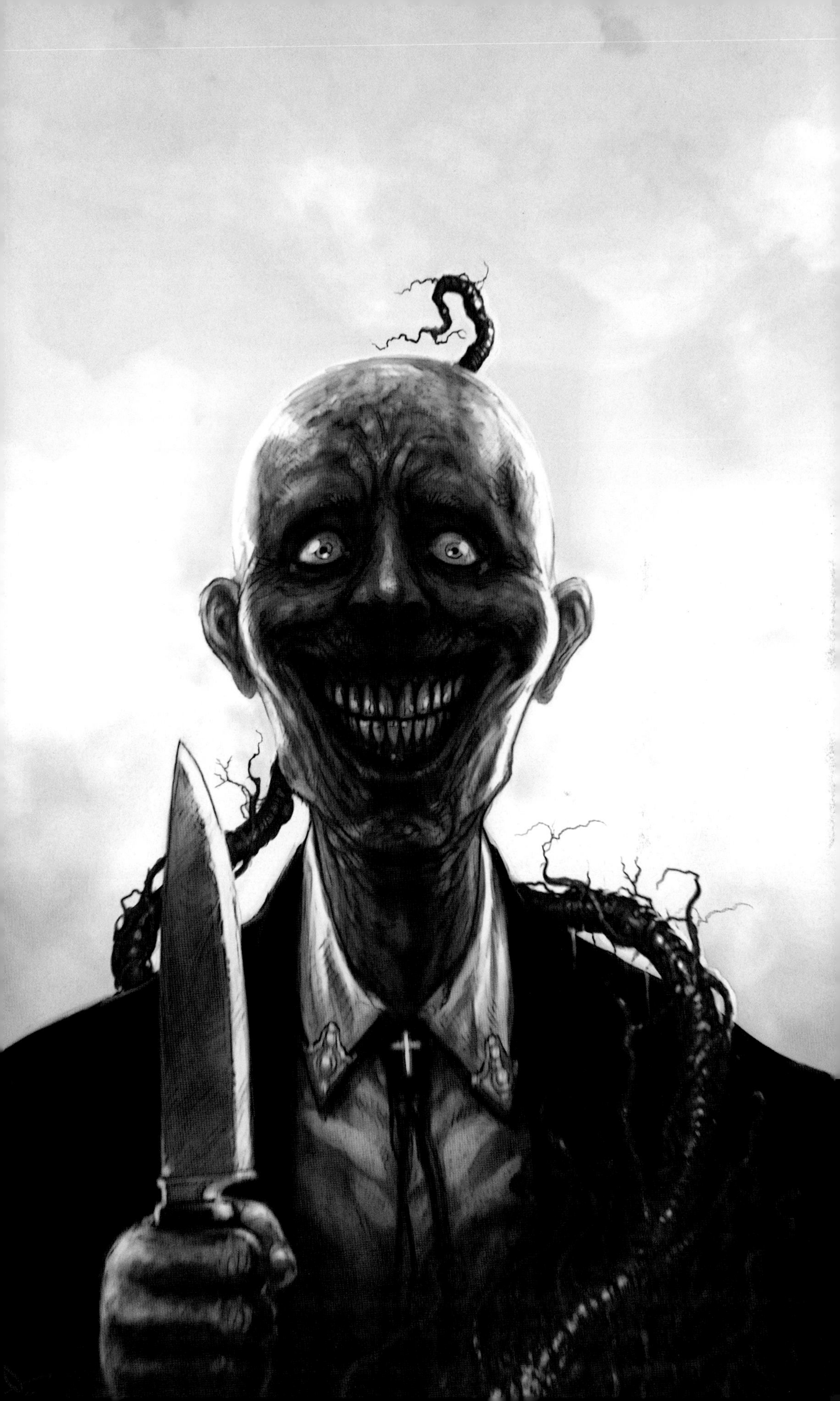

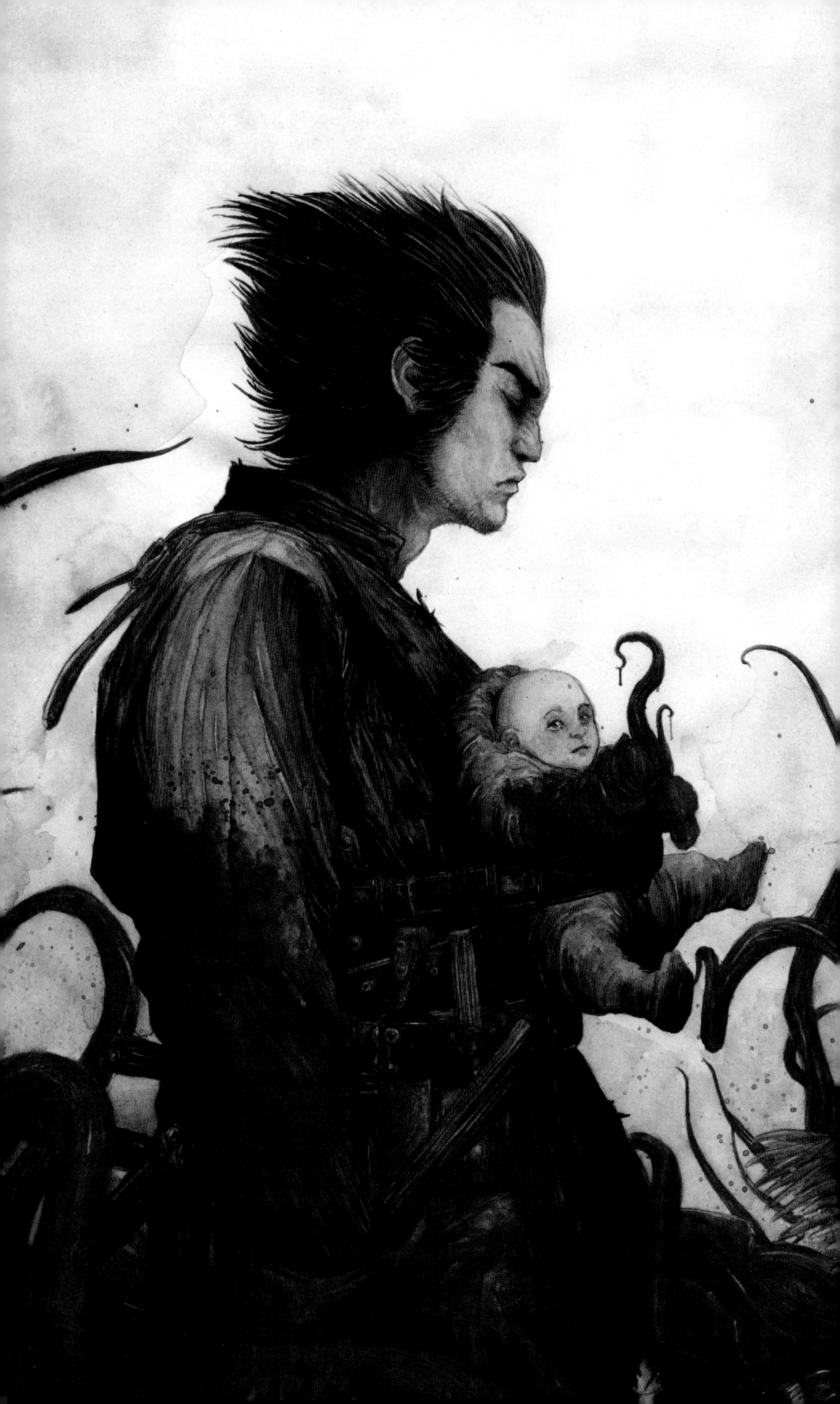

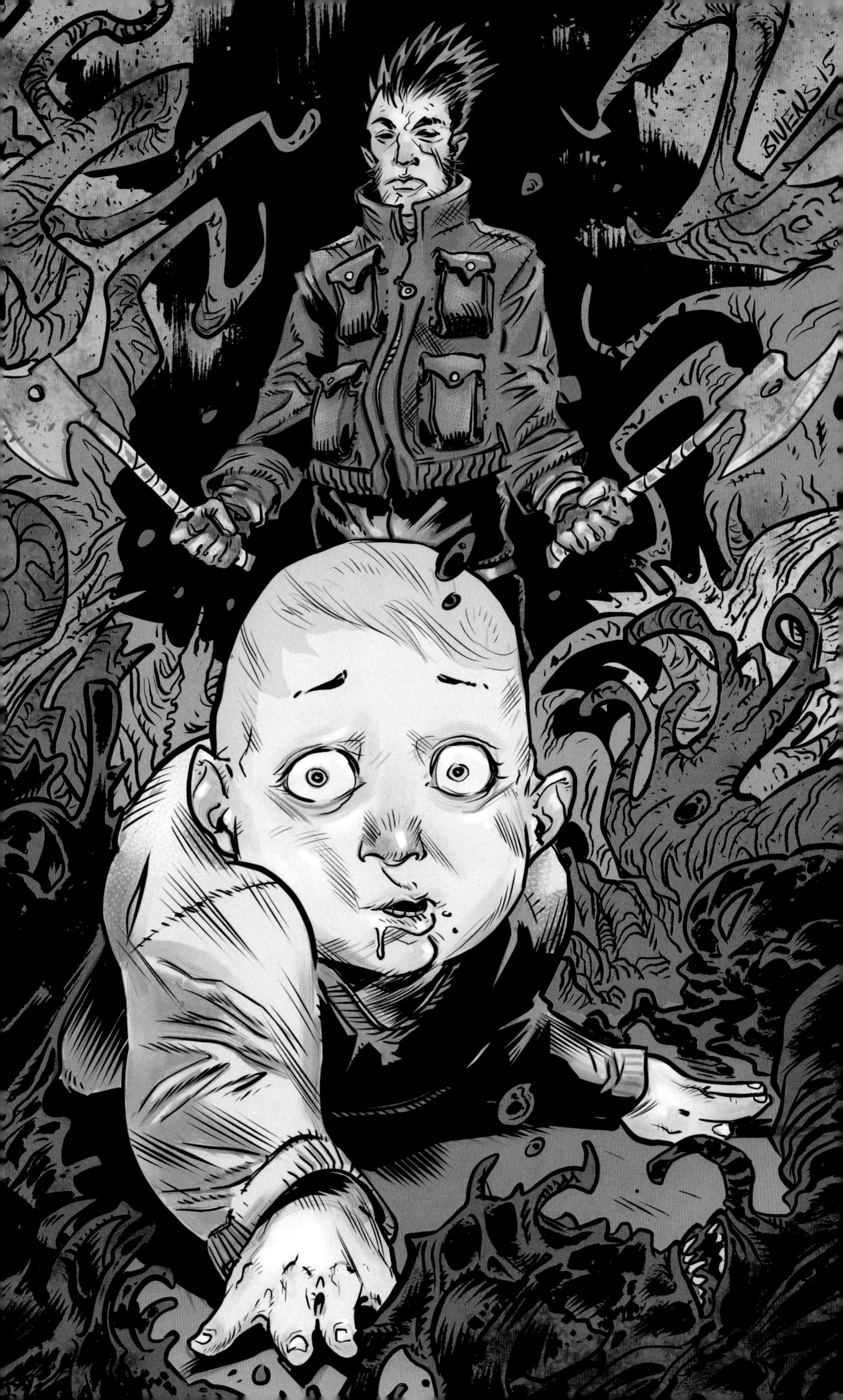
BIVENS 15

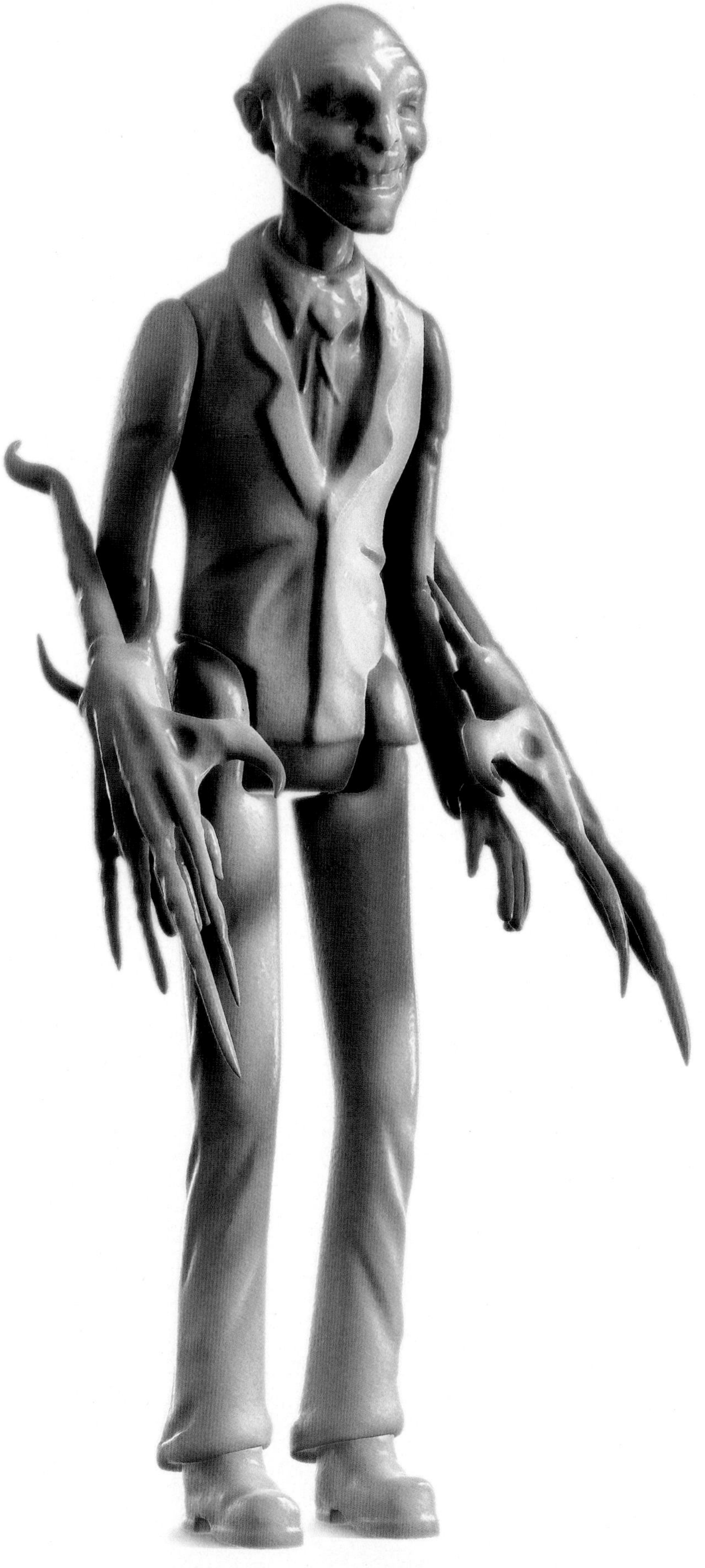

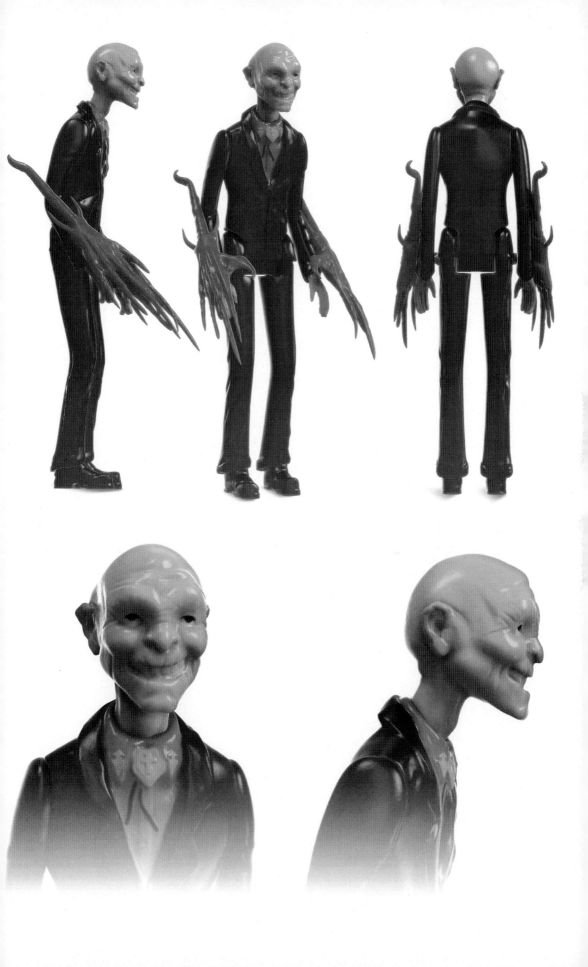

JUSTIN JORDAN

Justin Jordan lives in the wilds of Pennsylvania and writes comics. Lots of comics. Most notably the *Luther Strode* saga and *Dead Body Road* for Image.

Twitter: @Justin_Jordan
Email: JustinJordan@gmail.com

KYLE STRAHM

Kyle Strahm lives and works in a house in Kansas City, Missouri where he watches tv shows from back when they did it right and he rearranges old toys like a crazy person. You might have seen his work published by Marvel, DC, Dark Horse, IDW, Todd McFarlane Productions and various others.

Instagram: kylestrahm_art
Twitter: @kstrahm
Website: www.kylestrahm.com
Facebook: http://www.fb.com/krstrahm

FELIPE SOBREIRO

Felipe Sobreiro is an artist and colorist from Brazil. His work has been published, among others, by Image, Marvel, DC, BOOM! Studios and Dark Horse. He's the colorist of the *Luther Strode* saga.

Instagram: sobreiro
Twitter: @therealsobreiro
Website: www.sobreiro.com
Facebook: www.fb.com/fsobreiro

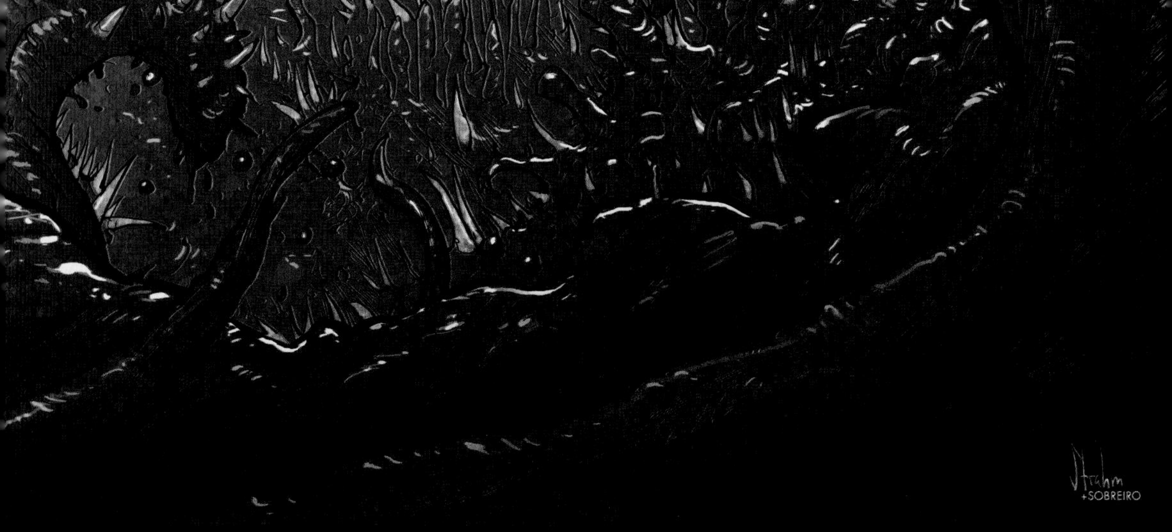
+SOBREIRO

CRANK!

Crank! letters a bunch of books put out by Image, Dark Horse and Oni Press. He also has a podcast with Mike Norton (crankcast.net) and he makes music (sonomorti.bandcamp.com).

Twitter: @ccrank

SEBASTIAN GIRNER

Sebastian Girner is a freelance editor and writer who has helped creatively guide and produce comics for such publishers as Marvel Entertainment, Image Comics, VIZ Media and Random House. He lives and works in Brooklyn.

Twitter: @SGirner
Website: www.sebastiangirner.com

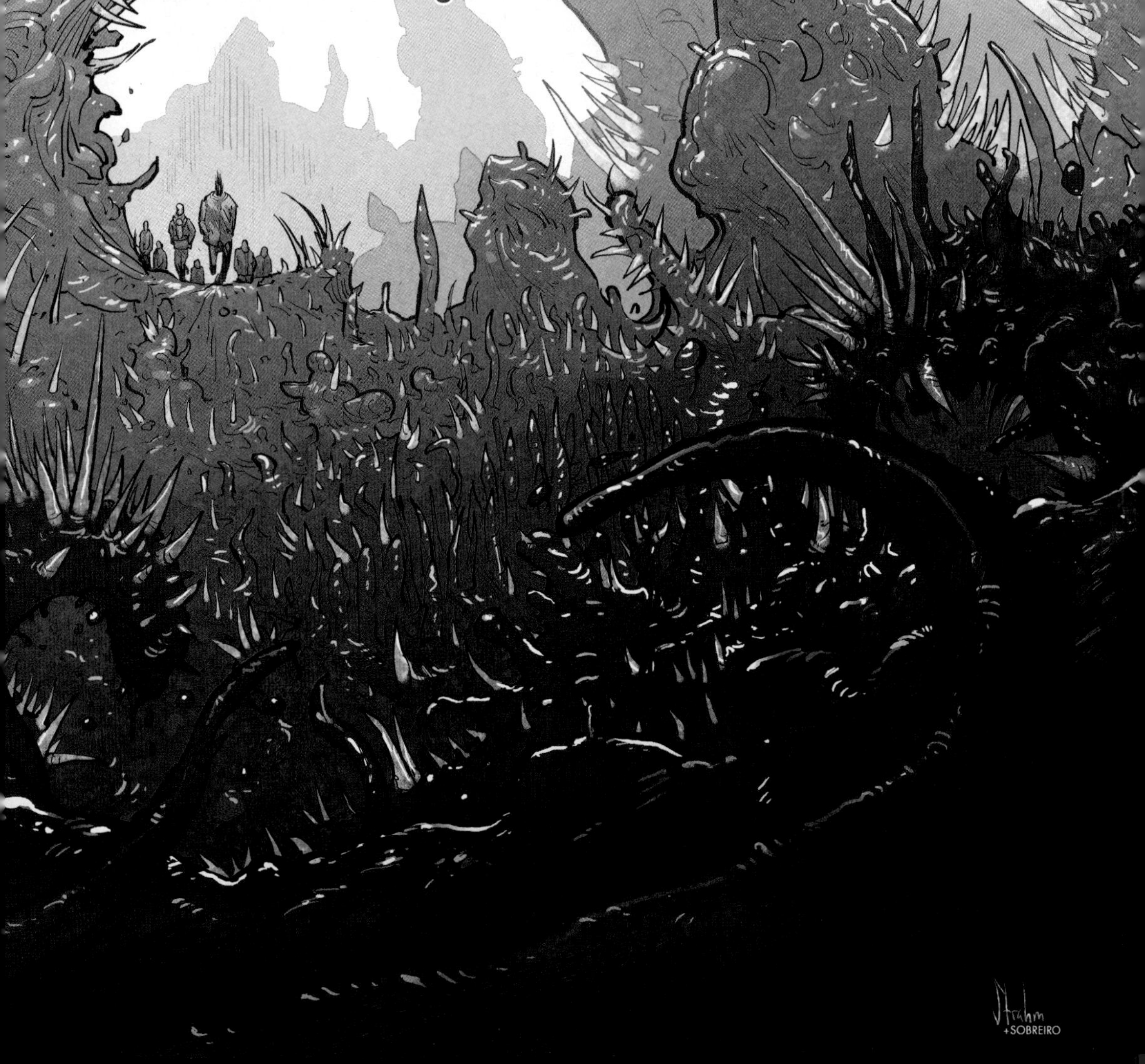
+SOBREIRO

SPREAD

WILL RETURN WITH VOLUME THREE.

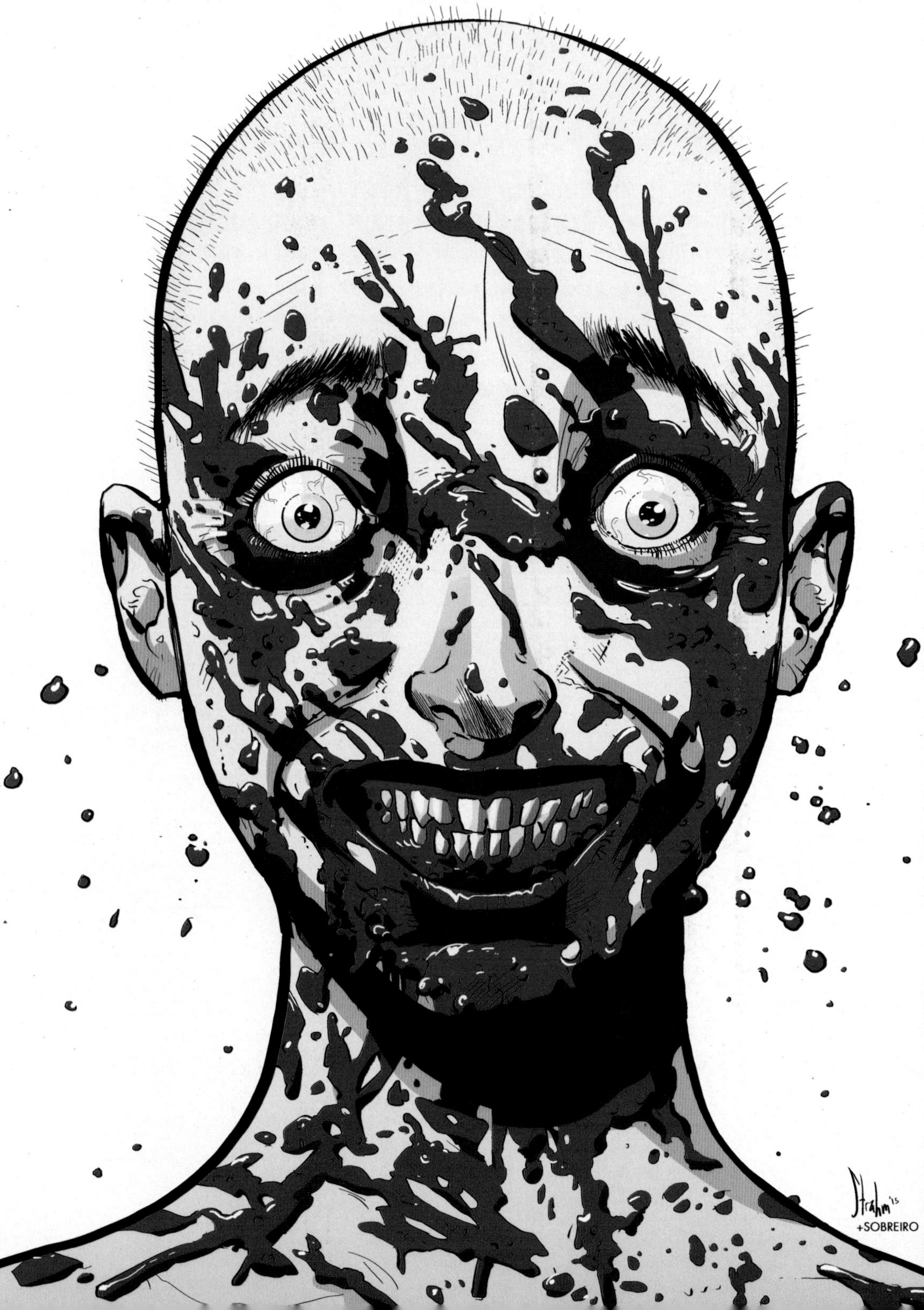

Strahm '15
+SOBREIRO